THE GOLF SWING TRILOGY

STAND AND SWING... GOLF CAN BE THIS SIMPLE!

SIR W. G. SIMPSON

ERNEST JONES

DARYN HAMMOND

DUTCHY GOLF TEAM

Copyright © 2012 dutchygolf.com

All rights reserved.

DEDICATION

To all the lovers of this grand game of golf.

To Sir Walter Simpson: A true appreciation for and understanding of how the Ernest Jones Method was inspired by Sir Walter Simpson's "The Art Of Golf" can only be achieved by reading the original work for yourself – BOOK I in this trilogy (edited, formatted and illustrated.)

To Ernest Jones and Daryn Hammond: A true appreciation for and understanding of how the Dutchy Golf Swing Trainer was inspired by the Ernest Jones Method can only be achieved by reading "The Golf Swing – Ernest Jones Method" for yourself – BOOK II in this trilogy (edited, formatted and illustrated.)

To the Dutchy Golf Team: we who have fallen victim to and been left paralysed (at times) by our crazy modern-day teaching systems. As a result we developed the Dutchy Golf Swing Trainer and related exercises – BOOK III in this trilogy.

In this Golf Swing Trilogy we present the original writings and illustrations from the 1880s and the 1920s. We are amazed at the clarity behind the thoughts of those times that unveil themselves to us as universal truths seemingly unaffected by the passing of time. And as readers have commented to us "some inconvenient truths about the modern day professional teaching system."

There is an inherent danger to studying our golf swing closely. Information by itself is dangerous, it can destroy our game. We swing our best when we have the fewest things to think about.

It's amazing how difficult this game is when we are playing poorly, and how simple it is when we are playing well.

Stand and swing.... golf can be this simple!

THE GOLF SWING TRILOGY

BOOK I   7
THE ART OF GOLF
BY
SIR W. G. SIMPSON, BART.

BOOK II   157
THE GOLF SWING
BY
ERNEST JONES
DARYN HAMMOND

BOOK III   285
THE DUTCHY GOLF SWING TRAINER
BY
DUTCHY GOLF TEAM

BOOK I - **THE ART OF GOLF**

BOOK I

THE ART OF GOLF

SIR W. G. SIMPSON, BART.

BOOK I - **THE ART OF GOLF**

'Pleasures are more beneficial than duties,

because, like the quality of mercy, they

are not strained, and they are twice blest.'

R. L. S.

THE
ART OF GOLF

BY

Sir W. G. SIMPSON, Bart.

"SACRED TO HOPE AND PROMISE IS THE SPOT."

First published 1887

BOOK I - **THE ART OF GOLF**

TO

THE HONOURABLE COMPANY

OF EDINBURGH GOLFERS

THIS BOOK IS DEDICATED

HUMBLY AS A GOLFER

PROUDLY AS THEIR CAPTAIN

GRATEFULLY FOR MERRY MEETINGS

AND

CORDIALLY WITHOUT PERMISSION

BY

THE AUTHOR

PREFACE

A Preface would be superfluous were it not necessary to say a word or two about the Illustrations. My aim was to show (for the first time, I believe), by means of instantaneous photography, the movements made by players with a classical style in the process of striking a golf ball. For plates in this book (with the exception of Nos. XII., XIII., XVI., XVII. and XVIII., which are the work of Mr. Alexander Nicol, Photographer) I have to, and do, cordially thank my friend Mr. A. F. Macfie, whose knowledge of the game, and whose skill with the camera, have enabled him to catch movements which are in many cases so swift as to escape ordinary observation. That the illustrations, therefore, truly represent the styles of the fine players who stood for them, no reader need doubt.

The authority of the text is another matter. It may be—nay, it has been—asked, 'What does he know about it?' Indeed (and alas!) I cannot speak from the highest platform. But if a poor cricketer, a hopeless billiard player, an execrable shot, begins golf by the doctor's orders after three decades, flounders hopelessly for years, and then by theory and experiment evolves a golf which I shall only characterise as infinitely better than his cricket, his billiards, or his shooting ever were, it is evident that he knows (whether he can say it) something of that department of brick-making which does not depend upon the quality of the straw.

3 Belgrave Crescent,
Edinburgh, May 1887

CONTENTS

PART I.

PRELIMINARY, AND PRINCIPALLY FOOLISH.

1	THE PRAISE OF GOLF	21
2	THE ORIGIN OF GOLF	27
3	THE NATURE OF THE GAME	31
4	OF SETS OF CLUBS AND OTHER GOLFING APPURTENANCES	35
5	OF CADDIES	41

BOOK I - **THE ART OF GOLF**

PART II.

OF PLAYING THE GAME.

1	OF DRIVING IN GENERAL	49
2	OF STYLE IN DRIVING	57
3	ADVICE TO BEGINNERS	77
4	OF PECULIARITIES AND FAULTS	87
5	OF TEMPORARY FAULTS	99
6	OF PLAYING THROUGH THE GREEN	109
7	OF BUNKER PLAY	113
8	OF APPROACHING	117
9	OF PUTTING	139
10	OF MATCH AND MEDAL PLAY	147

ILLUSTRATIONS.

PLATES.

Plate	I	ADDRESSING FOR A DRIVE,
	II	TOM MORRIS DRIVING (1)
	III	TOM MORRIS DRIVING (2)
	IV	TOM MORRIS DRIVING (3)
	V	JIM MORRIS DRIVING (1)
	VI	JIM MORRIS DRIVING (2)
	VII	SAYERS DRIVING (1)
	VIII	SAYERS DRIVING (2)
	IX	ADDRESSING FOR AN APPROACH SHOT
	X	JUST WITHIN A WRIST (1)
	XI	JUST WITHIN A WRIST (2)
	XII	SIXTY YARDS FROM THE HOLE (1)
	XIII	SIXTY YARDS FROM THE HOLE (2)
	XIV	LOFTING HIGH (1)
	XV	LOFTING HIGH (2)

BOOK I - **THE ART OF GOLF**

Plate	XVI	RUNNING IT WITH AN IRON (1)
	XVII	RUNNING IT WITH AN IRON (2)
	XVIII	RUNNING IT WITH AN IRON (3)
	XIX	PUTTING (1)
	XX	PUTTING (2)

DIAGRAMS.

POSITIONS OF THE FEET IN DRIVING.

Fig. 1 GETTING TOO MUCH IN FRONT
2 CADDY'S CORRECTION
3 STANDING 'IN FRONT'
4 STANDING 'SQUARE'
5 STANDING 'OPEN'

POSITIONS OF THE HANDS IN DRIVING.

Fig. 6 PROPER GRIP—HANDS 'OVER' OR 'ABOVE'
7 PROPER GRIP—HANDS 'OVER' OR 'ABOVE'
8 HANDS TOO FAR ' ROUND ' OR ' UNDER'
9 HANDS TOO FAR ' ROUND ' OR ' UNDER'
10 UNEQUAL GRIP, RIGHT HAND 'UNDER'

BOOK I - **THE ART OF GOLF**

PART I.

PRELIMINARY, AND PRINCIPALLY FOOLISH.

BOOK I - **THE ART OF GOLF**

1
THE PRAISE OF GOLF

There are so many good points about the royal and ancient game of golf that its comparative obscurity, rather than its increasing popularity, are matter for wonder. It is apparently yet unknown to the Medical Faculty. The golfer does not find it in the list of exercises recommended by doctors to persons engaged in warfare with the results of sedentary habits. He is moved to pity British subjects compelled to stir their livers by walking, horse-riding, or cycling. He knows how monotonous it is following one's nose, or flogging a horse and following it, compared with flogging and following a ball. For the wearied and bent cyclist, who prides himself on making his journey in as short a time as possible, he has a pitying word. Men who assume that the sooner the journey is over the greater the pleasure, evidently do not love their pursuit for its own sake.

With any other sport or pastime golf compares favourably.

With cricket? The golfer has nothing to say against that game, if you are a good player. But it is a pastime for the few. The rest have to hang about the pavilion, and see the runs made. With the golfer it is different. He does not require to be even a second-class player, in order to get into matches. Again, the skilful cricketer has to retire when he gets up in years. He might exclaim with Wolsey: 'Had I served my golf as I have served my cricket, she would not thus have deserted me in my old age.' How different it is with golf! It is a game for the many. It suits all sorts and conditions of men. The strong and the weak, the halt and the maimed, the octogenarian and the boy, the rich and the poor, the clergyman and the infidel, may play every day, except Sunday. The late riser can play comfortably, and be back for his rubber in the afternoon; the sanguine man can measure himself against those who will beat him; the half-crown seeker can find victims, the gambler can bet, the man of high principle, by playing for nothing, may enjoy himself, and yet feel good.

BOOK I - THE ART OF GOLF

You can brag, and lose matches; depreciate yourself, and win them. Unlike the other Scotch game of whisky-drinking, excess in it is not injurious to the health.

Better than fishing, shooting, and hunting? Certainly. These can only be indulged in at certain seasons. They let you die of dyspepsia during the rest of the year. Besides, hunting, you are dependent on horses and foxes for sport; shooting, on birds; fishing, on the hunger of a scaly but fastidious animal. The pleasures of sport are extracted from the sufferings of dumb animals. If horses, grouse, or fish could squeal, sports would be distressful rather than amusing.

Golf has some drawbacks. It is possible, by too much of it, to destroy the mind; a man with a Roman nose and a high forehead may play away his profile. That peculiar mental condition called 'Fifish' probably had its origin in the east of the Kingdom. For the golfer, Nature loses her significance. Larks, the casts of worms, the buzzing of bees, and even children are hateful to him. I have seen a golfer very angry at getting into a bunker by killing a bird, and rewards of as much as ten shillings have been offered for boys maimed on the links. Rain comes to be regarded solely in its relation to the putting greens; the daisy is detested, botanical specimens are but 'hazards,' twigs 'break clubs.' Winds cease to be east, south, west, or north. They are ahead, behind, or sideways, and the sky is bright or dark, according to the state of the game.

A cause of the comparative obscurity of golf is that the subject cannot easily be treated by the novelist. Golf has no Hawley Smart. Its Whyte Melville did not write, but played. You can ride at a stone wall for love and the lady, but what part can she take in driving at a bunker? It is natural that Lady Diana should fall in love with Nimrod when she finds him in the plough, stunned, brokenlegged, the brush, which he had wrested from the fox as he fell, firm in his lifeless grasp. But if beauty found us prone on the putting green, a 27 ½ embedded in our gory locks, she might send us home to be trepanned; but nothing could come of it, a red coat notwithstanding. No! at golf ladies are simply in the road. Riding to hounds and opening five-barred gates, soft nothings may be whispered, but it is impossible at the same moment to putt and to cast languishing glances. If the dear one be near you at the tee, she may get her teeth knocked out, and even between the shots arms dare not steal round waists, lest the party behind should call out 'fore!' I have seen a golfing novel indeed; but it was in manuscript, the publishers having rejected it. The scene was St. Andrews. He was a soldier, a statesman, an orator, but only a seventh-class golfer. She, being St. Andrews born, naturally preferred a rising player. Whichever of the two made the best medal score was to have her hand. The soldier employed a lad to kick his adversary's ball into bunkers, to tramp it into mud, to lose it, and he won; but the lady would not give her hand to a score of 130. Six months passed, during which the soldier studied the game morning, noon, and night, but to little purpose. Next medal day arrived, and he was face to face with the fact that his golf, unbacked by his statesmanship, would avail him nothing. He hired and disguised a professional in his own clothes. The ruse was successful; but, alas ! the professional broke down. The soldier, disguised as a marker, however, cheated, and brought him in with 83. A three for the long hole roused suspicion, and led to inquiry. He was found out, dismissed from the club, rejected by the lady (who afterwards made an unhappy marriage with a left-handed player), and sent back in disgrace to his statesmanship and oratory. It was as good a romance as could be made on the subject, but very improbable.

Although unsuited to the novelist, golf lends itself readily to the dreaming of scenes, of which the dreamer is the hero. Unless he is an exceptionally good rider, or can afford 300 guinea mounts, a man cannot expect to be the hero of the hunting-field. The sportsman knows what sort of shot he is, and the fisher has no illusions; but every moderately good golfer, on the morning of the medal day, may lie abed and count up a perfect score for himself. He easily recalls how at different times and often he has done each hole in par figures. Why not this day, and all the holes consecutively? It seems so easy. The more he thinks of it the easier it seems, even allowing for a few mistakes. Every competitor who is awake soon enough sees the necessity for preparing a speech against the contingency of the medal being presented to him in the evening. Nor is any one much crushed when all is over, and he has not won. If he does well, it was but that putt, that bad lie, that bunker. If his score is bad, what of it? Even the best are off their game occasionally. Next time it will be different. Meanwhile his score will be taken as a criterion of his game, and he is sure to win many half-crowns from unwary adversaries who underrate him.

The game of golf is full of consolation. The long driver who is beaten feels that he has a soul above putting. All those who cannot drive thirty yards suppose themselves to be good putters. Your hashy player piques himself on his power of recovery. The duffer is a duffer merely because every second shot is missed. Time or care will eliminate the misses, and then! Or perhaps there is something persistently wrong in driving, putting, or approaching. He will discover the fault, and then! Golf is not one of those occupations in which you soon learn your level. There is no shape nor size of body, no

BOOK I - THE ART OF GOLF

awkwardness nor ungainliness, which puts good golf beyond one's reach. There are good golfers with spectacles, with one eye, with one leg, even with one arm. None but the absolutely blind need despair. It is not the youthful tyro alone who has cause to hope. Beginners in middle age have become great, and more wonderful still, after years of patient duffering, there may be a rift in the clouds. Some pet vice which has been clung to as a virtue may be abandoned, and the fifth-class player burst upon the world as a medal winner. In golf, whilst there is life there is hope.

It is generally agreed that the keenest pleasure of the game is derived from long driving. When the golfer is preparing to hit a far clean straight shot, he feels the joy of the strong man that rejoiceth to run a race; that is to say, the joy we have authority for believing that the Jewish runner felt. The modern sprinter experiences none. On the contrary, there is the anticipation, through fatigue of as much pain as if he were ringing the dentist's door bell. For the golfer in the exercise of his strength there is neither pain nor fatigue. He has the combined pleasures of an onlooker and a performer. The blow once delivered, he can stand at ease and be admired whilst the ball makes the running.

There is no such being as a golfer uninterested in his driving. The really strong player seems to value his least; but this is merely because so many of his shots are good that they do not surprise him. Let it, however, be suggested that some other is a longer driver than he, and the mask of apathy will at once fall from his face, his tongue will be loosened, and he will proceed to boast. Even when a man cannot feel that he drives quite as far as the best, his pride in his own frame is not necessarily destroyed as by most other sports. The runner, the jumper, the lifter of weights, even the oarsman, is crushed down into his true place by the brutal rudeness of competitive facts. Not so the golfer. A. says, 'I drive with a very light club, therefore admire my strength.' B. smiles complacently, whilst you marvel at the heaviness of his —a brawny muscular smile. Little C.'s club is nearly as long as himself. The inference is that little C.'s garments cover the limbs of a pocket Hercules. D. can drive as far with a cleek as common men with a club. D. is evidently a Goliath. The inferences may be all wrong. A. may be a scrag, C. a weed, D. merely beefy. On the other hand, each may be what he supposes himself. This is one of the glorious uncertainties of the game.

To some minds the great field which golf opens up for exaggeration is its chief attraction. Lying about the length of one's drives has this advantage over most forms of falsehood, that it can scarcely be detected. Your audience may doubt your veracity, but they cannot prove your falsity. Even when some rude person proves your shot to be impossibly long, you are not cornered. You admit to an exceptional loft, to a skid off a paling, or, as a last appeal to the father of lies, you may rather think that a dog lifted your ball. 'Anyhow,' you add conclusively, 'that is where we found it when we came up to it.'

BOOK I - THE ART OF GOLF

2
THE ORIGIN OF GOLF

Golf, besides being a royal game, is also a very ancient one. Although it cannot be determined when it was first played, there seems little doubt that it had its origin in the present geological period, golf links being, we are informed, of Pleistocene formation.

Confining ourselves to Scotland, no golfer can fail to be struck with the resemblance to a niblick of the so-called spectacle ornament of our sculptured stones.

Many antiquarians are of opinion that the game did not become popular till about the middle of the 15th century. This seems extremely probable, as in earlier and more lawless times a journey so far from home as the far-hole at St. Andrews would have been exceedingly dangerous for an unarmed man.

It is not likely that future research will unearth the discoverer of golf. Most probably a game so simple and natural in its essentials suggested itself gradually and spontaneously to the bucolic mind. A shepherd tending his sheep would often chance upon a round pebble, and, having his crook in his hand, he would strike it away; for it is as inevitable that a man with a stick in his hand should aim a blow at any loose object lying in his path as that he should breathe.

On pastures green this led to nothing: but once on a time (probably) a shepherd, feeding his sheep on a links—perhaps those of St. Andrews—rolled one of these stones into a rabbit scrape. 'Marry,' he quoth, 'I could not

BOOK I - **THE ART OF GOLF**

do that if I tried'—a thought (so instinctive is ambition) which nerved him to the attempt. But man cannot long persevere alone in any arduous undertaking, so our shepherd hailed another, who was hard by, to witness his endeavour. 'Forsooth, that is easy,' said the friend, and trying failed. They now searched in the gorse for as round stones as possible, and, to their surprise, each found an old golf ball, which, as the reader knows, are to be found there in considerable quantity even to this day. Having deepened the rabbit scrape so that the balls might not jump out of it, they set themselves to practising putting. The stronger but less skilful shepherd, finding himself worsted at this amusement, protested that it was a fairer test of skill to play for the hole from a considerable distance. This being arranged, the game was found to be much more varied and interesting. They had at first called it 'putty,' because the immediate object was to putt or put the ball into the hole or scrape, but at the longer distance what we call driving was the chief interest, so the name was changed to 'go off,' or 'golf.' The sheep having meantime strayed, our shepherds had to go after them. This proving an exceedingly irksome interruption, they hit upon the ingenious device of making a circular course of holes, which enabled them to play and herd at the same time. The holes being now many and far apart, it became necessary to mark their whereabouts, which was easily done by means of a tag of wool from a sheep, attached to a stick, a primitive kind of flag still used on many greens almost in its original form.

Since these early days the essentials of the game have altered but little. Even the styme must have been of early invention. It would naturally occur as a quibble to a golfer who was having the worst of the match, and the adversary. In the confidence of three or four up, would not strenuously oppose it.

That golf was taken up with keen interest by the Scottish people from an early day is evidenced by laws directed against those who preferred it to archery and church-going. This state of feeling has changed but little. Some historians are, however, of opinion that during the seventeenth century golf lost some of its popularity. We know that the great Montrose was at one time devoted to it, and that he gave it up for what would now be considered the inferior sport of Covenanter-hunting. It is also an historical fact that Charles I. Actually stopped in the middle of a game on Leith Links, because, forsooth, he learned that a rebellion had broken out in Ireland. Some, however, are of opinion that he acted on this occasion with his usual cunning—that at the time the news arrived he was being beaten, and that he hurried away to save his half-crown rather than his crown. Whatever the truth may be, it is certain that any one who in the present day abandoned a game because the stakes were not sufficiently high would be considered unworthy of the name of a golfer.

The rest of the history of the game, is it not written in Mr. Clark's book?

BOOK I - **THE ART OF GOLF**

3
THE NATURE OF THE GAME

Golf belongs to that large class of human games in which a ball plays the principal part. Balls of all sorts and sizes amuse men—hard ones, soft ones, large ones, small ones. These are treated in a variety of ways. They are struck, used to strike with, pushed against each other, knocked into holes, rolled as close as possible to things, battered against walls, knocked over nets, cuffed with the hand, jerked with the finger and thumb, struck with an instrument, kicked with the feet, etc. In some games the ball is buffeted whilst in motion, in others whilst at rest. In some, one player's aim is to make it go whilst others try to stop it, or both may want to keep it moving, each hoping that the other will fail to do so. In games where it is the adversary's object to stop the ball, he keeps his face towards it and catches it with his hands; when he loses by doing so his back is turned, and he runs (except in war, in which the adversary does not wish to be struck, but should nevertheless have his face to the ball). In some games there is but one ball, about which there is a continual struggle; in others, each has it alternately. There is a common element in them all—rivalry.

Now golf is a game in which each player has a small hard ball of his own, which he strikes with a stick whilst it is quiescent, with the intention of putting it into a hole. Abstractly he wishes to do this with as few blows as possible, concretely in fewer than his opponent. A round of the green is called a match. A match is the best of nine, twelve, or eighteen games. Each game is called a hole, because it ends at the bottom thereof. The tee is not, as in many other games, the object aimed at, but the point started from. It consists of a small pile of sand placed on the ground, and solidified by the palm of the hand. On this the ball is placed. Each blow or miss is called a stroke, that is to say—a stroke is constituted purely by intention. A stroke is not the same thing as a rub, which is usually a blow received by a third party, but it is nearly identical with a shot. The latter, however, does not include a miss in the same impartial way as the former.

The distance between the tees and the holes is from a hundred to five hundred yards. After leaving the tee, you are not allowed to do anything to the ball except strike it or swear at it until you have either given up the hole or got to the bottom of it. In each hole there is a flag, so that its whereabouts may be seen from a distance. This is temporarily removed when the player gets near it. The flags are little bits of cloth or a bunch of wool at the end of a stick or wire; but on greens where they are not habitually stolen, the whole flag is of iron, with the name and number of the hole printed on the top. These names are for the most part either geographical, personal, gastronomical, or arithmetical. The geographical names are suggested by peculiarities of the ground around or in front of the hole. If there are none, a wall or a bathing-machine in the neighbourhood may suggest a name. Holes called after people have usually been planned, laid out, and added to the course by their godfathers, who for the first ten years earn anything but gratitude, as these new holes are for a long time very rough and bad; a public-house or a refreshment stall in the neighbourhood of a hole is always recognised as its most important feature, and it is christened accordingly. The last hole is called the last, the one at the extremity of the links the far-hole, unless a public-house be there to make such a consideration unimportant; for it is admitted on all hands that the state of a man's stomach has much to do with his game.

The grounds on which golf is played are called links, being the barren sandy soil from which the sea has retired in recent geological times. In their natural state links are covered with long, rank benty grass and gorse. These get worn away by sheep and golfers, and short springy sandy turf is disclosed. The part of the links thus worn is the course. Links are too barren for cultivation; but sheep, rabbits, geese, and professionals pick up a precarious livelihood on them. A good course ought to be from 50 to 100 yards wide, the ground undulating or even hilly. The finer the turf is the better; but it is never perfect, because golfers are always slicing bits of it out with their clubs, quicker than the green-keeper can replace them, which is not saying much. When you find your ball lying on one of these scrapes, you bemoan; but it is only when breaks in the turf are found within twenty yards of the hole that the green-keeper is inexcusable.

On every course there ought to be plenty of hazards—that is, places where a shot is lost unless the driving be far enough, straight, or high. Off the course there are rabbit-holes, gorse bushes, railways, ploughed fields, gardens, and green-houses for crooked drivers; on it, bunkers or sand-holes for topped and short balls. The best kind of bunkers are natural. Those which are often visited usually have names, being called some man's nose or grave, or merely his bunker. To have a bunker named after you is a *monumentum aere perennius*. People like being godfathers to bunkers, although it is not usually complimentary to their driving. Where there is a lack of natural bunkers, artificial ones are dug. Walls, roads, ditches, and cops serve as hazards on the course, but these are not recognised as so desirable as bunkers.

BOOK I - **THE ART OF GOLF**

4
OF SETS OF CLUBS AND OTHER GOLFING APPURTENANCES

A SET of clubs may be defined as that assortment which the player's caddy carries in a cover on wet days. On fine days the player carries one club himself, either that which he has just used or the one he is about to employ.

I propose here to give a descriptive list of all the clubs which may or may not be in a set.

Nearly every one carries a play club, an instrument consisting of many parts. It has no legs, but a shaft instead. It has, however, a toe. Its toe is at the end of its face, close to its nose, which is not on its face. Although it has no body, it has a sole. It has a neck, a head, and clubs also have horns. They always have a whipping, but this has nothing to do directly with striking the ball. There is little expression in the face of a club. It is usually wooden; sometimes, however, it has a leather face. Clubs, without being clothed, occasionally have lead buttons, but never any button-holes. Clubs' heads are some black, some yellow, but colour is not due to any racial difference. From this description it will be easy to understand, without a diagram, what a club is like.

Spoons in most respects resemble clubs. Their faces are somewhat more open. There are long, short, and mid spoons, so called according to the length of the spoon.

BOOK I - **THE ART OF GOLF**

Brassies differ from spoons and play clubs in that they have brass bottoms which are screwed on.

Irons and cleeks have no sole. Their toes and noses are one and the same thing. They have iron faces. They are never whipped. They have sockets instead of necks. Their mode of locomotion is called 'approaching.' This is a short swinging gait. Sometimes, like play clubs, they drive, but no kind of club ever walks. There are different kinds of irons. A driving iron is used when it is too far to go without doing so. Lofting irons are more light-headed; they look like their work, but do not always do it. Cleeks are cleeks; they are not marked out from their creation for special uses. You may carry a driving and an approaching cleek, and a cleek for putting; but if some one steals your set, or if you die, your putting cleek may be used for driving, etc., etc.

Then there are putters. A good one ought to have the name 'Philp' stamped on it by somebody who must not tell you that he did it himself, or it must have belonged to some one else before you got it—either an old golfer who is dead (no matter whether he was a good holer-out or not) or else to a professional. No golfer with any self-respect uses a putter which he has bought new out of a shop for four shillings.

The niblick is too vulgar-looking for description in a polite treatise like this. He is a good fellow, however, ever ready to get you out of a hole.

These are the ordinary clubs, but there are many more. There are clubs with vulcanite heads, with german silver faces, with horn faces, clubs with bamboo shafts, clubs with cork grips. Old gentlemen use baffy spoons.

The 'President' is a niblick with a hole in it, which might be a very good niblick if it were not a president. It is called a president because the hole makes it clear-headed.

There are putting irons which are not irons but putters. People who putt badly use these, and are happy, although they only put it out of their power ever to putt well. There are putters made like croquet mallets, and there are perfectly upright ones. The latter are of no use to corpulent persons, as they cannot see the ball. Even the emaciated holeout better without them.

PART I - CH. 4 — OF SETS OF CLUBS AND OTHER GOLFING APPURTENANCES

Old-fashioned irons look like the missing link between a meat cleaver and a kitchen spoon. They all originally belonged to somebody's grandfather, and are only now to be found in glass cases or in the sets of very bad players, who, according to whether they had a golfing grandfather or not, expiscate or purchase them. The player, when getting this instrument from his caddy, does not ask for an iron in the usual way. He says 'Give me *my* heavy iron,' in a tone which causes the inexperienced adversary to despair. In reality, using an old-fashioned iron is the last expedient of those who cannot loft a ball with anything else. Even this expedient often fails, but defeat is at least avenged by the destruction of the green.

In addition to ordinary and extraordinary, there are special clubs (most of my own invention), few of which have as yet come into general use.

The automatic self-adjusting tee is a simple little contrivance whose name explains it. It prevents toeing, heeling, and topping, correcting errors in the swing of the club, acting somewhat in the same way as the compensating balance of a watch. It is a convenience to attach the automatic tee to your button-hole by a string which can be used to lift it to your hand after each shot, just as the organ-man jerks up his monkey when about to move on.

The portable platform for the feet, when the stance is bad, cannot be recommended. A spade to level the ground is more easily carried, and equally efficacious.

The 'Dynamite' is a very powerful weapon. It is a club in the face of which is inserted a small cartridge which explodes when the ball strikes it. With this club a good driver has been known to get past the long hole at St. Andrews in one shot. Loading for each drive is, however, so inconvenient that the dynamite has not come into general use. Besides, the trouble, the expense, and danger connected with it are so considerable as to make it unpopular. It would be rash to start on a round without a surgeon to carry the clubs, and surgeons of course charge more than ordinary caddies. If dynamites came into general use the rules of golf would require to be slightly altered. As they stand at present, holes would occasionally be lost because the player could not come up to time. Ten minutes is scarcely enough to allow for trepanning, which would often be necessary, as the cartridge frequently fails to go off till the club has reached the level of the head. With a dynamite it is safer to jerk

BOOK I - **THE ART OF GOLF**

than to take a full swing. The author does not recommend the dynamite. It reduces golf too nearly to the level of grouse driving or covert shooting.

The putter scale is a light iron tripod, into which you adjust an ordinary putter, placing the tripod so that the head of the putter rests behind the ball. On the tripod there is a scale showing the distance the putter is to be drawn back and let fall for each length of putt. Of course the player has to guess the said length for himself.

We now come to the subject of golf balls, of which, as of clubs, there are many kinds—not, however, like the clubs, to be used for different shots. There are twenty-sixes to twenty-nines, guttas, eclipses, black, white, and red balls, and the magnet ball. The numbers twenty-six to twenty-nine are purely sentimental. White balls are used when there is neither snow nor daisies, red ones when there is either, black ones by the poor and the stingy. Black eclipses are less objectionable than black guttas, for at least they are round. With a black eclipse one is allowed to pretend that the love of money is not the root of the evil. The magnetic ball is one of my own many inventions. It is simply an ordinary ball containing a small magnet which enables the player to hole-out with great precision, the iron in the hole (the 'tin,' it is called) attracting the magnet. For driving north the magnet ball is very good, but in driving east or west some allowance must be made for the skid of attraction. During a thunderstorm the carry of these balls is really astonishing.

'But,' cries the beginner despondingly, 'must I buy all these things?' He certainly may if he choose. Like some patent medicines, if they do no good, they will do no harm. The usual course, however, for the tyro is reluctantly to be persuaded to buy a cleek and a driver, and to get the loan of a ball. This is sure to decide him to go in for the game, and he buys a full set—namely a driver, a long spoon, a mid spoon, a short spoon, a cleek, an iron niblick, a putter, if he goes to a club maker. If he buys a friend's spare clubs, they will be a more necessitous-looking lot, the shafts either twisted or too thick to twist. This does not much matter, as the whole set will be broken several times over before the tyro begins to develop notions of his own. With an old coat, nailed boots, and someballs, he is ready to start. Gloves for blistered hands, pitch to make the gloves grip, sticking-plaster for frayed fingers, a knife for sharp nails, elastic wristlets for started sinews, may be purchased either at once or as the necessity for them arises. As soon as the tyro is

PART I - CH. 4 — OF SETS OF CLUBS AND OTHER GOLFING APPURTENANCES

admitted to a club, it is his duty to buy a golfing umbrella for the use of the members.

Bad players always carry a very large set, but the converse of this proposition is not true, many good ones doing the same. Still, there are certain inferences to be drawn from sets of clubs. One need never be afraid to give a shade of odds to a player who carries three spoons. It is safer not to bet with a man who has none. Why bad players carry all these spoons I have never been able to make out. Perhaps it is to encourage themselves with—to use and discard as each in rotation proves itself ineffectual. It is certain that one or other becomes for the time being favourite. It is the best club he ever had; he can drive further with it than with a play club (a doubtful advantage, one would think. Would a man praise a putter which sent a two-yard putt three past the hole?) The largeness of a bad player's set is usually due to excess of wooden clubs. Approaching, being all a fluke, he leaves to chance. The good player with notions, on the other hand, runs riot in irons and cleeks, mashies, niblicks, and putters, each of which is supposed to have specialties in the way of loft, length of carry, etc. etc. That constantly changing does not ruin his play is because of the extra care needed to hit accurately. The man of one iron is apt now and then to miss from too implicit trust in the familiar face which has never deceived him for many a round.

BOOK I - **THE ART OF GOLF**

5
OF CADDIES

Caddies are persons employed to carry golfers' clubs. Some people call them 'caudies,' others try to do without them; but experience teaches that a bad one is better than none.

On the older greens, where carrying is established as a free trade, there is a very miscellaneous selection of caddies—boys, ragamuffins just out of prison, workmen out of a job, and professional carriers. All but the last ought to be avoided.

A good boy to carry is not a bad thing in its way. From him too much must not be expected. If the tees he makes are not over two inches in diameter, if each time a club is required he is not further than three minutes' walk from his master, if he knows the names of the clubs, he is a good boy. But on free greens, where there are professionals, the boys do not come up to this standard. They are, however, cheaper than professionals. The workman out of a job is not cheaper, besides being more inefficient than a boy.

From men who have adopted carrying as a trade, the golfer is entitled to expect the highest standard of efficiency. If he carries for you regularly, the professional ought to know what club you intend to take, and to give it without being asked. When you are in doubt about how to play your shot, he ought to confirm you in the opinion you have formed regarding it. He must never show the just contempt he has for your game.

Carrying clubs is one of the most agreeable trades open to the lower orders. In it an amount of drunkenness is tolerated which in any other would land the men in the workhouse. A very low standard of efficiency and very

BOOK I - THE ART OF GOLF

little work will secure a man a decent livelihood. If he is civil, willing to carry for three or four hours a day, and not apt to drink to excess before his work is done, he will earn a fair wage, and yet be able to lie abed till nine in the morning like a lord. If he does not drink (this is a hard condition, as he has little else to do), he is positively well-off; if he makes balls, and can play a good game himself, he may become rich. A caddy who, in addition, employs his leisure (of which there will still remain a great deal) in acquiring the elements of an education, may rise to be a green-keeper or a club-master, and after his death be better known to fame than many a defunct statesman or orator.

As a rule, however, the professional caddy is a contented being, spending what he gets as soon as he gets it, a Conservative in politics, a heathen in religion. He is a Conservative because he likes and admires gentlemen, who, according to his idea, are the class which plays golf and overpays him. He is a heathen, churches being to his mind as sacred to gentlemen as clubs.

A caddy's occupation being connected with a sport, he hates anything which would tend to make it a steady, regular wage-earning business. Accordingly badges, tariffs, and benefit societies he abominates. Clubs or eating-houses got up for his advantage he will have nothing to do with, if conditioned with the payment of a periodical sum, however small. A coffee-house erected for him unconditionally is well enough. It can do no more harm than the gift of a suit of old clothes too ragged to wear. A caddy is always grateful for, and solicitous of, suits of old tweeds. If you offer him a frock-coat, he suspects you of quizzing. The sumptuary laws in his set make the wearing of frock-coats or knickerbockers impossible. Nor is a gift of shirts appreciated by caddies. Our shirts are too light in colour for their fashion of wearing one till it is only fit to send to the papermaker.

On free greens the question of paying caddies is rather a troublesome one. There is usually an understood tariff. But as ragged children, miners out of work, discharged coachmen and butlers, drunkards who have spent their all, and ex-criminals are entitled to be paid on this scale for very inferior work, the professional carriers naturally expect more. What this more ought to be no man knows. It is useless to ask a friend what he pays, for he will not tell the truth. He will understate the amount. He dare not admit to having overpaid his caddy. Since John Stuart Mill and others made the law of supply and demand popular, the morality of stinginess, except where your name is to

PART I - CH. 5 – OF CADDIES

appear in a subscription list, has been fully admitted. Therefore to pay a caddy as much as will be accepted without grumbling, and to announce it, will lead you into an argument. Here is a specimen of the kind of thing I myself have gone through:—

'How much did you give your caddy?'
(Rather ashamed) 'Four shillings' (having given five).
' What nonsense! Three shillings are more than enough.'
'Perhaps' (rather mildly, but feeling right).
'Just spoiling the market. Three shillings for three hours' work!—more than any skilled work man can earn. Besides, it does no good—they just spend it.'

I submit; but alone in the evening I have it out with my hard-headed friend. I say:—

'Sir, when you accuse me of spoiling the market you are merely degrading free trade principles to the position of handmaids of your selfish avarice. Free trade can live alongside of charity. If not, I go for charity. You seem to have heard of Adam Smith's *Wealth of Nations*, but not of his treatise on the *Moral Sentiments*. You have evidently read neither; or, if you will argue on the selfish principle, it is politic to overpay caddies. Cheapening golf is debasing golf. I wish it were compulsory to pay a sovereign a round. These school-boys and mechanics, and pot-hat golfers with a club and a cleek, are a nuisance. I wish gutta-percha balls had never been invented, and, as for eclipses, they are simple communism. They rob wealth of its advantages.

' "The caddies will only drink the more if overpaid," you say. Indeed! and to what good purpose do you apply the money you grudge to the poor? Is there something nobler in your gout and dyspepsia than in my caddy's red nose. Or no! I do not despise your gout (I feel a twitch myself), but your incapacity for taking pleasure in giving it (cheaply) to others is what I contemn. An Epicurean with the vices of a Stoic, and none of his virtues! I shall grossly overpay my caddy in future.'

On the newer greens, private ones, and those far from a town—in short, where it has been possible to reduce the carrying proletariat to subjection—the player will find a crowd of boys, with a sprinkling of meek men, near the club-house, from whom to choose a caddy. Under these circumstances a boy should be chosen. The men are no better than they, and, being grown up, not so scoldable. From boys, as I have said, the same standard of carrying cannot be expected as from professionals, but a well-chosen boy is satisfactory enough. He must not be too big. The big ones are usually louts who cannot stay the distance. He must not be too intelligent-looking. The bright-eyed, eager boy is apt to be admiring Nature whilst you are waiting for a club, and his interest in the game being awakened by a sharp word, it becomes for the moment too intense. He arranges the clubs whilst you are putting, or wanders into inconvenient situations to see you hole-out. The intelligent boy is sometimes himself a golfer. For the first half-round, whilst studying your game, he is a perfect treasure. After that, with the arrogance of youth, he assumes that he knows more than you do, and clubs are offered before asked, advice given in regard to distances, etc. Another kind of boy is chatty, and his anecdotes, autobiographical and local, which at first amuse, become intolerable as the match closes in darker and darker each hole. An embryo village plumber or carpenter, neither clever nor stupid, will carry best.

On his home green the golfer soon settles upon a professional or a boy to his mind, according as his is a free or a controlled green. On the latter, when he is merely on a visit, there is not much trouble either. Any person has the moral courage to pay off a child at the end of the day if he does not suit, and to try another. It is different when you have once employed a man. Steaming, say to St. Andrews, the player is filled with anxious thought regarding caddies. He makes up his mind what manner of man to employ; but scarcely does he set foot in the station before he is bewildered by a dozen clamouring volunteers, unless he has had the forethought to disguise himself as a commercial traveller or as a tourist. Even disguise will only delay the inevitable for a few moments; when the tell-tale club box comes out of the van he is discovered. It is of course possible to flee before it is laid on the platform, leaving secret instructions with a trusty porter. But if the player has ever visited St. Andrews before, disguise and flight are of no avail. Years may have elapsed since his last visit, nevertheless he will be greeted by name. Several will assert that they carried for him before. He must either be more than humanly firm, or else be diplomatic, asserting, for instance, that he has a sprained wrist and does not intend to play, or before he has got to his lodgings he will find himself the thrall of perhaps the same being who poisoned his last visit. It might seem that the simplest course was to employ a boy so small that the weakest of men could dismiss him if unsatisfactory. But somehow there are none such at St. Andrews. There are carrying persons with

PART I – CH. 5 – OF CADDIES

the outward semblance of boys, but these chew, smoke, and drink. It seems as if education or something bridged the space between childhood and manhood.

Should the player escape to his lodgings unpledged, his best plan is to get down to the club as unobtrusively as possible, and make a selection from the window with an opera-glass. A caddy once engaged, most men make the best of him. Should he disappear for a day or two, having gone on the spree, you are not necessarily free from him. You have probably furnished the means for the debauch by paying some days' wages in advance, and it seems hard to sacrifice the money entirely, more especially as the miscreant will return humble and apologetic.

Yet it is not so difficult as it seems, even for a man of average will, to dismiss a caddy who is not to his taste. The best plan is to pay him at the end of the day, and say nothing about it, making some excuse for taking your set into the club-house instead of leaving them in his charge. Next day you take on a fresh caddy by simply handing the clubs to him, and it is astonishing how little demur the old one will make. Caddies are a race as proud as they are improvident, and, however sycophantic under ordinary circumstances, they will take no other revenge for this insulting sort of dismissal than to assert that they left because underpaid, and because it is too wearisome to carry for such a bad golfer.

To summarise my advice in regard to caddies on greens to which the golfer is a temporary visitor, I advise him, where there is a corps of badged and licensed caddies, to choose the smallest boy who seems capable of getting round, and to keep him, if he stands still during play, and is generally within earshot when a club is required. It is necessary that he should not leave the ball in the hole, nor lose clubs on the way round. On free greens, persons having the outward semblance of boys are to be avoided, and a professional chosen if a good one be known to the player. If, however, he is a complete stranger to the green, his safest course is to select a decrepit old man. His age proves him not to be an inconveniently excessive drinker, whilst being steady and still a carrier of clubs further proves that he is a meek, mild, mindless creature, who will trudge round without interfering.

BOOK I - **THE ART OF GOLF**

PART II

OF PLAYING THE GAME

PLATE I. ADDRESSING FOR A DRIVE

PART II - CH. 1 – OF DRIVING IN GENERAL

1
OF DRIVING IN GENERAL

It is a common complaint that, with so many things to be thought of at golf, accuracy is almost impossible. This is not the way to state the case. It should rather stand: If points of style are thought about and trusted to, bad shots will be frequent. That there is some secret which, if discovered, would make our driving infallible is a belief which dies hard. Nostrum after nostrum is tried day after day. Hope is quickly followed by a despairing desire to break the whole set or spitefully to present them to a friend, so that he too may suffer. Time after time the golfer thinks he has discovered what he was doing wrong. He gushes about it, or gives half a crown to the professional who has found it out. Alas! there is no side road to golf. It can never be certain. With careful aiming for each shot, it may become pretty steady, but even with this there will be better and worse drives. It would be going too far to say dogmatically that nothing but aim must have a place in the golfer's thought, although it is perhaps best so; but certainly if stance, or swing, or address are dwelt upon it must be as subsidiary points. 'There is something wrong about my style,' says the golfer, 'which is causing me to drive so short.' 'Not at all,' say I; 'aim more accurately.' Hand and eye and body must concentrate themselves on, restrain themselves to, hitting cleanly, fairly, firmly; not greedily, wildly, gaily. The golfer cannot afford to allow a favourite muscle to disport itself. The eye is officer, the muscles liners, each doing the duty required of them and no more. The tongue only may wag as it will without doing harm or good.

There is no alternative. It is of no use to say to the ball, 'I will make thee magnificent gifts if thou wilt yield thy secret. I am ready to wrench and thump for thee, to stand nearer or further from thee, to bend the knee. I will imitate

BOOK I - THE ART OF GOLF

the swing of a Morris to conciliate thee.' The ball wants none of these self-glorifying gifts. Abandon body and will to hitting, and the hidden secret of the mystic 27 ½ shall be revealed.

Still, the amateur golfer must be allowed to theorise to some extent. It is a necessary concession to him as a thinking animal. Within the indicated limits, it will do little or no harm; but because he does not think the professional is better than the amateur, the uncultivated beats the educated player. The former finds enough intellectual pabulum for his duller brain in the prosy principles of simply slogging. To grasp the idea of doing so, sufficiently occupies his thoughts. For an educated man to confine himself to so narrow a range is irksome. The professional's theorising does not go beyond, 'I hit lazy —I heeled— I topped—I sclaffed—I toed.' To perceive so much is an effort of observation. The amateur must consciously exclude thought, if he is to confine himself to such elementary facts. It is noticeable that he (in distinction from the professional) asks, 'Why did I heal—top—sclaff—toe?' —and if golf is to be a pleasure, not a business, he must be allowed to ask these things. The amateur, if keen, is inductive, deductive, inventive. If not, he is apt to give up the game as too simple. On the other hand, if he does not recognise 'hitting the ball' as his business, theory as his recreation, he becomes so bad a player that he nearly gives up.

'Keep your eye on the ball,' is the categorical imperative of the golfing world; below which there is room for much harmless digression. Say that I am playing very well, but that there is some irrational difference between my style with short spoon and driver. A professional would not know this of himself, or, if told, would not care. It is outside the range of his ideas. 'I'm driving fine,' he would say. But your amateur cannot rest till he has corrected one of the styles into uniformity with the other, or found a rational cause for the difference. If A. drives high, B. low, is it possible that A. with a university education, can rest satisfied with merely observing this fact? No. He will try to find out why, and, having done so, will either modify his style, or register to himself the conclusion that he prefers to drive high. The amateur ought to think. The man who buys a baffy because he can't drive with a cleek has not a cultivated mind. If he carry both—if his set is composed of a lot of preposterous inventions of his own, all of which he uses in turn, he increases the difficulties of the game indeed, but is nevertheless noble in not accepting defeat at the hands of any club.

PART II - CH. 1 – OF DRIVING IN GENERAL

Experiment, so long as the major premise is not lost sight of, is the recreation which may be allowed to the golfer whilst attending to his business. It is a necessary concession to human nature; it is the spoonful of jelly with the Gregory's mixture; it is the working man's half-holiday, and a great many other analogous things. By all means let us have our clubs long or short, heavy or light, upright or flat. The golfer may be trusted in the long run to give up anything which is too fanciful, although for a time he may spoil his play with a fad. It is harmless to buy clubs from professionals for gold, no better than what are for sale in the shops for four shillings.

The player may experiment about his swing, his grip, his stance. It is only when he begins asking his caddy's advice that he is getting on dangerous ground. A professional can play. It does not follow that he can teach others. He can comfortably assimilate foods and drinks (more particularly the latter) which would prostrate those he carries for on a bed of sickness. Is he therefore an authority on dietetics? But being constantly asked for advice, the professional has a few stock prescriptions which he gives recklessly, doing more harm than good. So anxious is the golfer to learn without plodding that he uses these eagerly. The truth is, your caddy is a good judge of distance and direction. He can advise well what club to take, but as to how to use it, he may show, but ought not to be asked to advise. For instance, the player is persistently driving to the right or to the left of the line he wishes to follow. Let him correct his stand, but let him do so accepting the fact that he is standing wrong because his eye is at fault. Let him try to see straight. He ought to come away from his ball, and take up his position afresh with careful reference to his intended direction. But the usual thing is to accept the caddy's dictum (stand 'more behind' or stand 'more in front') blindly, and, without looking up, to scuffle about with the feet. When told, 'That will do,' the player either misses, being stiff and twisted; or—what is more common—he scuffles back to where he was at first, like a sitting hen moved from her eggs, and drives off the line. Having done this latter a dozen times, it seems that the position the caddy advises must be the solution of the difficulty. He, who has been driving persistently to the right, has got into the position shown in Fig. 1; in other words, his left foot has got nearer the ball than the right, which it has a strong natural inclination to do, and the tendency is to drive in the direction of the arrow, and not of the dots. What ought really to be done is that the player stand up naturally and aim carefully. The result of applying a

BOOK I - THE ART OF GOLF

correction such as 'stand behind' will not make the ball go straight until the awkward position of Fig. 2 is reached.

It may seem that if the advice, instead of being, as it always is, 'Stand more behind,' were 'Change the position of one of your feet,' the result would not be to produce the style of Fig. 2. But this would alter the player's distance from the ball, and, instead of being the beginning of a cycle of fatal and deceptive good driving, would inaugurate a round of tops, heels, or pulls, to the immediate discredit of the caddy. If I wished to be cynical, I should say, therefore, 'Change one foot' is the better advice. But no! the proper thing to do is to try again. Anything else is absurd. Were a caddy to say, 'You would drive better with my arms,' or were he to offer the loan of any other limb, the nonsense would be evident. Yet the absurdity of using his eyes does not seem apparent. The player allows himself to be put in position like a lay figure. Even suppose he understands the orders, and does pose as the caddy intends, a lay figure cannot hit a ball. One man's mind cannot work another man's body.

The following is a specimen of what may be expected if a player hopes to drive by taking advice instead of aiming at the ball with his own eyes.

Player (1st shot).—' Why did I heel that?'
Caddy.—'Drawing in your arms.'
Player (2d shot).—'Why did I pull that?'
Caddy.—' Drawing in your arms.'
Player (heeling again).—'There ! I did not draw in my arms that time.'
Caddy.—' No sir, ye cut it.'
Player (4th shot).—' There 's that confounded heel again.'
Caddy.—'Ye didna cut it. Ye hit it clean enough that time; but ye were stanin' that way.'
Player (examining his club face after a vicious top).—'Right off the heel too. What on earth is the meaning of it?'
Caddy.—'Ye 're fallin' in on the ball.'
Player (6th shot).—'Another top.'
Caddy.—'Ay, ye fell right back.'
Player.—'Oh, hang it! with so many things to be thought of all at once, steady play is almost impossible.'

PART II - CH. 1 – OF DRIVING IN GENERAL

Having heard all that passed I here remark with a smile—meaning sardonic and oracular—'Not almost, but quite impossible.'

Another error, nearly as bad as to take advice blindly, is for a player, when standing wrongly, to try to pull or push the ball according to the correction for direction desired. Let him rather correct his stance. Faults covered by faults do not cancel each other. The second fault only gives the ball an additional chance of escape from the way it should go. Far the wisest course is to apply a direct remedy. The player whose driving is feeble should hit harder, unless it is because he is nipping, or not hitting off the middle of the club, in which cases he ought not to nip, or should aim for the centre of the head. It must be admitted, however, that it is much easier, for the moment, to apply indirect corrections, and few indeed are the formed golfers on whose style the cicatrices of early patchings are not visible. Some of these are almost harmless; but others may cripple the player permanently, although at the time, like new brooms, they sweep away the ball clean. For instance, there is a class of stereotyped faults whose origin is traceable to a miserable time when every ball was hopelessly heeled. If the wretched man (oh, how despondent he was then!) had only attributed his misery to the true cause—namely, that he was heeling—the fault would have corrected itself. But he found a royal road to the middle of his club. You see the former victims of heeling either standing nine feet from their ball and taking a header at it, or so crouching on their haunches that you are astonished, when the stroke is made, to find player and ball are not both left seated. If you see a golfer draw his club so slowly back that ten is easily counted before it begins to return, as a tyro he has been one of those who fervently wished that balls had no top. Again there are men who face the east when they mean to go north. The sole ambition of these has been to drive a very long ball. They are victims to the truth that a ball so struck will sometimes go further north than one aimed to that part of the compass. But what does it profit when it as often goes east or west ? Such fill men's gardens with golf balls, and lose many more in the waves of the sea.

Do I maintain, then, the reader may ask, that every one ought to have the same style? By no means; on the contrary, for you or me to model ourselves on a champion is about as profitless as to copy out Hamlet in the hope of becoming Shakespeare. If we have a neat style, so be it; and if we have begun before our hair is grey or gone, it probably so is. But for a fat man to model himself on a swank youth is frivolous. We cannot ignore our deformities.

BOOK I - THE ART OF GOLF

Your shoulders are heavy, your fore-arm puny; it is useless to rebel. A very easy long swing is impossible with such a configuration: you may play well—beat the swank youth very likely,—but only if you are content with a stiff style. Are you lank and loose-limbed?—So will your driving be, if left to develop naturally.

On the other hand, there is no more fruitful source of bad golf than to suppose that there is some best style for each individual which must be searched out by him if he is to get the best results out of himself. In a broad and general way, each player ought to have, and has, a style which is the reflection of himself—his build, his mind, the age at which he began, and his previous habits. The ex-cricketer reflects cricket. The rowing man has a straight back, and there are characteristics in each golfer the history of which it is more or less difficult to trace. This is his style; and, however much he may feel he modifies it, to an onlooker, it will remain the same—because it is the same. It is not the general principles that a man has before him (of these he is seldom conscious) when trying to find out his absolutely best. It is some minor detail of which he exaggerates the importance—some particular twitch, which has arrested his attention after a very satisfactory drive. This will be stubbornly pursued till it is exaggerated into a mannerism to which it is secretly believed everything good in driving is due. If golfers could only become convinced that no mannerism is of the slightest value, that there are fifty different styles (by style I mean here the petty variables of which alone we are conscious) in which a good shot can be made, that it is not indispensable to repeat in the next the same movements felt in one good shot, bad ones would be less frequent. There is, I repeat, a categorical imperative in golf—'Hit the ball;' but there are no minor absolutes. There is no best shape, or weight, or lie of clubs—no best stance, grip, or swing. From the nature of the case, one does not change his driver during the round; but the other things may vary every shot—nay, will, unless one makes a point of preventing them, sacrificing ease and accuracy to a consistency which, if stubbornly insisted on, may permanently cramp driving. There is no better proof of this argument than to watch a boy of about twelve, who hits every ball clean and (for his strength) far, of whom there are very many. At this age even the broad features of style are unsettled. At one moment he swings round his neck, at the next round his shoulder, his feet near together or wide apart, according to the unconscious fancy of the moment. And yet each ball flies away with unerring certainty. This should teach us that when we think we see what we are doing wrong-, or what we are doing right, that when we cling to this bit of style or avoid that, we are merely distracting our attention from the main issue.

BOOK I - **THE ART OF GOLF**

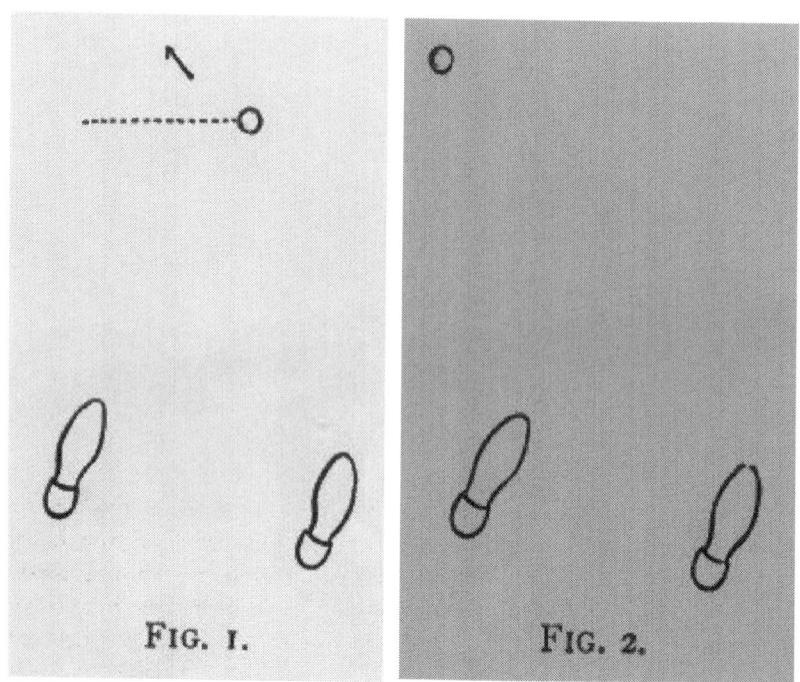

PART II - CH. 1 – OF DRIVING IN GENERAL

2
OF STYLE OF DRIVING

For the purpose of analysis the swing of the golfer may be divided into three parts: 1st, Position; 2nd, Address; 3rd, Swing proper.

Position.—Some treatises on the game tell us in feet and inches the distance the player ought to stand from the ball; in degrees, the angle at which it ought to be placed between his feet. Such information, whether true or not, is unpractical. Arithmetic is required to count the shots, but cannot assist us in making them; and as for mensuration—well! a six-inch scale marked on the putter shaft often prevents disputes. Roughly speaking, however, it may be laid down that one ought to stand what professionals call square to the ball— that is to say, facing at right angles to the direction it is meant to drive in. Any decided deviation from this position is a mistake, although scarcely any one adheres to it absolutely. Many place the left foot nearer the ball than the right, commonly called standing 'in front' (though different from the fault of doing so illustrated in Fig. 1), and lean more weight on the former than on the latter. This is because the left leg of most men is the stronger. Some of the finest players stand to their ball in this way; but on the whole it is to be avoided, because it tends to produce wildness and uncertainty of driving. Obviously the position offers facilities for a long swing back, and those who are lured on by the charms of an occasional raker will adopt it. Why occasional? The reason seems to be that when the heel of the left foot leaves the ground most of the weight of the body is supported on its toes, which unsteadies the player's balance, and consequently his driving. The remedy is scarcely to let the heel leave the ground at all—a correction made by all steady drivers who have acquired this style. The segment of swing thus chopped off is, however, lost entirely. It cannot be added to the other end, as, of course, the stance which takes the right shoulder out of the road brings the other more forward. The result is shorter driving if steady off the tee, but not from bad lies; for this stance, by enabling the player to get 'his shoulders well into it,' is very commanding. On the whole, however, it is better to stand square or open as in Fig. 4 or 5. This gives freer scope for a full second half to the swing, which, I shall insist further on, is of more importance than the first half. Exaggeration, even conscious posing, in either direction, will produce, in the first case, pulling, wildness, topping; in the second, heeling, skying, or at best feebleness.

If we observe a player who stands 'square' about to strike, it will be apparent that his ball is at a more obtuse angle to his left than to his right foot. If the player stands 'in front' (Fig. 3), as it is called, the ball is more nearly still in a line with the left, the opposite being true when the stance is 'open.' But in practice he ought not to attempt to measure this angle, for the all-sufficient reason that his measurement will be wrong. To prove this, we have but to ask an experienced player who stands 'square,' at what angle he poses to his ball. He will say at an equal angle from each foot. We have but to watch him play to be convinced that he is mistaken. That he cannot measure it will be made evident by a little experiment regarding another point. Some players turn their toes in, some out. (Which is right? Either, provided the position be not strained.) Now if you place yourself opposite a ball, at what some books call the proper angle, it will be found that by pivoting on the heels, although your place, or its, is in no way changed, a drive would be impossible without lifting one foot and putting it down somewhere else.

As the angle at which the player ought to stand can only be determined by instinct, as a comprehensive glance at feet and ball will give no information even to engineers accustomed to mensuration, so there is no measurable proper distance at which we ought to be from the ball. Much depends on the lie of the club, its length, that of the man, and his style. Yet the varying of it is a common cause of bad driving. Quite suddenly, from unconsciously changing it, a player goes off his game: without knowing it, he begins to hold his hands too far reached out, or to stoop forward with his body. It is useless for him to note his proper distance some time when he is driving well, for he may maintain that and yet be all wrong. For instance, he may be cancelling his overreach by standing very upright, or stooping and tucking in his arms. Always to take a natural pose towards the ball must be the result of habit.

PART II - CH. 1 – OF DRIVING IN GENERAL

Even the best players go wrong occasionally from getting into the way of standing at the wrong distance. The worst of it is, stooping or overreaching soon feels natural, and the bad driving is ascribed to some other cause. In its proper place, I will point out a few of the results as regards the ball, which ought to awaken suspicion that our position has got wrong.

How far apart the feet ought to be is the next point. About this, as about so many other things, there is no hard and fast rule. It is sufficient to point out that the closer they are, the freer will be your swing; but when they get too near together your driving will become feeble and uncertain in direction. On the other hand, a wide stride stiffens the player, thus shortening his driving, although it gives him power. In a bunker, or in a bad lie, it is politic to straddle more than usual, if you remember at the same time to swing short.

Address.—After taking their stance, most players are in the habit of making some preliminary motions with their club before proceeding to drive. In some cases these flourishes are slight, in others more free: but, whichever they be, they are only reasonable and advantageous, if made, to waken up the muscles, and to let the hands settle to their grip. With too many players, addressing the ball is merely an excuse for other thoughts. One will take this opportunity to scuffle round his ball, another to get nearer it or further from it, another to lift his toes and assure himself that his heels are well on the ground, another to look at his feet or the position of his hands, another to hunch up a shoulder, another to turn in a toe. In other words, the time during which the player should be getting concentrated on the work of hitting, many waste in thinking of the quackeries which they hope will take the responsibility of aiming off their shoulders. Some of those who thus waste the precious moments make no pretence of shaking themselves together. They stand stock-still. What are they thinking of? Are they bidding a fond adieu to the ball, shrewdly suspecting that the club head may not be passing that way on its return journey. Slowly and reluctantly at last club and ball part, when suddenly whack! From others there are storm warnings. The club rises, and returns solemnly—Once! twice! Thrice! The player seems to say, 'I warn you, look out. Look out once! twice! thrice! Very well, take that, and off you go! Then there is the elbow twitch, which seems to say, 'I am just shaking my clothes loose to go for you, and getting my arms free to follow you.' It is a bragging kind of address, which threatens a strong blow, and is really preliminary to a weak one. The confident twiddle which makes no pretence of aiming, but commandingly points out to the ball the direction of the hole, and is followed by an angry quick swing, such as comes unawares behind a disobedient child, is not so sure to strike home as the blow it is compared to.

Some twiddles are complimentary to faults which the player proposes to avoid. A long, slow straight motion over the ball foreshadows a determination to follow it well. A stiff small one means that the player is bent on gripping tight. A quick jerky one betrays the intention of driving a screamer. There is the sanguine, the phlegmatic, the healthy, the headachy flourish, and a thousand more. None of these, except in so far as they suggest that the player has a right or a wrong idea as to how the fact of a palpable hit is to be accomplished, are essential. But placing the club behind the ball for an instant after them is essential, if the shot is not to be more or less bad. Although the address is usually a shadow of things to come, it is no guarantee of them. Free preliminaries are quite compatible with a cramped performance, and vice versa.... It may be said, then, Why not abandon them altogether? Why not place the club behind the ball, and strike at once? In these cases, where addressing the ball consists in merely making ornamental flourishes, or when they are gone through to give the player time to speculate on the chances of a miss, or to call up before his imagination a view of the bunker in front which he has just taken a last glance at, they would be better dispensed with. But, properly apprehended, they have their uses, some of which we have indicated: the chief one, I wish now to insist upon.

'How ought I to grip my club?' is a question which causes lifelong trouble to, and bars the progress of, many players. Addressing the ball means working their hands into some cramped position. They arrange the left hand tight, the right loose or tight, in the palm or in the fingers, under the club, over it, or with the knuckles pointing in some prescribed direction, according to whose disciple they are. There is scarcely a modification of holding with two hands which some one has not adopted as his grip, each giving its owner a sense of command over the club, so long as it is at rest, behind the ball. That a player should give attention to this important matter is right enough; but the mistake usually made is to get the hands into the most efficient position for dealing a heavy, instead of a swift blow, without reference to the most essential point in a grip—namely, that it be so arranged as to prevent the club either slipping or twisting in the palms during any part of the swing. If a player gets his hands under the club handle (see Figs. 8 and 9) it is impossible to take more than a

PART II - CH. 1 – OF DRIVING IN GENERAL

half swing without letting go. If (see Fig. 10) he have the right more under than the left, and tight (a grip one is apt to adopt when a 'screamer' is contemplated), anything but a swing round the waist must bring the club head back to the ball turned in (which is the secret of the screamer when it comes off, and also the cause of its failing so often).

If any one by chance has read this last paragraph carefully, he will feel pretty certain that I am about to describe the proper position and tightness of each hand. But he will be wrong. On the contrary, my view is that players may take great liberties with their grip,—at least with that of their right hand,—without affecting driving. The club may be sunk in the palm, to save a sore finger, or held in the fingers If the palm be painfully horny, without prejudice to play, so long as it is so held as not to slip or turn one hair's-breadth throughout the shot. Nay! in the right it may be even allowed to turn. In fact, if a player grip as in Fig. 10, he must hold loose with the right, and allow the club to slip round if his swing be perfect, otherwise his wrist becomes locked. Of this a trial swing will convince any one. It is only possible with a grip as in Figs. 6 and 7 for the right hand to remain glued to the club throughout a perfect swing. 'How is the grip to be tested for adherence during the swing?' is the real question, which the address ought to solve thus:—Having placed himself opposite the ball, let the player take hold of his club loosely, but so that, if held short, the end of the shaft would pass under the wrist bones (somewhat as in Figs. 6 and 7). Let him swing it backwards and forwards freely over the ball, describing an elongated eight, whose length is limited by the locking-point of the wrist joints. After two or three such continuous figures have been described, the hands, still holding loosely, will settle themselves into a proper relation to each other, and to the shot. The club will then be placed behind the ball, the grasp tightened just as it is, and the blow delivered. Whether both should be tightened, or only the left—whether it is into the fingers, or the palm, these movements are to adjust the club—are immaterial points, which may be left to individual taste. Nor ought the amount of tightening to be treated as important. Some only tighten a little, some as much as they can; all that can be said is, that the limit of permissible looseness is overstepped when, in the course of sweeping away the ball, there is any slipping or turning in the left hand at the very least. The preliminary flourish under discussion will be detected in the driving of the best and, freest players. Should an elongated eight be found on any ancient Egyptian monument, it is certainly the symbol for golf, and will prove that venerable nation to have played the game. I say this flourish can be 'detected' in a good style; but a practised player does not require to pass over his ball more than once, or he may even pretermit all, except the merest rudiment. He has a proper hold at once, without searching for it, and can at once proceed unhesitatingly to strike. There is no pause, after the club has been placed behind the ball, to allow a final and fatal alteration to be made. It is interesting confirmation of the soundness of what I am advancing, that fine players, many of whom are proverbial for the instantaneousness of their address, are often more elaborate in a big match. Whereas a mere rudiment of a flourish is all they ordinarily indulge in, this becomes one or more complete eights, when a single mistake might be fatal. It is as if they said, 'I am almost certain to grip rightly; but it is as well to test it.'

Whether this plan of preliminary flourish is or is not the best, there is no doubt the grip should be found by some sort of trial swing, not by placing the club behind the ball, and settling down as comfortably as possible. The true grip is that which accommodates Itself to a free swing, not to a commanding stance. Indeed players may be divided into two classes, according as they act upon or ignore this principle. The one arrives at the position of the hands typified In Figs. 6 and 7, and perhaps Fig. 10; the other is prone to the fault shown in Figs. 8 and 9. The one makes its flourishes, places its club for an instant behind the ball, and without hesitation strikes. If they allow it to dwell longer, it is not comfortable perhaps. Nor need it be. Ease whilst swinging, not whilst at rest, is the essential thing. The other finds its grip whilst the club is at rest, and then proceeds to flourishes. Take the case of a player of this class who makes the orthodox figure-eight gyration. He takes his grip, makes a motion over the ball, and, unless by chance it is a true one, disturbs it by so doing. You may see him pause a moment to rearrange it; the other accepts the disturbance as a proper correction. Whatever the prowess of the player, his class in this respect can be detected by watching whether, after putting his club finally behind the ball, he hesitates or strikes at once. Nearly all bad players belong to the class which does not arrive at its grip by experiment but dogmatically; not that all in it are bad, however. Their grip may by chance be good, or they may have the tact to accommodate their swing to the conditions they have imposed upon it. But assuredly this common error of taking hold of the club in the most comfortable way for being photographed striking, rather than for the blow, has to answer for many monstrous styles, efficient and otherwise.

PART II - CH. 1 – OF DRIVING IN GENERAL

Swing.—'My swing' is a constant theme for conversation with the young golfer. He is for ever making it quicker or slower, longer or shorter, some skilful player being in his mind's eye, whom he fancies he is imitating—or rather, whom he is imitating in every way except one—the only one which will give him a true style;—not thinking about it when playing, which the good player never does. His one problem is to sweep the ball away with speed. This is done by his body remaining a firm fulcrum for the lever composed of his arms and club. His swing back ends when the contact of his left biceps with his chest prevents it going further, his wrists remaining as taut as he can keep them. Not that he thinks of this, or of anything but sweeping the ball away. Let the beginner devote himself to the same problem. For a long time he will have a short swing; but it will lengthen quickly enough. There is not the slightest danger of its not doing so, unless he fall into the error of supposing that the more gently he hits the surer he is.

Many begin in quite another way. They see the professional's club swishing round his back, and they determine, at all costs, to get theirs as far round. By a variety of schemes they accomplish this, and become the proud possessors of a concatenation of contortions, in which no one but themselves recognises the resemblance to a full swing. Some swing naturally to a certain point, then, letting their wrists bend, drop the thing down their backs, draw it up again, and proceed to drive the ball. In the meantime their position has almost certainly changed in some way, so that the club head does not return to the ball along the same imaginary line it went from it. Others avoid the natural check of the biceps against the body by sticking out the left elbow and passing the arm round the neck, which, being thinner, allows the hands to get as far as the back of the head. To play in this way it is usual, or at least better (if I may be allowed to use an approbatory adjective at all in reference to such a matter), to employ upright clubs, although they will not overcome the inevitable uncertainty of direction. To get the club to the back of the neck, it must be drawn away at a tangent to the direction the ball is to be driven in. To prevent it going to the left, the player has to resort to some counter modification. He must, after impact, let his arms away to the right. Should he be lucky enough to catch the ball at the exact instant when his curve is practically parallel to the direction it is meant to go in, although 'cut' the shot will be straight; if he reaches it a hair earlier, it will be 'pulled'—a hair later, it will be 'heeled.' These are the terms the player would use. It would be more

BOOK I - **THE ART OF GOLF**

exact to describe the three drives as a cut to the right, a cut to the left, and a straight cut. Some who drive in this way stand well in front of the ball, and thus reduce their curve more nearly to a straight line; but I have seen none get rid of the cut entirely, which they might do by turning their back altogether to the line of fire.

The left elbow joint, as a joint, has no part in a true swing. But it is a prevalent habit to close it a little after the club has circled back as far as it naturally should. This is not quite so silly a way of giving one's-self the sensation of swinging far as is dropping the club over the shoulder by means of the wrist joints. But it is foolish enough, particularly if the player begins his swing with straight instead of slightly bent arms, in order to have more elbow-bending to do afterwards. Any one can see, when it is pointed out, that this joint work is merely a break which has to be mended before the sweep forward commences. Yet good players often take to it for a time if their driving is not satisfactory, feeling, in spite of commonsense, that they are lengthening their reach.

It would be profitless to describe more of the endless twists and twiddles with wrists and elbows which golfers acquire, seeking for a long swing in the wrong way, which is the same thing as seeking for it at all. Hundreds of balls are daily 'foozled' which would be struck but for these little spasms after the club has reached its proper goal. One sees them all over the links. They remind us sometimes of hairs which have grown too long arid split at the ends; sometimes they suggest blind men groping their way.

It must strike any one who thinks of it, as curious that so many should wander so far from the main road in search of a swing. Qne reason is, as already indicated, that swings are among the things which, according to Longfellow, 'are not what they seem.' Hence the errors of imitators. The professional appears to wind his club round his back. It is not so. It is the club which winds round him, not because he wishes it to do so, but because his muscles, though knit, have their natural elasticity. The player is in the centre of a circle, at a point in the circumference of which is the ball. The more nearly his club head describes a perfect segment whilst driving, the better. But it is not possible to make a true circle swiftly with a springy wire, which the player is, or a springy club shaft, if you will. He is even a bad shaft, weak in some places —for example, at the wrists. Let a player look upon his

PART II - CH. 1 – OF DRIVING IN GENERAL

left arm as a part of a club. He can see at once that it will not lengthen his driving to have a break in it somewhere. He might as well expect to lengthen his swing by putting joints in the actual wooden shaft, strengthened (say) with strong india-rubber bands, spliced over them, to imitate human joints. In other words, every joint of the fine driver's left arm below the shoulder is as taut as the extensor muscles (I rather think these are the ones) keep it without undue attention to the point. I have said the left arm. I should say nothing about the right, were it not that I might be supposed to mean that it too was to be treated as part of the shaft, and that I was advocating that stiff dunch from the shoulder with arms not naturally bent but rigidly straight, by which many late beginners remove their ball from the tee. In true driving, the left arm has to accommodate itself in the swing back. It is loose and obedient. Its elbow joint has to flex, and it is not until it is brought back to within a foot of the ball that it joins with the other in the work of driving—not till after impact that it becomes master, the other slave.

Fine players are not only apt to lead others astray by appearing, to the superficial observer, loose and flexible in every joint, but knotless contortionists, who are really so, look stiff and ponderous. Learners are thus doubly impressed with the idea that a free and a flabby swing are one and the same thing. Nor is it easy for them to be disabused of their error. No man can see himself strike, and thus learn that the swing he has adopted, the flexibility he feels, is visible not as ease but as awkwardness. Nor is there much chance of finding out his errors by comparing his sensations with those of good players, who, as a rule, pay no attention to such matters. Curiously enough, if pressed to say something, it will often be (I have got this answer from many professionals), 'My longest balls are when I feel I've got my wrists into it.' This misleads the tyro terribly, although it is true. The professional gets this sensation from a full, taut, indiarubbery swing. It is the result of his determination to get back to the ball as soon as possible. The other takes it to mean that he ought to get as far from it as he can by allowing the club to master his wrists. One day an adversary sought my praise for the way in which he was driving with his iron. I said (which was apparent), ' You have a fuller swing with it than with the play club.' 'You mean the opposite,' he answered. I repeated my commentary, and he rejoined, 'That is curious. I've been off my iron play, and am getting into it again by taking a half swing.' But I was right, which he admitted after experimenting in the matter. In driving from the tee this player had a long—a very long—swing, if by that is meant

BOOK I - **THE ART OF GOLF**

the distance the club head meandered away from the ball before coming back to it. In addressing, his arms, instead of having the natural bend, were straight as bars. They took the club a long way off, flexion of the left elbow took it further, flexion of the wrists another foot. By stretching, over-reaching, relaxing, his journey was the longest possible; but travelling far and swinging long are different matters. With his iron he described a true segment of a circle, every muscle as stiff and taut all the time as when the ball was struck.

In short, then, a good swing seems to the onlooker swift and flexible; but if the player feels supple, he exhibits an awkward, stiff, straggling movement. The player ought to be, in his own hands, a stiff bow which he bends and shoots with. Of course, by practice, he learns to bend this bow with ease, and to shoot with accuracy. But when he goes off his driving the remedy is not to lengthen and loosen the string, but rather to tighten and shorten it.

Hitherto I have spoken chiefly of errors in swinging developed in the region between the shoulders and the point of the club. Those that can be made with the rest of the body are of a simpler nature, because, in regard to them, swings for the most part are what they seem. It is without dispute that the shoulder joints are to be used with perfect freedom and flexibility. If a man is reaching too far with them he does not need to be told. He feels his neck sink into his body. He knows that the more freely his trunk oscillates on its supports, the better. He knows that, his position once taken, his body ought not to sway to the right nor to the left, forward nor backward. Not that he can count upon its never doing so. We often get into tricks of falling backwards, swaying away to the right, etc., but we are conscious of them. Every one knows that whether he play with straight or bent knees, they must remain straight or bent throughout the shot. The necessity for standing firm on the feet, however, although admitted, is not universally appreciated. There is a prevalent disposition so to plant them as to make sure that the left heel will come away from the ground, as if this were of as much importance as a firm foundation. Indeed, I am inclined to think that it is of none at all. That the heel of good players does come away from the ground, there is no doubt; but, in the case of many of the very best, how reluctantly!—and merely as if torn from it by the force of the swing. As I have said before, most fine players (I might say all who began young) have no theory, and can give but scant advice. One of the very best, when pressed for answer as to a certain peculiarity in his stance, said, 'Do I stand so? I didn't know (said as if it

PART II – CH. 1 – OF DRIVING IN GENERAL

meant, 'I don't care'). The only thing to think about is planting your feet in the ground—it doesn't matter where, so long as they are glued down.' I said, 'But your heel leaves the ground when you swing.' 'Does it? Are you sure? I don't think so.'

A chapter on *Swing* would be incomplete without some reference to the maxim 'Slow back.' Every one acknowledges and feels that it is a sound one; but many fail to put it in practice, particularly those who have a slow, ponderous style. This seems to be a contradiction in terms, but it is true nevertheless. The fact is, 'slow back ' is not an accurate term for what is meant. Those learning the game get puzzled. The professional does not appear to practise what he preaches. He seems to swing, and does swing, swiftly. What is really demanded by 'slow back' is not absolute but relative slowness. If we compare the true swing to an india-rubber band, 'slow back' means that it is to be stretched more slowly than it will recoil. By practice, men learn to set the spring quickly, and the rate is of no importance provided there be nothing approaching to a jerk or wrench back. You must not be able to hear the club swish through the air as on the return journey. 'Stiff back,' 'taut back,' or 'sway back,' would be a more explicit phrase. Whatever it be called, the thing itself is a sine qua non of fine driving. When a player is merely pushing his hands round his neck instead of swinging, however slowly, and twitching them forward again, his caddy will be tempted to tell him he is too quick back, as much as if he is jerking it up round his shoulder. A good player who has temporarily fallen into any form of (to invent an ugly word) unpendulumness, on being warned that he is too quick back, will understand that he is not tightening all the muscles properly used in swinging equally— that he is merely flopping at the ball with his arms. A bad player, who has never learned what a true swing is, may only be made worse with 'slow back.' It may induce him to lift the club up softly and gingerly, with the kind of slowness necessary to grab a fly on his right ear, but which has nothing to do with driving a ball. A true swing is not like flashing a sword through the air, but as if forcing it through a strongly resisting medium.

Whilst the minds of golfers are, for the most part, unduly exercised about their swing before impact, tricks, jerks, and false curves in the other segment of their circle are scarcely thought about or observed. We wonder that A., with a short, spasmodic twiddle, should drive further and more steadily than B., who gets credit for quite a professional style. But if we look (not a natural

BOOK I - **THE ART OF GOLF**

thing to do, because the eyes instinctively wink when club and ball click together) B. will be seen 'to follow,' whilst A. pulls up short. Of the two evils, crampedness after striking is perhaps more fatal than before it, or rather it would be more accurate to say that no one is contented to swing short back as many habitually do forward.

It is unnecessary to enlarge upon this part of the swing. What has been already said applies equally to both halves of it. The second part ought to be, as far as possible, a reflection of the first. In the case of good players who stand square to the ball, it is so in every respect, being a little shorter or longer proportionately according as a man stands 'in front' or 'open.' Falling in, falling back, etc., are as apt to occur in one half as in the other. Swaying the whole body forward after the ball is as likely to cripple driving as swaying away from it when taking the club back. It is not so common to let the right heel leave the ground too much at the end of a stroke, as it is to rise too much on the left toe. Nor do men need to keep a tight hold of themselves lest the club wander away by itself in search of a long swing. Loose-jointedness here rather betrays itself by a check a foot past the tee and a finishing twitch with the wrists.

PART II - CH. 1 – OF DRIVING IN GENERAL

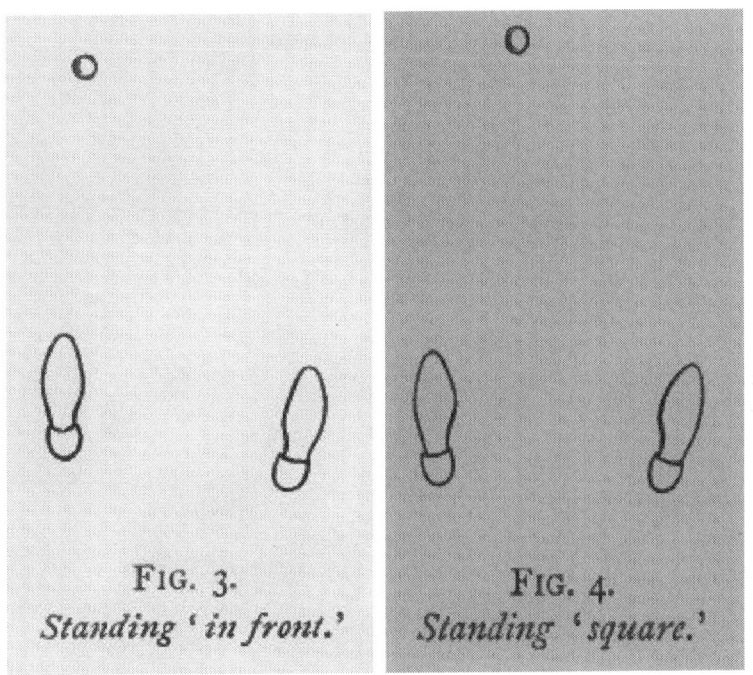

Fig. 3. *Standing 'in front.'*

Fig. 4. *Standing 'square.'*

BOOK I - **THE ART OF GOLF**

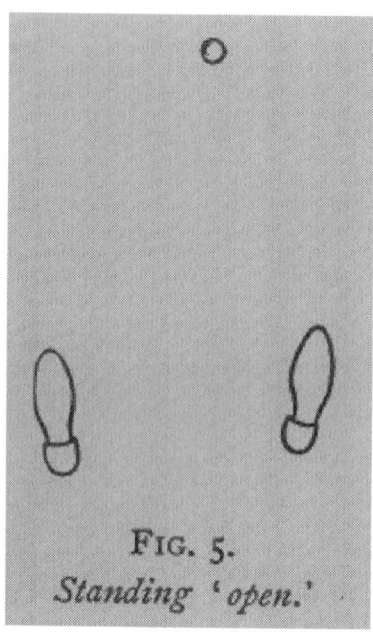

Fig. 5.
Standing 'open.'

PART II - CH. 1 – OF DRIVING IN GENERAL

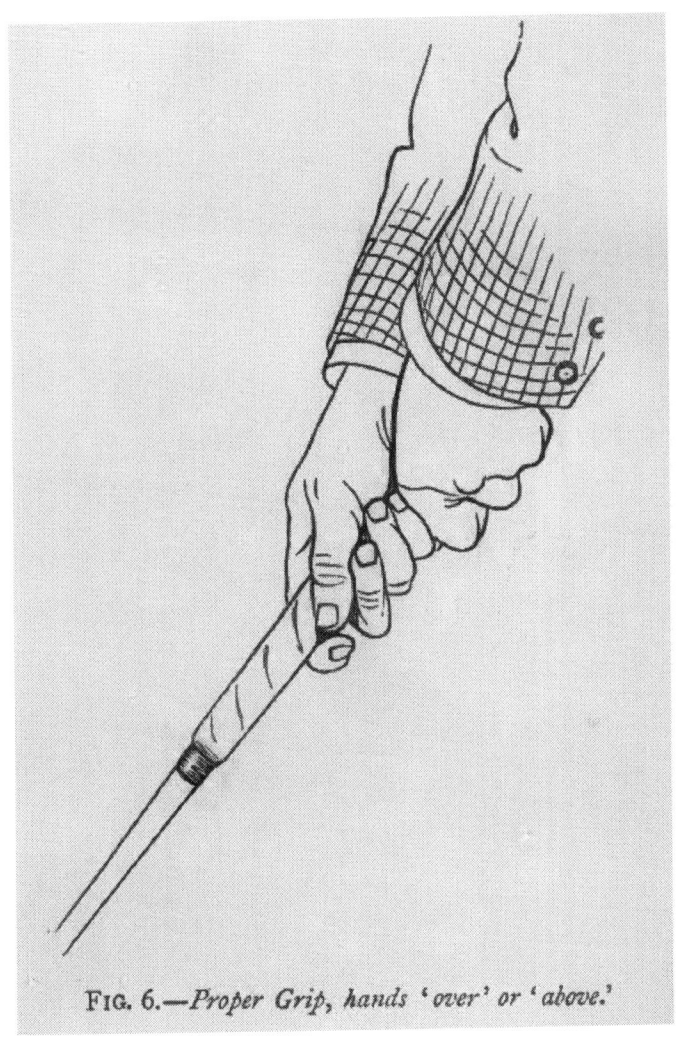

FIG. 6.—*Proper Grip, hands 'over' or 'above.'*

BOOK I - **THE ART OF GOLF**

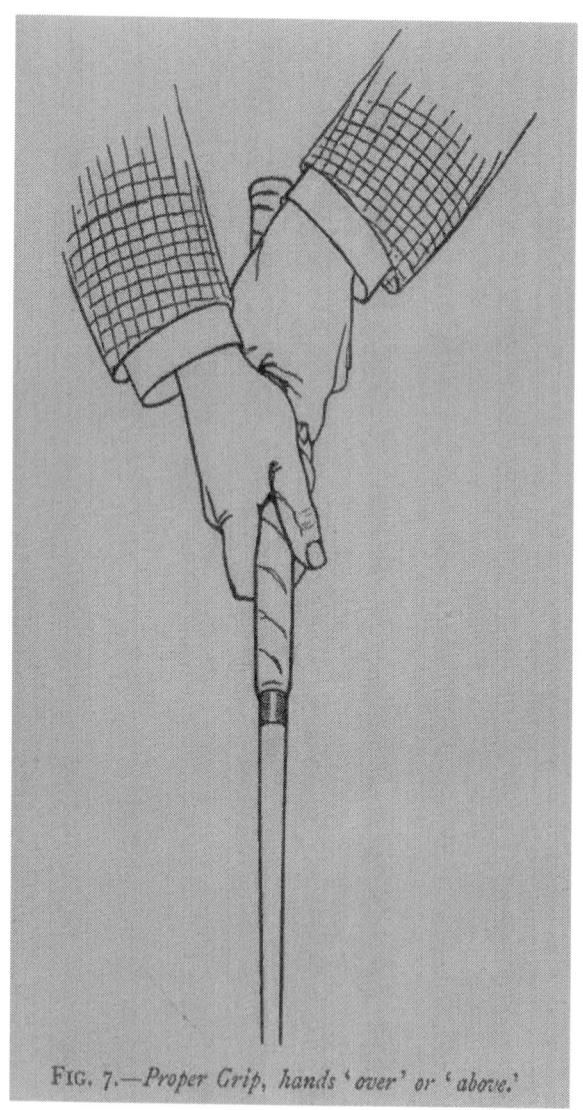

FIG. 7.—*Proper Grip, hands 'over' or 'above.'*

PART II - CH. 1 – OF DRIVING IN GENERAL

PLATE V. JIM MORRIS DRIVING (1)

BOOK I - **THE ART OF GOLF**

PLATE VI. JIM MORRIS DRIVING (2)

PART II - CH. 3 – ADVICE TO BEGINNERS

PLATE VII. SAYERS DRIVING (1)

BOOK I - **THE ART OF GOLF**

PLATE VIII. SAYERS DRIVING (2)

3
ADVICE TO BEGINNERS

The beginner who has read the foregoing chapters will be apt to re-read the first sentence, and to agree with those who complain that accuracy is almost impossible with so many things to remember; or, if he sees that it is not intended he should think of them all, he will still be puzzled to understand which are the elementary, which the more advanced, instructions. Accordingly I propose in this chapter (even at the risk of some repetition) to write a little sermon for the young player.

Let the beginner shake himself down naturally before the ball, and hit. Till he has done this for a good many days, no advice has either use or meaning. During this first stage it is probable that he will be quite delighted with his driving, and with good reason. His attention being entirely directed to hitting —his curiosity about how to hit not being so far aroused—he makes good shots. In many respects a man naturally attacks the ball in the proper way. He stands up, stands firm, does not force; and although his swing is of course stiff, it is not artificial. From the very first some players, however, make the mistake of treating the ball as a heavy object, whilst in reality it has, for practical purposes, no weight, and ought to be swept away, not jerked. In a bunker or a hard hole it becomes heavy, and nothing will do but a jerk; but from the turf the problem is to shave it cleanly off. Again, early cricket, and many other games with balls, start most beginners on their golfing career with a wrong grip. The handle of the club is opposite the third waistcoat button instead of being as low as the length of the arms naturally let it go. They wish to drive as much in cricket form as the shape of the club will allow. Not that any one thinks of literally golfing with a straight bat. They are freed from that restraint, and enjoy swiping across the wicket. But this cannot be allowed. A

BOOK I - THE ART OF GOLF

bad cricketing style is not a good golfing one. The beginner must learn that golf is the very opposite of cricket, that he must get his hands as much down at it as up at the other. He must use his club like a scythe; must sweep, not strike the ball. In my opinion the extent to which the player gets his hands over the club cannot be exaggerated. To have them well over is a *sine qua non* of an easy style. Beginners and others do not like the position until they have proved it, until patience and experience convince them that the grip which is most convenient for catching the ball a hammer-like thud is not the best either for far or sure.

I say, 'until they have proved it.' Lucky for them, if they ever do. A very large percentage of players live and play and die with their knuckles pointing too much towards the ground, with their club at too obtuse an angle with their arms, and consequently without the possibility of ever having a perfect swing (Figs. 8 and 9). Seen from the front, a perfect player's arms and club appear at the angle to each other shown in Fig. 6. Imperfection lies between that and a straight line from shoulder to club head. Why getting the knuckles too far round is so common, so almost universal (see Figs. 8 and 9), is (besides that it gives the hammering power already referred to) that it prevents the wrists being used, and leads quickly to fairly steady driving, whilst the true position enables them to be employed with consequent feeble and uncertain hitting. I would therefore strongly impress upon beginners the advisability of having their hands well over the club,—of becoming steady by keeping their wrists taut, rather than by so gripping the club that their joints cannot bend. I say 'hands.' It should rather be 'hand' —the left hand. The right will look after itself. If the tyro acquires a grip which prevents him seeing his left knuckles, and which shows him instead more than the first joints of his fingers (compare Figs. 7 and 9), if his club handle point to his waistcoat instead of well below that garment, there is no reason why he should not become an effective, but he never will be a pretty, driver—a true, full style of the orthodox sort is impossible. The fault must be compensated by either a short, a broken, an overhead swing, or by some other modification, pronounced, or slight in proportion to the cause. Let any one grip in this way, swing a club back to his shoulder, examine the constrained position of his right wrist, and he will see that one of these things is inevitable.

PART II – CH. 3 – ADVICE TO BEGINNERS

If he acquire a grip as in Fig. 10, it would be hypercritical to interfere. As I have said, great latitude may be allowed to the right hand in this matter, particularly if it grasp loosely. But should any one be so misguided as to hold disproportionately in the opposite way—that is, with the right hand over and the left under—farewell to all chance of even passable driving.

It is not generally till after the first week that the golfer begins to think about his game—to wish to know how it is done, in order that he may improve. With these inquiries his troubles begin, and let us hope that, with patience and commonsense, he will get through them without crippling his style.

He will soon hear on all sides, 'Keep your eye on the ball.' Of course one must see the thing which is to be struck; but it is a mistake to insist upon it as if it were very difficult. If the beginner glares at the ball too determinedly it will mesmerise him, so that the hammering will be a distraction, and cuts from former tops appear to be fatuous mouths smiling derisively.

Then it comes to be a question with the beginner whether he ought to go in for a full or for a half swing. If he must have an answer—if he must have a name for, and an ideal on which to mould, his blow, let it be a half swing. It will be some time before his unpretending thump can be classed at all; but no matter. It ought to be more like a half swing than anything else; it will grow into that, and from that into a full one, unconsciously, as the fetters of awkwardness fall from his limbs; but if he try for a full swing at once, he will not get it,—he will merely acquire the habit (difficult to correct later on) of allowing his club to wander aimlessly about his back and shoulders.

In the laudable endeavour to drive far (and no man should ever accept the position of a weak player), the beginner has to stumble through many errors before mastering the secret of where and how to apply his force. There is one the beginner is certain to fall into. In order to get a good sweep at the ball, instead of causing his trunk to revolve on its own axis, he sways it back over his right leg. One feels as if tremendous force were acquired in this way. So there is, but of the wrong sort—slow, ponderous, clumsy. Even a ball clean hit, and getting the full result of this swaying motion, does not go far. But it seldom is hit, and no more wonder than that it should be missed if struck at whilst the player is walking. Swaying thus is a standing walk, a term which

BOOK I - **THE ART OF GOLF**

may be objected to, although it ought to be as intelligible as the accepted phrase, a 'standing jump.' It is perhaps as well to advise young golfers to have both hands close together; at all events, it is but fair to warn them that every inch which separates them takes ten yards off the length of their shot.

These few hints are ample theoretical equipment for many months. But the beginner will get many more, to which I advise him to turn a deaf ear. Every old hand will be ready to advise him that his own last crotchet is the one thing needful. He will be told that the great point is to keep his hands tight, or not to keep them tight, or one slack, his elbow in, or his elbow out, to let the club follow the ball, or his arms follow the ball, etc., etc. Naturally he thinks these people know. He tries one and all, getting as confused as if he were selecting a new religion. The fact is, there are more bad teachers than good, and if the beginner must have advice, let him consult a really first-class player, who will probably tell him he knows nothing about grips, or elbows, or following, and that all he has to do is to stand firm and smite hard.

If the beginner is liable to be confused by his friends, his danger is much greater from his caddy. The former only give advice when it is asked, the latter volunteers it, and insists. There are such things as good professional coaches, but they are rare. On the whole, it is better not to allow your caddy to interfere. Most of them advise a thousand and one things within the hour. They feed babes with strong meat, and expect to, or at least try to, make them full-grown golfers within an hour. Besides things good enough in themselves if they could be digested, two pieces of advice which they mostly insist upon are positive poison. One, already spoken of in the last chapter, is that the player should rise upon his left toe. The swing not yet being so full and free as to tear the heel from the ground, by acting on this advice the beginner is simply left with a few spare inches of leg which he does not know what to do with. He may double them under him out of the road, but most likely he will use them to sway his body away back over the right leg, his caddy thus actually encouraging him to commit this common and fatal mistake of beginners. The other is, insisting on the right thumb being over, not on, the club. If (which is likely enough, as we have seen) the beginner is holding his club as uprightly as possible, both hands too much under the club, it is absolutely impossible for him to strike at all if he obeys. His grip well over, he may do it; but ought not to unless it is natural—perhaps not even then, as at this early stage it foreshadows an intention of driving with the wrists, and

PART II - CH. 3 – ADVICE TO BEGINNERS

opens the way to these wanderings of the club round the back—these so-called long swings of which I have already said a good deal. Leave the thumb where it is. By degrees, if the player allows himself to acquire his art without prejudice, it will slip into its proper place, getting out of the way to allow a fuller swing. But at first it is needed to guide the stroke, and if not allowed to be used, the beginner will effect his purpose by some other means, perhaps burying his club in his palm so as to work with the end of the second joint instead of with the point of the thumb. This inevitably 'turns in the nose' of the club, and it breaks. His faith in his caddy costs many a beginner much money and many sad rounds, in which his set gets reduced to some irons and some headless shafts. It is lucky for his golf if in the end he rebels against the oracle. If he does not, his grip with the right hand is a difficulty ever after. It remains twisted, and to do any work at all, the body and legs have to twist too.

For some time the beginner (I am speaking of men, not boys) makes marked and regular progress, until suddenly one day there is a break-down, which crushes his sanguine hope that his march towards perfection was to be smooth and rapid. It is the first of many which will occur from time to time so long as he is able to hold a club. To avoid them altogether is impossible, but their number may be lessened, their severity checked, by wisdom and care. When the beginner is getting on swimmingly, let him not be carelessly confident, for pride goes before a fall. Nor when his driving is very satisfactory ought he to attempt to note what he is doing, so as to be able to return to it if a relapse occurs. This in itself is the beginning of backsliding. Golf refuses to be preserved like dead meat in tins. It is living, human, and free, ready to fly away at the least sign of an attempt to catch and cage it. It will confute your logic if you, as it were, stand aside and try to produce it by causes. With patient attention to hitting, not relaxed even when we are in the full pride of good play, our relapses will be fewer and less severe; but there is no means by which we can secure uniform progress. In proportion as the wave of advance is great, so will be the back draught. Let not the learner be discouraged by it, and begin to doubt lest the tide has turned. Golfers often speak of their game. The best the learner has ever played is his game, even supposing it is a third better than what he has relapsed to. It will come again soon, unless, indeed, he begin to ask, 'What am I doing wrong?' 'How did I stand?' 'How did I swing then?'

BOOK I - **THE ART OF GOLF**

It is impossible to say how good a player a man may become; but every beginner ought, as much as possible, to play with better golfers than himself. He will unconsciously by that means aim higher. It should be his ambition to beat somebody, and, having done so, to attack a still stronger adversary. Many half-crowns will be lost in the process, but what of that? It is cheaper and pleasanter than to employ a professional coach.

In the early manhood of his golfing-life, the earnest and promising player's mind is apt to be much exercised as to the weight, length, lie, and spring of his club. He will feel sure that a best club for his style is to be found, and to find it will for some time appear a matter of the last importance. After many experiments, he will be in possession of a mass of conflicting evidence, and a box full of clubs more remarkable than useful. From extreme hope and faith he will fall back into a condition of dogmatic unbelief. He will try to use any club—even the rubbish accumulated in his days of faith. Truth lies between these two extremes.

In the matter of lie, a tall player's club ought to be upright, a short man's flat. The reason is that for all sorts and sizes of men about 3 feet 6 inches is the proper length. That a longer club will not drive further, that a shorter one drives as far, is proved to be true. Theoretically, the long club reaches the ball with greater velocity, but as each inch adds to the difficulty of being accurate, it has to be taken easier. It is not your strong man who can wield a long club; on the contrary, it is your pocket Apollo, whose long driving is due to precision and neatness. An exceptionally short club, on the other hand can be, and instinctively is, swung with much more force. The objection to their general use is that they break a man down, not so much from the fatigue of over-exertion as from the loss of self-control which results from it.

As for weight, so long as the specific gravity and absolute weight of the head is greater than that of the ball, the carry will not be affected by it. Within this limit the lightest club will drive the longest ball, because it can be swung more swiftly than a heavy one (with what lightning accuracy one sweeps off daisy heads with a walking-stick!). The danger with a very light club is that muscles having so little strain are apt to grow frisky and wanton. Theoretically, therefore, a heavy club ought to steady a wild, pressing player. It does not do so. It ought to act as a bit in his mouth. He takes it in his teeth. Practically, the golfer with an ambition for lead handicaps himself terribly. He

PART II - CH. 3 – ADVICE TO BEGINNERS

cannot play easily in proportion to the weight of his weapon, for part of his ambition is sure to be to drive a long ball. This he will do occasionally; but he must hit perfectly clean, or else make an egregious foozle. There is no reserve force in him if he sclaffs. His club sticks in the mud, or is twisted out of his hand. To avoid the ground he is apt to top. Sometimes when he does hit clean, the club runs away with him to the right or left. And all this on account of a crude, erroneous idea that the heavier the club the further it will drive. It is a mistaken idea, otherwise the man who could swing a 16-lb. hammer would beat the record. It is evident that even Goliath would make a very feeble shot with such a club or with his own; but with a Philp he might have outdriven the champion.

The spring of a club has more to do with comfort than with carry. Nobody likes stiff shafts. Many charges are laid at their door; the only just one is that they jar the hands. Each man will drive, not further, but better, with the club he likes best. A 'fozy' handle will do very well if you have a sweeping, scythe-like swing. If your style is jerky, such a shaft, or one with the spring under the rind, will prove itself useless to you at once; the club or the jerking must be abandoned. For all kinds of forcing players (those who let in when they get to the ball), the spring must be confined to the neighbourhood of the skeer. If you wish to compel yourself to drive easily, buy a 'wabbly' club; it will either teach you or top your ball. It is pleasanter, however, to play without a master. In short, my advice is—use a stiff club, whatever your style, with just enough elasticity to make the ball go off sweetly, and give up all idea that spring here or spring there will make you drive further. If you don't want to abandon this notion, no matter. Your club with an ideal spring may drive further on account of your confidence in it.

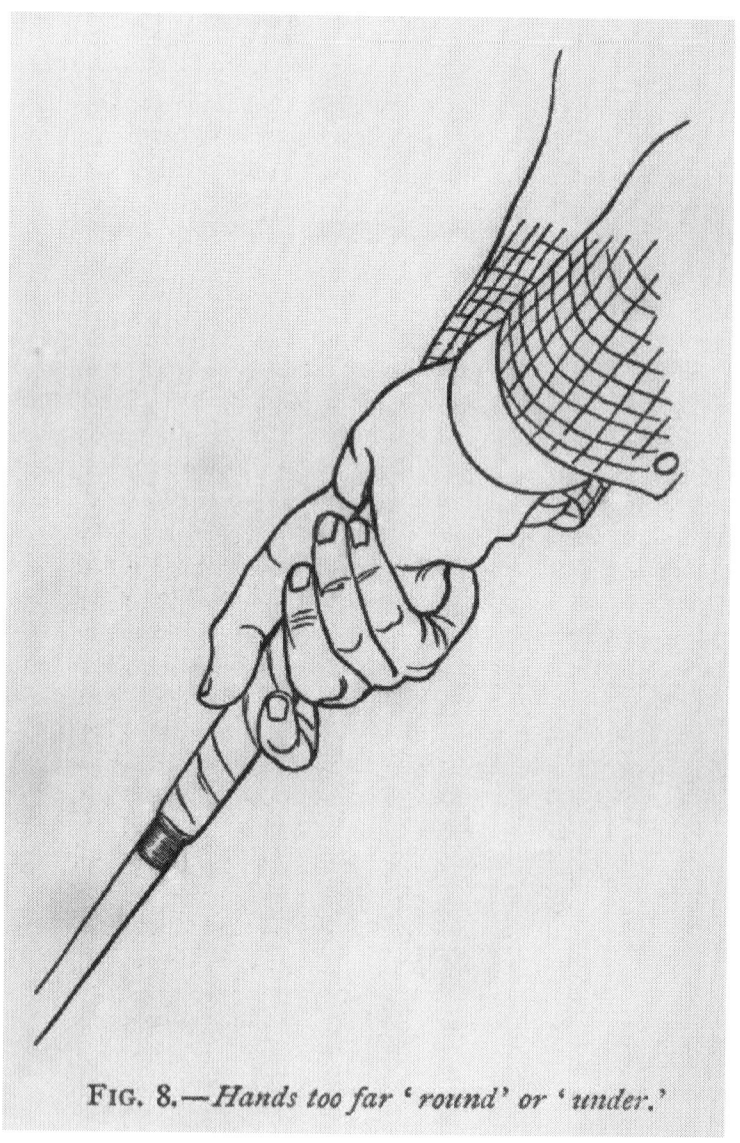

FIG. 8.—*Hands too far 'round' or 'under.'*

PART II - CH. 4 – OF PECULIARITIES AND FAULTS

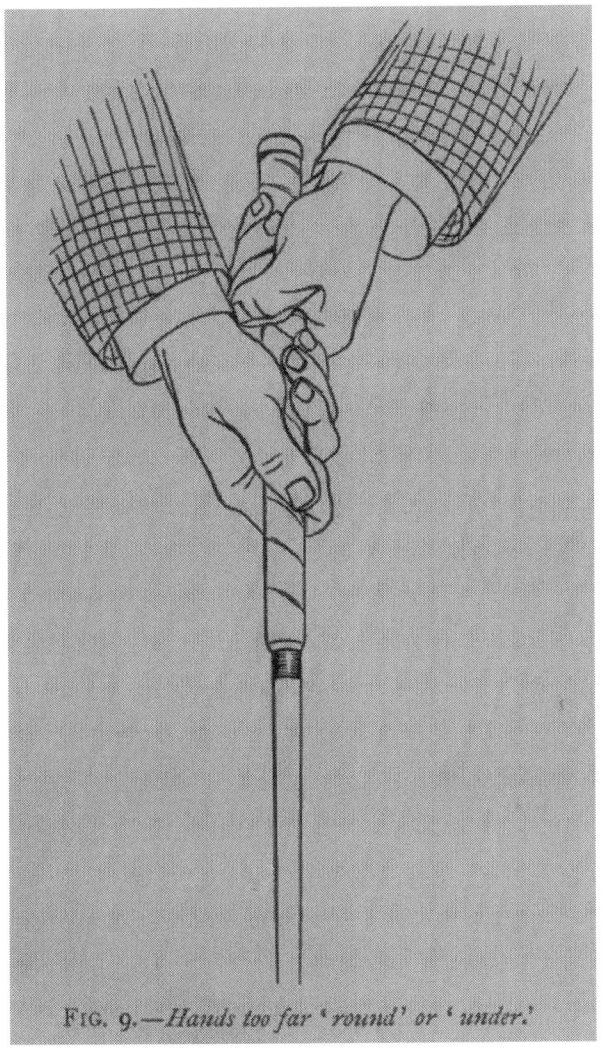

FIG. 9.—*Hands too far 'round' or 'under.'*

BOOK I - **THE ART OF GOLF**

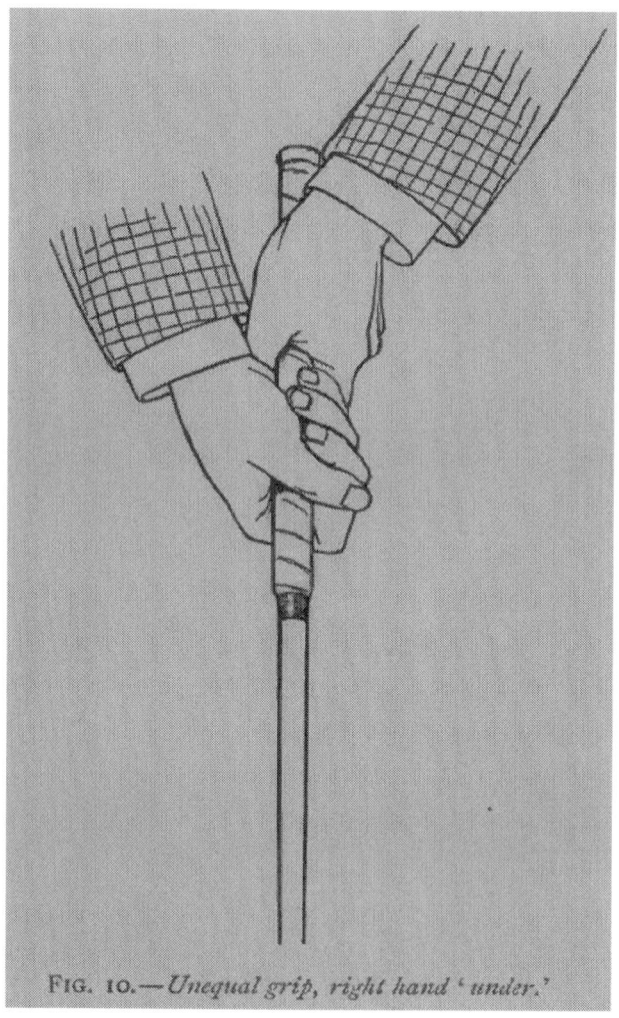

FIG. 10.—*Unequal grip, right hand 'under.'*

4
OF PECULIARITIES AND FAULTS

There is a general—I might say universal—tendency among golfers, to exaggerate the importance of style. From the best to the worst, when off their driving, they begin at once to alter something, assuming that the cause is to be found in a wrong stance, grip, or what not. And yet the experienced know well enough that their driving will never come back so long as they pursue this line of research. Style, in other words, is not nearly of so much importance as accurate hitting. Take a batch of first-class players, and we find that they all drive practically about the same distance, notwithstanding infinite variety in their way of doing so, and even greater differences in physique. It is usual to attribute the powerful driving of small men to the excellence of their style; if this be the cause of it, how does it happen that there are big men twice as strong, and with as easy swings as their little rivals, who as often play the odds after the tee shot as not? A batch of second-class players drives, on an average, some ten yards shorter than those who can give them a shade of odds (I do not include those who are second-class because they are beginners, or incurably careless). The same slight superiority exists in the approaching of first over second-class players; and I am inclined to believe that this is also true in regard to putting, although it is the fashion to credit many bad drivers with skill in this department. Where are those fine putters on the ladies' green? How is it, when there are prizes there for men, it is some golfer known to fame who usually wins? No. Strength and style are of minor importance compared with accuracy. I do not mean that the first is of no value at all; but to ordinary physiques of five feet six inches up to gianthood it gives no advantage, except from bunkers and bad lies. Even from these a Hercules is not necessarily the best. Precision is the main thing. When a man's eye is in he may address the ball in a dozen different ways with the same result; when it is out, no shifting of position will mend matters. First-class play is compatible with ugly style. A third-rate biceps may drive a long ball; but a second-class combination of hand and eye will prevent a man being both far and sure. To be a steady player, a man who finds he cannot hit a screamer every time must either play more easily or more coarsely, the latter preferable. Men learn their position instinctively. Watch an eminent golfer in the prime of youth, a prudent liver, or not old enough to be affected by imprudence, driving against, perhaps, a stronger man, who either never did aim exactly, or whose more delicate machinery is a little shaken by the wear and tear of life. How coarse and sclaffy the latter's shots are by comparison! One drives like a new hansom, the other rattles like an ill-built or old four-wheeler.

As we are accustomed to see dissimilar swings producing about the same result, so, on the other hand, cases of the exact converse are not uncommon —cases of two men with apparently the same style, one a powerful driver, the other incapable of sending the ball a hundred yards. Here comes a player who gets his hands under the club, swings it over his head, stands with the ball close to him, and yet sends it flying. Behind is another, his exact counterpart, except in the matter of results. Why is this ? Why is the one a good player, the other not? If we take up a club of the first man, it is found to be very upright. Why he adopted this lie, whether by accident or on purpose, matters not. There it is, and he plays well, because his style is a natural product of a single-minded concentration on hitting clean. The duffer got his swing in another way, namely, by mimicry. The copy is fairly good, but not quite exact. The hands are Esau's, but not the club, which, being flat, compels him to add some movements not indulged in by his master. He has to bend down to adjust its head behind the ball, to rise during the swing, and subside again at hitting-time. Not that this omission in the copy of externals matters much. His play would be no better with his ideal's club, because they differ utterly in their thoughts. The one thinks of hitting, the other about his manner of threatening to do so. Here is another good driver coming up to the hole where we critics are standing—another with an ugly style, as anything with peculiarities is called. He stands with his feet far apart—stands 'open'—and swings round his biceps, not his neck. Why is he driving well, and his partner and reflection so badly? Again, a flaw in the copy gives a hint as to the origin of the leader's peculiarities. He has his hands very much under the club and at the same time exceptionally near the ground, whilst the other is evidently proud of his 'proper' grip. The intelligent onlooker (if I may be allowed so to speak of myself) retires a little off the course to drive imaginary balls, to discover that, given this particular grip, the rest follows as a natural consequence, and to speculate that probably the leader accidentally took this grip when he began to play, and thought no more about it.

The most natural manner in which to address a ball is, of course, to stand with legs straight and firm, and with no more stoop of the body than is absolutely necessary to enable the player to direct his eyes straight on the ball from the middle of their sockets. But good golfers, in the laudable endeavour to stand well away from the ball, acquire in great numbers the habit of stooping forward more than is necessary. These instinctively apply a corrective. For instance, some bend their knees. There are good golfers who stoop so far forward, and have cancelled the effect of doing so to such an extent by bending their knees, that they would fit a chair if placed behind them when driving. Some of the stupid imitators of these think the secret lies in the stooping, some in the knee-bending, with bad golf as a result in either case. Other good players, who stoop over their work, keep their bodies steady and their grip of the ground firm by placing the left foot nearer the line of fire than the right. They stand as in Fig. 3 exaggerated. Some of the stability given in the line of fire by keeping the feet apart is used to prevent falling in. One of the best—if not the best—player in the world at the present moment, in this way cancels the bad effects of his stooping forward to his work, and, as might be expected, at the sacrifice of a little of the straightness which a 'square' stand gives. At this moment his miserable imitators swarm on every golf green in the Lothians. They all copy his peculiar stance, some have grasped some other point; not one has improved his game. They have a little of Pygmalion's art; not one of them can animate their work. The ass of fable dressed like a lion they address like one. When the beast brayed he was betrayed; so it is when they swing.

Some day we may have a great player who has fallen into the habit of cancelling his stoop by placing his right foot near the ball, his left back (why not?), and then there will be a revolution among the mimics.

The examples of mimicry I have taken are of imitators of eccentric styles. Those who make copies of the orthodox swing are not so common, although there are pretty players who miss as often as not. Most who try it make an unrecognisable caricature, which is not to be wondered at, as caricature of persons with no salient feature is very difficult. Some again, who try to learn

BOOK I - **THE ART OF GOLF**

golf on imitative principles, have merely an imaginary ideal. In their case one can only infer from their exceeding bad play that they aim at a style instead of at a ball. Under this head come those who secretly determine to jerk instead of sweep the ball away, either through ignorance or stubbornness, or both. The ignorant flounder on, misdirecting their energy because they never have tried to strike in the right way; the stubborn, because they often jerk a long ball, and prefer the sensation to the gentler joy of feeling it slip away almost by itself which a proper shot gives. The latter are hopeless. Golf is not a game for men who find more pleasure in brute force than in the exercise of skill.

It is usual to attribute peculiarities, whether of good or bad players, to their only having taken to the game late in life; but this neither explains them, nor is it quite in accordance with the facts. It is true that there are more artlessly artful players amongst those who have been on the green more or less since they could handle a leadless club two feet long, but it is quite a mistake to suppose that a man who takes his first lesson after his beard has grown, or even when the hair has all flitted from the top of his head to his chin, is too old or too set or too something ever to swing easily. Why it is more exceptional for him than for the other to do so, is due to another cause. The boy begins differently from the man. He lets fly, indifferent as to a hit or a miss; or, rather, he means a clean, swishing, smashing blow. All others, from a glober to a fair shot, are merely misses, to which he pays no attention. They do not put him out; he expects them, and does not count the proportion of them to good shots. The bad ones do not matter, for his pleasure is to drive balls, not to play holes. Hence his style is quite free. A man has not patience for this. Just as the boy finds a round monotonous, so the man aims at striking steadily, leaving the rest to develop later.

It thus appears that the chances in favour of the former having a free style when he grows up almost amount to certainty, and yet, except that he has acquired a certain amount of skill, the boy beginner, as soon as he is old enough in mind to settle of his own accord to match-playing (I do not include those little boys who are forced into double harness with their fathers) is in the same position as a grown-up beginner. The man playing his first shot, and the golfer of (say) twenty-one, are equally ignorant of how much or how little it is safe to play consciously. The former thinks of what he is doing from the first, the latter begins to do so about this time of life. Either may go astray, or either may discover the golden mean before becoming set in the tricks they have excogitated. If this were not so, there would be fewer of those boy players, who are expected to do wonders in two or three years, who at eighteen can beat any one, and who at one-andtwenty disappear, either for ever, or to come to the front after an interval, with or without peculiarities, according as they used or abused their new-born consciousness. A perfectly unconscious style in a grown man is very rare. It will oftenest be found among professionals whose education does not tempt them to think. There is one illustrious and venerable champion of whom it is proverbial that not even a whole round of bad shots can tempt him to consider his position. 'I've missed the ba',' is all he says. To hit it again, is all he tries. It is wonderful how soon he succeeds, too—much sooner than if he were to begin asking why.

When a man first attempts to play, he is stiff and awkward indeed, but he has no mannerisms. They begin to show after his first breakdown, and after each succeeding one a mark is apt to be left on his game. When that is full-grown and set, the cicatrices of old wounds remain as excrescences, which, unless inconvenient, are better not excised. There is a risk of hurting the constitution of our golf if the operation is attempted. But as when an ankle has once been sprained, it is inclined to give way occasionally, so people with 'wonderful' styles are apt to crack unexpectedly, and when out of practice they take a long time to come into their game. Some people are lucky enough to have developed their abnormalities on non-vital spots. Though ugly, the ball yields as readily to their style as to something more elegant. You strike your shoulder, your thumb or thumbs are down the shaft, you bend your knees, shuffle with your feet, get your hands so far under the club that a full swing is impossible, etc., etc. These things will give no trouble. But if by playing for a pull, by gripping the club in a way that, although become natural, was acquired at a time when there was a wrong conception of how to make a ball fly, etc., you are wild and uncertain, there is nothing for it but to begin again. It is of no use to attempt patching; other faults have grown up alongside of the original one. They were necessary to put life into it at all. Say, for instance, you have a nipping style. You realise that. In consequence, your driving is short. It is useless to force yourself to follow the ball; you will only top. Stance, grip, and attitude have adapted themselves to the conditions originally imposed. There is nothing for it but contentment or a fresh start. For the latter, experience gives you an advantage over the real beginner. You know the true theory, viz. to stand opposite the ball and sweep it away by describing a true radius, on which it is a point. At first you will flounder, miss, and be uncertain; but a new and better game will grow to its full strength at last.

If we consider the plausible and insidious means by which these tricks insinuate themselves into a golfer's affections, it is not so much to be wondered at that he is conquered. By their aid he finds himself suddenly steady, able to beat adversaries previously dreaded, and to win handicap electroplate with strokes to spare. At first they do not even shorten driving, the diseases taking some time to get into the system and cripple the other members. By the time they have done so, it is too late to get rid of them. The player works through stages of foozling, and, after as long a period as it would have taken to be a pretty golfer, he comes out a robust cripple, ungainly, although perhaps strong. This is the prognosis in the most favourable cases, but some would-be golfers are restless in the use of remedies. They employ device after device, add fault to fault. No sooner is their driving weakened by assimilating one, than another, and yet another, infallible 'steadier' presents itself, and is accepted, till at last there is not a chance of their cleanest hit ball going more than fifty yards. These call themselves the steady old players. Steady, indeed! They top and puff just as often, if not oftener, than those who have acquired their game with less prejudice. They are steady only because it does not matter to their partners whether they hit or miss, and straight, because wildness is not appreciable in very short distances. Any morning we can see men out teaching themselves crippled swings by driving daisies. A trial swing now and then, especially before starting, may do no harm. There are even good players who indulge a good deal in the amusement. Them one can distinguish from the deluded creatures who are teaching themselves styles by the free, thoughtless way in which they let out. The others—earnest, careful, apparently concentrated on the blade of grass in front of them—do not hear 'Fore—stop that—hurry up,' shouted behind them; for their mind is busy committing to memory their last patent gyration. If the fools would but reflect on a certain passage of Scripture they might learn that neither leopard nor golf spotting can be managed by taking thought, and that thought will not add cubits either to their stature or driving. From the latter it will take some off.

These remarks do not apply to the petty variations in their style which many, or most, golfers are conscious of, from day to day. Little vagaries are

PART II - CH. 4 — OF PECULIARITIES AND FAULTS

not part of us. Our knowing of them proves them external. If not made a serious point of, they do no harm. One of them will amuse for a round or so, and being the only thing which, for the moment, divides our attention with the essential of aiming, it may even improve our driving, and then be forgotten, modified, or smoothed out. The points under discussion are so superficial, or even imaginary, that no one notices them but ourselves. They are quite another thing from playing *à la* Morris, or Fergusson, or Martin, which is revolutionary, and never attempted, except in jest.

Even minor sensations, too earnestly attended to, may, however, do a great deal of harm. When, by patiently keeping his attention fixed on hitting, the golfer has got into his best driving form, he is tempted to luxuriate in the sweet balls; to note how he gets his shoulders into the work; or how he feels like a whipcord, from the point of his toe to the head of his club; or, how, without effort, his palms feel glued to the rind of the club; and to determine that in future these joys shall be repeated every shot. Fool! he might as well expect to repeat the pleasure of appeased hunger by a second dinner, or make a pleasant dream more vivid by wakening. Pursuing these agreeable sensations he will lose them, and go off his game besides. Disappointed, he will return to the drudgery of hitting the ball, when lo! some, or all of them come back too. Again he will be off in pursuit of the will-o'-the-wisp, and again break down. It takes long, long experience to convince a golfer that he must give up all the pleasures arising from a shot, except that caused by results, if he is to drive far and sure. Imitating one's own style is only less bad than copying a neighbour's. 'Know thyself' may be good philosophy; it is bad golf. Some players remain with the marks of sensation-hunting on their style for life. For instance, A. makes himself knockkneed when he addresses the ball. Once, long ago, when he drove a beauty, there was a feeling of gripping the ground with the balls of his big toes. If you question him warily, he will tell you the year in which, and the hole at which, the sweet shot was made, that he has grown knock-kneed in endeavouring to repeat. B. sits down, because once, when he had a habit of falling forward (very likely he now falls back), it restored his game. C. turns in his toes because it cured him of swaying his body. Of course, it was stopping swaying, not standing like a crab, which restored his driving; but he did not know at the time what he was doing wrong, and so he has made a fetish of his toe, which, he thinks, is the god of driving. I know a golfer who does all these things, and a good many more. In his case they have long ceased to have any meaning or effect upon his play, earning him only the reputation of the ugliest-styled good player in the world.

BOOK I - **THE ART OF GOLF**

Besides the innumerable kinds of missing to which we are liable, certain players get into a way of driving exceptionally high or unusually low. Those who have acquired the latter peculiarity are not, like their opposites, dissatisfied, although they ought to be; for, of the two, they are likely to be the worse players. The high driver is inclined to be impatient at finding himself always playing the odd; but the other, although never steady, is reluctant to part with his reputation for length from the tee, and therefore seldom reforms. Nor is it so easy for him to do so as for the other, whose fault is due to simpler causes.

High driving is the result of too upright a swing. I do not mean that the onlooker sees the club go over the player's head, or anything of that sort; but he may detect that the club reaches, and also follows the ball at too steep a gradient. The typical high driver has a neat style—a little too easy, perhaps. He stands open, and with the ball too much opposite the right foot, on which he very decidedly leans his weight. The position makes it difficult for him to take a sweep back near the ground, and his easy, flipping swing tends to make the departure more abrupt still. Of course, many a skier does not stand in this way. So much the better for him; he will have less trouble in describing a full segment of a circle, and of a larger one. It is not the position, but the way of coming down on the ball which skies it. A man standing for a pull, and pressing, often skies. If he asks his caddy how that was, he will say, 'You swung too quick.' So he did, but in this case quickness was the result of lifting the club too straight up, in his hurry to be back. I have often noticed that when a long, pulling shot is intended, the sky can be foretold if the player place himself with the ball less opposite the left foot than it should be for a bow-shaped raker.

In driving low, it is essential that the weight of the body rest more on the left than on the right leg, and that the hands pass over an imaginary line between the eye and the ball, in advance of the club head. If he is in the habit of standing square to the line he is going, it will be observed that a low driver has his ball more nearly opposite his left foot than is orthodox. This manner of address is not the cause of his abnormal trajectory, but a correction necessary to make his scheme of hitting succeed; as his hands are to pass over the ball before the club head (not at the same instant, as in the case of a true

PART II - CH. 4 - OF PECULIARITIES AND FAULTS

driver), he must thus stand behind, because if he did not, there would be no room between his grip and the ground for the club to continue its course after impact. By standing behind, the limit of arm's reach is touched immediately the ball is struck, and the hands sweep up to the level of the shoulder, leaving room between them and the ground for the club to follow. There would be no objection to this mode of driving, so efficient when it comes off, were it not bristling with difficulties. For one thing, a hook must be expected from time to time. The ball is too near the extreme point to which it is possible to sweep the club along the line of fire, the point at which the hands must do one of three things—stop altogether, rise towards the level of the shoulder, or sweep round the body. The first contingency has nothing to do with golf. If the hands are at the rise before the ball is reached, so is the club, and we have a skimmer off the horn, or a top. If they are kept down to prevent it, the club must sweep round and hook the ball. To see that this must be so, take an exaggerated case. Let the player stand normally—that is, parallel to the line of fire; but let the ball be placed as far in front of the left foot as it ought properly to be behind it. By leaning well on to that leg, it may be driven straight, but it would be easier to drive it at right angles. Low driving is prone to deride its votaries in another way. For them, a topped, or a
 heeled, or a toed ball is the same thing as for others; but woe betide the low driver if he take it thick. His adversary's 'sclaff' will send as far anything else, provided he has his grip firm. A little grass and earth no more checks a club than a little skin a razor. Let the other touch ground, and his ball will spout into the air, and land twenty yards from the tee; or he may give a wrench, turn his club, and drive away to cover point. His hands being in advance of it, they are nearer to the ground than the club's length, so that it jams, stops, and jerks the ball up feebly; or else it carves out a new course for itself away to the right, round the gate the hands have closed, and there is a raker to whatever country lies in that direction. With a hook to begin with, and a shot like this to follow, the player, after two long shots, may find himself again at the tee. Instead of standing parallel to their intended direction, low drivers, and those who are so foolish as to try to be against wind, sometimes get rid of the risk of sticking in the ground by standing for a pull. They sweep the ball round, the club passing over the ground as does a scythe, instead of straight over it. The great disadvantage of this expedient is its wildness. The ball must go off at a tangent from the circular sweep, and there is only one which is straight. For low driving an upright club is best. It is easier to stand over it—an essential. If you play for a pull, the arc of the circle described over the ground is larger, and the tangents at which the ball flies off

more nearly coincident with It. The lowest driving club is the putter, because it is so upright; but of course it is too short to carry far.

Getting both hands well under the club also produces a low carry, and fairly long shots against wind, or where the ground is favourable. But players in this style are not long drivers under ordinary circumstances. Indeed, but for their balls flying low they would be short, this grip, as already shown, making a free, full swing impossible.

Although short drivers are scarcely a class by themselves, it is convenient now to treat consecutively some of the causes of shortness not already incidentally mentioned. Amongst those who are born late into the golfing world (whose period of gestation has endured, say thirty years), many deliberately confine themselves to a half swing. Very properly beginning with this, they put a check upon their growing suppleness, and trust to powerful clubs and clean hitting. There is much to be said in favour of such procedure. They sooner arrive at maturity, and they escape (by keeping back from them) all the man-traps laid for the long-swing hunter. A half swing will never enable a man to say that he has driven the longest ball on record—at least truthfully, which is doubtless different—but it is effective, and will last. What a slogger loses in carry by shortness of sweep, he nearly regains by tautness of muscle. The slogger has a great advantage in this, too, that he is never tempted to press through wounded vanity. If he is outdriven a little, what of it? Is it not wonderful that he should get so far? How strong he feels. Better still, how strong he is admitted to be. It is a simple proportion sum. A. drives 200 yards with one shot, B. 190 with half a shot; how much stronger is B . than A.? Whilst his biceps is being admired, A.'s, which is, perhaps, bigger, must remain in its sleeve; or if produced, what is it? Bad meat, evidently, to judge by the driving. A. may indeed, perhaps, be evidently a clumsy player, and his reputation for strength will, in consequence, be saved; but it is a poor alternative to choose between being an awkward Samson and a puny fellow. Of all short drivers the slogger is the happiest; whilst his converse—he whose swing is short after impact—is the most contemptible in the matter of strength. As I have before pointed out, no one notices where a man's club goes after hitting the ball. The reversed slogger is merely written down a fraud if he has broad shoulders. The onlooker will conclude that they are tailor-made. To make it worse, his driving is even shorter than the slogger's. For

PART II - CH. 4 – OF PECULIARITIES AND FAULTS

some reason, which I do not know, the second part of a swing is the more telling of the two.

We have seen that if a man has not a first-class combination of hand and eye, he will not have a game at all if he aims at very long driving. At the same time, many err on the side of hitting too easily, especially at first. Both mind and muscle accustom themselves to a conception of how the thing is to be done, of which they never get rid. Once formed, it is of no use for them to hit harder, unless they make a fresh start altogether. These are usually neat players, who stand too near the ball. But it is no use to get further away. Their muscles have accustomed themselves to work in a certain way.

A common cause of short driving, apart from eye (of course, in these paragraphs I am speaking of players, not duffers), is a loose grip. There is confusion of opinion as to how tight one ought to hold. One fine driver will tell you that he grasps his club lightly; another, that he clings as firmly as possible. The difference of opinion arises from quality of hands, and it may be assumed that neither lets the club move in the least degree from the beginning to the end of a stroke. A soft, well-padded hand, or a strong one, is firm unconsciously; a bony one must hold tight; a weak, bony hand, no matter what its owner is otherwise, conduces to short driving. If it holds tight, other muscles become sympathetically too rigid, and the ball is nipped. If it holds naturally, the swing must either be easy, or else the club slips a little. All three conditions of matters produce short driving. The golfer with weak hands must learn to hold tight without telegraphing the exertion to other muscles—a very difficult feat—or accept shortish driving as his lot. If he does this, the second alternative—to hold naturally and swing easy—is the best to adopt. To the first he cannot settle, the third will rub and blister his hands.

BOOK I - **THE ART OF GOLF**

5
OF TEMPORARY FAULTS

A man's golf, like the rest of him, is subject to many temporary ailments. By simply living as usual, his body will recover; by golfing, his golf will. For colds, golf, and biliousness, the less doctor's stuff we can do with, the better. Yet prescriptions used in moderation may hasten the restoration of health or game, if it is the right medicine. That is the danger.

Young golfers have often a sad time of it from hitting hard in the wrong way. The common phrase, 'Putting your back into it,' misleads them. The experienced player understands by this that from his foot to his hand he is to be one springy, supple sapling—that he is to be all of a piece—the stronger muscles accommodating themselves to do the same work as the weak, the greatest power of the weakest being the limit of force required of the strong. The young player misapprehends what is meant, and puts his back into it as the blacksmith does wielding his hammer, or the athlete putting a weight. In consequence, he commits many fatal mistakes—falling forward towards the ball, back from it, or swaying sideways over the right leg in swinging back. These things are done in order to catch the ball a terrible thud. One has seen (or even felt) boys flicking peas off the backs of their hands. The peas would not fly as far if driven from the shoulder. A golf ball is, indeed, too heavy to flick; but it is equally too light to putt like a 16 lb. cannon-ball. I have already warned the beginner against swaying side-ways; no more need be said about

BOOK I - THE ART OF GOLF

that. The second time he is bitten with the desire to squeeze, there will be an epidemic of falling forward. He will not know what he is doing, but the consequences will be apparent—hitting off the heel, club-breaking, ground-thudding—particularly the first. Most likely his caddy will make things worse by bad advice; attacking the symptoms, not the cause of the disease. His caddy will say, 'Stand further away.' This sounds like common-sense, but it is not, any more than taking a foot-rule to measure the height of a mountain would be. The player tries it, falls in more, and heels as much. Desperately, he stands so that the ball is two feet beyond his reach whilst addressing it. The result is the same. Evidently he is not too near. Cynically he gets quite close, and lo! there is an epidemic of toeing and more club-breaking. Now he thinks he has discovered a secret, viz. that toeing is to be cured by standing further away, heeling by getting nearer. With this valuable piece of knowledge he expects, in no time, to find a stance which will compel the middle of his club and the ball to meet. But he does not, and never will until, after long grief and pain, he comes back humbly to the point from which he began to go wrong. The worst of thumping at a ball with the weight of the body is that now and then—just often enough to lure on its victim—there will be a long wild shot; occasionally, even a long straight one—longer than any he has driven before, the ball happening to be caught with a sweep which has been quickened to reach it before the player has quite lost his balance.

A ball hit off the toe is usually pulled, and one off the heel skids to the right. When an experienced player hits in either of these ways, it is to be hoped that he will recognise them as accidents due to faulty aim, instead of asking, 'What am I doing wrong?' It is as foolish to attribute these occasional shots to style, as it would be were they complete globers. But all pulled balls are not off the toe, nor heeled ones off the heel. You may have an epidemic of either unstraightness without wandering from the middle of the club. Pulling in this way is due to the grip of the hands having got out of proportion. The right may have got too much above the club, or the left too much below it. Nature, i.e. a free address and careful aim, will provide a remedy, if the matter is left in her hands. If not, the disease grows worse, till the player finds his elbow sticking up before him so much that he can scarcely

PART II - CH. 5 – OF TEMPORARY FAULTS

see the ball if the left hand is at fault, whilst there will be symptoms of cramp in that wrist if it be the right. Sometimes heeling (I still mean skidding to the right off the middle of the club) may arise from too timid a care not to pull, consequent checking of the swing by pulling in the arms, or by throwing one's-self back. If the golfer has done one of these last two things, he will be conscious of it after the shot. Not so if his heel is due to another cause—placing the ball too nearly opposite the right foot, and catching it, consequently, before the club head has got into the straight.

It is true that skidding to right or to left, hitting off the toe or off the heel, may come from actually being too near or too far from the ball but if it is discovered that either is the case, it is, nevertheless, dangerous to get further away or nearer. Rather, for the next shot, one should shake himself loose, and address the ball without prejudice. To get nearer or further away, is almost certain to demoralise driving altogether. The former stiffens the player, till he feels like the poker swinging the tongs; the latter tempts him to crouch over his work, so that he cannot do it for fear of toppling forward.

Although getting nearer, or further away, are useless as devices for making the ball go straight, they are mistakes that one is constantly falling into. It is within most golfers' experience that suddenly, and unaccountably, they go off their game entirely. They become feeble, uncertain, and, above all, uncomfortable in their address. When such a breakdown occurs, the cause of it is often standing at a wrong distance. The player does not feel that he is wrong. The error has crept gradually and insidiously into his style. He has been unconsciously varying his distance, inch by inch. Not that a foot nearer or further than ordinary affects play. In fact, everybody varies at each shot in this respect; but there is a point at which one's game suddenly collapses. If the breakdown be complete, it is not easy to detect the cause of it, for the feeling that one is going to foozle is so paralysing, that one is likely to go entirely to ruin beyond hope of recovery—for that day, at least. But there may be nothing more than an evident incapacity to make the ball go a respectable distance, however cleanly hit. If this is the result of standing too near, the player will presently notice that he is inclined to do one of several things in

BOOK I - **THE ART OF GOLF**

addition to driving feebly. For instance, swinging back, there is a tendency to strike the shoulder; but it is more particularly after impact that the consequences of a wrong stance will reveal themselves. The player will be inclined at one shot to throw himself back; at another, his swing may end with an uncomfortable twiddle. Some shots he will jerk, stopping the club altogether; or, being quite determined not to do this, I have seen a golfer actually break his shaft by striking his left shoulder. These are the symptoms if the player laudably persevere in hitting with the middle of his club. Should he determine to let out at the ball whatever happens, he will founder it off the heel. If he has crept too far away, and is covering the extra distance by stretching out his arms, there will be a tendency to swing over the head rather than round the neck. If he is stooping to reach it, he will be inclined to fall forward, to jerk into the ground, and fail to follow (which may cause him to imagine that his fault is a loose grip), or there will merely be a general sense of decrepitude, proving itself not imaginary, by short, puffy shots. If the player make up his mind to let into it, he may hit off the heel, just as in the case of being too near, but with this difference, that he may make a fair drive, either straight or hooked— hooked, to his astonishment, off the heel. It is quite true that, standing too far away, a player may hit off the toe; but this is usually an isolated accident (caused by taking a careless stance), which will not be repeated unless he is foolish enough to apply a corrective next shot.

Sensible golfers, either of experience, or who have devoutly accepted my previous remarks upon caddies' advice, know the folly of forcing themselves to do, or not to do, these things when told they are standing too much in front, not letting their arms away, not getting their shoulders in, etc. They (the sensible golfers of both sorts) know from experience, or from this book; that direct surgical treatment is of no use, and that, although their caddies' comments are quite just, they are better to keep hammering on, leaving the cure to nature, than to attack the symptoms. If they are very sensible, it is, however, no harm that they should know the causes of these things. We get too much front (see Fig. 1) when the sweep we picture ourselves giving the ball is concave, like a scythe-cut, instead of straight. It is very common to drift into this mental attitude towards the stroke. Our club describes a semicircle

PART II - CH. 5 – OF TEMPORARY FAULTS

through the air. Why not another over the ground? Why not, indeed, when there is a feeling of greater power, too? There is nothing to be said against this so long as all goes well; but sooner or later there will be a wild shot or two, a consequent loss of confidence, exaggeration of the position, and a general breakdown. What the player should do under these circumstances, is to set himself to what ought never to have been abandoned—the sweeping of his club straight in the direction the ball is wanted to go. Let him not think of his feet; they will follow his intention.

When we are not letting our arms away, it is useless to begin pushing them out after the ball. It is rather the time to nip it firmly, and, above all, to remember that the best of our force must not be expended in swinging the club back. At once things will come right, unless one of the results already spoken of reveal that we are too near the ball.

We do not get our shoulders in when it is the idea to follow the ball upwards the instant it is struck. There is nothing more tempting than to do this. We feel that it is our place to lift it; that otherwise it must grub along the ground, which of course it would, were it not for friction, or gravitation, or some such thing which the golfer naturally forgets about, if he ever knew.

It is extraordinary, but nevertheless true, that the most serious, complete, and persistent breakdowns are due to elementary aberrations. Very often a long run of exceptionally steady play will force on us, in spite of previous experience, the conviction that at last we have discovered that will-o'-the-wisp, the secret of driving, and that, by remembering it, we will be steady for ever. We are temporary victims of the illusion which the bad player never shakes off at all, with this difference,— that by certain extraneous expedients he hopes to play, and never does, whilst we, playing well, hope to stereotype the means by which we are doing it. Yesterday we were driving far and sure; to-day we are determined to play with hands and feet placed, and club swung exactly in the same manner. We do not quite get a hold of it; search, and break down; search more, and break down worse. There are few of us wise enough to learn, once and for all, the lessons here taught, viz. :—1st, that as

BOOK I - **THE ART OF GOLF**

soon as any point of style is allowed, during the shot, to occupy the mind more than hitting the ball, a miss, more or less complete, will result; 2nd (and this is less obvious), that nobody can acquire complete uniformity. If we are driving well, do not let us trouble ourselves unduly about how it is done. Let us rather bear in mind that slight nuances of difference in grip, or stance, or swing, are of no importance. For instance, I am driving well, and cannot help observing that I have my hands more than usually over the club. Just because I have noted the fact, there will be, next time I take my stance, an inclination to alter this. It would be a mistake to balk myself. If we are not thinking of style at all, being too intent upon the match, there will be little variation; but if we are, let us give way to it, saying to ourselves, 'All right, do what you like about that—I am busy with the main issue.' I do not mean that we can overswing or get into a constrained position with impunity; but there is no danger of extremes so long as differences of attitude, mental or bodily, towards the ball, are not expected to drive it. It will be within the experience of many, that when an adversary, after playing a few holes, explains that he feels he is going to drive well to-day, because he has hit upon the proper something or other, he ends by being an easy victim. But if he says, 'I feel that it does not matter how I go up to the ball,' we may be sure that nothing but good play will secure us the victory after a hard-fought battle.

It does seem as if, when a breakdown takes place from attempting to stereotype a successful style, nothing were simpler than to recover. But this is not always, nor, indeed, usually, the case. Of the best players it has often to be said for months that So-and-so is not playing well. Nay, a breakdown may last so long that a first-class player becomes an acknowledged second, and remains so for years or for ever. This is not a common case; but retrogression, more or less complete, of from a day to three months is. It seems as if periods of bad play ought never to last long. The player does not anticipate it. Nothing seems easier than for him to recollect the manner or manners in which he hit when steady. He tries for them, one after the other, and fails.

PART II - CH. 5 – OF TEMPORARY FAULTS

Although a shot is made in a moment, there are many which remain green in the memory, and of which the player can recall, long after the particular sensation, how his shoulders seemed to get into that one, his feet to grip the ground for another, his hands to have held the club as if made for it for another. A man has always a dozen pet shots in stock, to the sensations of which he tries (and fails) to return when a breakdown comes. Then he says, 'Never mind; perhaps I am thinking too much of how to hit, and too little of hitting.' This is sure to be true; but he still fails. During his spell of good play all the elements of driving, such as sweeping the ball away, placing the club behind it, etc., became second nature. During his period of style-hunting some vicious tricks have got grafted on to them. The name of these is legion. He may know, and be told by his caddy, that he is swinging too fast, without knowing that it is so, because he is lifting his club too straight up. A lack of confidence may have twisted him into some uneasy attitude, or (this is almost certain) he is hitting too hard, which he was able to do successfully when in form. It looks as if I were now admitting (what has already been denied) that there are a thousand and one things to remember at every shot. This is not so. The very reason of the continuance of the breakdown is that the player (although he tells himself he has) has not purged himself of these things. When playing well he swung swiftly and stood firmly, but within the limits of ease; now there are quickness and stiffness without ease, and, above all, impatience to recover. At last he will humble himself utterly. He will give up mending his style. To his feeling, his swing will be short and stiff, his hitting weak and careful. The recovery will be rapid, but not immediate, as all this time he has been trying to make it. His lost confidence will cause many a miss; but after a round, or even less, there will be a recovery of fitness for freedom. He will by degrees tighten his grip, and let them have it. But let him take care. Let him beware of noting his symptoms, so that the way to do it may not escape him again. If he does so, another relapse is certain. It is only when each shot is treated as a separate act, in no way guaranteed by previous good ones; when each time he addresses the ball his chief care is to hit it— not far, not in this way, not in that, but hit it; when how far it is to be struck is scarcely thought of; when, during the swing, there is no consciousness of how he is swinging— that there will be an almost continuous record of palpable

BOOK I - **THE ART OF GOLF**

hits. That nobody almost ever plays a dozen shots equally clean, exactly as far as each other, is because they cannot absolutely do this. The experienced player knows that his last shot was perfect because his mind was applied to it, and to it alone; and yet he cannot prevent himself from trying to make the next as good, not in the same way, but by repeating the last. One can watch the process in any adversary who has played a strong, steady game for (say) half a round. He is thoroughly stretched, supple, confident, and consequently out comes one of those extra long shots. If you and he both leave him alone, he takes no heed, and other extra ones follow at intervals. But, if you are a cunning player, flatter him about his shot, point out that his next is as long, and, if he takes the bait, the third may be long too; but your experienced eye will detect that he has staggered and over-exerted himself to produce it. It is a question of your tact against his sense, whether you get him broken down altogether, or whether he returns to hitting steadily and without prejudice.

In conclusion, I will summarise the times we are in most danger of relapses. One is, as just explained, when we are in a particularly good vein of play. Pride goes before a fall. The slightest shade of retrogression from a perfection we have come to consider normal may make us impatient, or lead to an examination of the cause, and either impatience or examination are fatal. To be beaten in an important match, to be distinctly out-classed by a player not considered our superior, when playing our best game, is very trying. On the other hand, an uninteresting match, which we can win as we choose, may start us on a fatal course of experimenting. Lastly, after a long absence from the green the risk is great. There is a false axiom that a man cannot play well under these circumstances, which is often made true because it is accepted. We return to work expecting to do ill. We play carelessly. We hit hard, trusting to Providence before our muscles have got accustomed to their duties; and, in about three days, when our form ought to be returning, it is further away than ever. No wonder! for two days have been employed in acquiring vices. When a man has had a holiday, let him settle down to each shot as if a match or a medal depended on it, and his game, or a better one than he ever played before will be his in no time. Men often absent themselves from the green because they have broken down. These usually

PART II - CH. 5 – OF TEMPORARY FAULTS

recommence humbly, and find their game restored. All returning prodigals should do likewise. The folly of sowing careless shots on fallow ground, in the expectation of reaping good golf, is unspeakable.

BOOK I - **THE ART OF GOLF**

6
OF PLAYING THROUGH THE GREEN

After an accurate tee shot, the second has usually (a grumbler would say, sometimes) to be played from a light lie on soft sward, and is but a repetition of the first. Some people, however, maintain that you should hit as hard as possible from the tee, and take it easy through the green. The wisdom of this is doubtful. It seems to me to be better to hit boldly and with a will in both cases. To attempt to strike harder than hard is, for most men, to top, whilst softer than hard causes a heel or a draw. What club should be used through the green—driver, brassy, or spoon—may be left to individual sentiment. It is common to hear it said, 'I cannot use my play club through the green.' The answer to such nonsense is, 'Learn, then.' But if a man says, 'I prefer my brassy,' then brassy let it be. He is probably the owner of one which happens to suit him well. It is very likely that, in six months, the favourite will be broken, three or four rejected copies will be lying in his box, a pet driver reigning in their stead. Between a driver, brassy, and long spoon, the difference is practically fanciful. It is another matter if a short spoon or a cleek is constantly used for full shots from clean lies. You may be sure you have to do with a poor player if he cannot use the proper club, and does not try to learn.

But, alas! the ball does not always lie well. Then brassy, cleek, iron, and niblick sprawl themselves, fanshaped and derisively, before the mental vision, with a mark of interrogation after each. On the border-land, between good and bad lies, is the hanging ball. One of these with a face a yard or two in front of it, is a bad ball, which can only either be dunched along the ground a short distance with a brassy, or popped equally far with an iron. When there is no face in front, a hanging ball ought to go as far or further than another. Why it baffles many golfers is that they try to raise it instead of playing it downhill, leaving nature to raise it. A caddy will say, 'Turn in the face.' This is good advice if taken to mean that the club is to lie naturally towards the slope it is to drive down. If it is placed hopefully, in accordance with the general lie of the green, a shot similar to what results from turning up the face when the lie is normal must follow. A good general maxim for a bad lie is, when in doubt between two clubs, take the meaner. The violent do not take the hole by force. It is the patient who are rewarded. With a bad lie there is more need than ever of a firm grip and an exact aim. These are the means by which the ball can be forced. A violent swing and a terrific blow may force a clean ball; but a cupped one derides such treatment. There are bad lies and bad lies. Even a thick tuft of legitimate grass is not so bad as it looks. It will scarcely do more than leave a green mark on the club face. But these little sandy patches, half-bred between a bunker and a putting-green, are treacherous indeed. One little teaspoonful of sand taken with the ball, and your adversary gains half a shot. Beware of a cup, however small. If you expect to demolish it by means of a little extra powder, you are mistaken. If the higher side of this innocent little inch of slope is in front of you, the chances of a clean drive are very small—much less than if there is only a lump behind. A careful aim will slip you in between the latter and the ball. Clean balls, lying to you or from you ever so little, must be allowed for, if you are to go straight. These are very deceptive. Sometimes the declivity is not even noticed, and something else is blamed when we fly away off the line. The worst of bad lies are caused by a few sparse shoots of long, wiry grass. I do not know the botanical name of that diabolical stuff; most likely it is christened in a way which it would be impolite to write. These grasses, like cholera, are more virulent in autumn. I say, beware of a few of them. If there are many, the bad lie is self-evident, and we humbly take a niblick. But a few are just as fatal. They whip themselves round the shaft and arrest its progress, like the toasted cheese which clings to your feet in a nightmare, when you are within a hundred yards of the city of refuge, and the avenger at your heels. But bad lies have their bright side. Sometimes, by taking thought, one makes a shot, even with a niblick, which rejoices and surprises. They, moreover, make one grateful for a clean-lying ball. Best of all, the adversary may be the unfortunate. There are few more restful, hopeful, happy moments at golf than those in which he is hesitating about which club to use, cursing his luck, consulting his caddy, changing his stand. It is better even than to see him in a bunker or up against a fence. You know that it is any odds to one that he will take the wrong club, and that the loss of the hole will be due to his own fault. Up against a fence, one's joy is tempered by an uncomfortable feeling that Providence is interfering too much.

BOOK I - **THE ART OF GOLF**

7
OF BUNKER PLAY

Before leaving that part of the game in which sending the ball as far as possible is desirable, it is necessary to consider for a moment a very painful subject—Bunker Play.

The mere appearance of a niblick suggests doubts and fear. Other clubs are graceful, smiling, elegant things. The niblick is an angry-looking little cad, coarse, bullet-headed, underbred. Its face looks up as if to say, 'I will raise the ball into the air.' Its smile is treacherous. It does fulfil its promise sometimes; but just as often it smothers its laughter in the sand, leaving you and the ball nonplussed.

No one is ever proud of his bunker play. Some men of strong shoulders are more successful with the niblick than others; but they do not glory in their strength. There are men who give up the hole when they find themselves in sand, preferring to pretend that they seldom get into any to more substantial advantages. So little is force exerted in a bunker regarded, that men who act thus are not credited with weak physique.

There is at the best little pleasure in niblick play. When you are compelled to ask for that implement, it is under a sense of humiliation at having put yourself into sand. Even if you get out, you are an unprofitable servant, not quite so far on with your work in two shots as you ought to have been in one. Perhaps the feeling nearest akin to pleasure derivable from a niblick shot is a

BOOK I - THE ART OF GOLF

partner's sense of relief when you get the ball out. This the player does not share. With the hopefulness inherent in the true golfer, he expected to succeed. Besides, the twenty yards or so the ball has travelled seem a small result, considering the extent to which his withers are wrung.

If there is small joy to be got from bunker play there may be great sorrow. The ball may not be got out in one shot. Indeed, after six it may be worse in than at first. This may entail nothing more than the giving up of the hole. But supposing your adversary to have played two or three more before you got in, how sickening! In medal play or a stroke match, in which you have backed your score against others, can anything be more awful than to feel a sovereign vanishing at each blow. It is a providential arrangement that a niblick is so coarse an implement. If it were a club that could scarcely be replaced, men would often add shame to woe by breaking it. But a shaft which can infallibly be replaced for a few shillings is useless as a safety valve. On the other hand, a niblick is a formidable weapon of offence, and I have seen the life of an adversary, who counted the oft-repeated shots aloud, in serious danger.

It is worthy of observation that bad players are *ceteris* (i.e. muscles) *paribus* as effective in a bunker as the best. This is because nobody has any theory about his swing or his stand, or this or that, when addressing himself to a common ordinary bunkered ball. Every one simply thuds at it. Men who, on the green, must needs shuffle, bob, and writhe, each in their own manner, as much as if coming into the presence of the Llama of Tibet, the ball waiting for them as calm and stolid as he, will hit freely and naturally with the niblick. Another reason why one man is as good from an ordinary sand cup as another, is that the ball is best dislodged by a jerk. A lot of sand must be forced away with the ball, so that it is really a heavy object for the nonce. As we have seen, it is because it is not always so—because it is so light—because hard thudding will smother it—that skill in driving is an art, and not a mere question of strength.

Most bunkered balls, then, are best dislodged by a good coarse jerk. It is usual to take a full swing with a niblick; but my own opinion is that a half one is more effective, particularly if you use a light club. Whether a heavy or a

PART II - CH. 7 – OF BUNKER PLAY

light one should be carried may be left to individual fancy. The weight of the former makes up for any loss of applicable force.

Sometimes a bunkered ball presents peculiarities which make it unadvisable to apply the common thud. If there is a high face to loft, or if there is a mound of sand close in front of the ball, the shot to be described in the next chapter is advisable. That miniature face in front is particularly apt to cause disappointment. If there is one behind as well, the player grasps at once the horror of the situation, but not if all is clear in that direction. Yet if the ball be struck in the ordinary way, when there is a face only in front, it is as unlikely to be treated successfully as when entirely surrounded. A mound behind, with flat sand in front, is not nearly so serious. By getting in front, and chopping down close to the ball, or simply by driving mound and ball together, satisfactory results may be expected. The above shot is also the only one that will do in a hard, deep, clay-bottomed bunker. If there is no face to get up, it is different. The ball lies then as well as if on the green, except (and it is a considerable exception) that the club cannot be placed behind it. Be cautious with a teed ball in a shallow sand bunker, however. It is very nearly a mad thing to take a wooden club. Even a cleek or an iron must be selected with much solemnity. But if there is a face to rise over!

BOOK I - **THE ART OF GOLF**

8
OF APPROACHING

When the player's ball is within less than a driver shot of the hole, approaching commences, and new qualities—the sense of weight, how to weigh it, appreciation of distance, etc., are called into requisition. The least amount of difference between driving and approaching exists when the distance is still so great that a full shot from a cleek or an iron is advisable. Some players find it easier to drive with wood than with iron; but this is not because the latter should be wielded in a different way. The difficulty is either sentimental, or due to some false attitude of mind. A feeling that an iron club will sink into the ground, or the opposite view, that it is more capable of cutting through it, may incline a man on the one hand to top, on the other to puff the ball. A man's iron shots may go too high because he lays the club unnaturally back, or because, looking upon it as more powerful than a wooden club, he, intending to hit harder, swings too quickly, therefore too straight up and down, therefore lofts too high. These results are not due to the clubs, but to the player's treatment of them. There is one real difference, however, between wood and iron. A golfer who is inclined to cut the ball will find his tendency to swerve to the left greater with the latter, probably because of the more polished face. Long driving with iron clubs is the result of clean hitting, as with wood, except sometimes in the case of beginners, many of whom congratulate themselves on what should be a cause of regret and a hint that something is wrong—namely, that they drive as far with a cleek as with a play club. This something is the possibility of treating the ball as a heavy object with a cleek, and so treating it effectively. A jerk with iron

BOOK I - THE ART OF GOLF

endows it with something of the elasticity of wood. But a jerker can never reach a first-class standard of steadiness. This will dawn on the beginner as he improves, and his jerks will be reserved for cupped balls.

The nomenclature of true approach shots—those requiring less than a full swing, is somewhat indefinite. Half, three-quarter, quarter, wrist shot, etc., mean each something to players who employ the terms, but they have no generally recognised manner nor status. It cannot be laid down that if a full shot goes a hundred yards, a quarter shot goes twenty-five, etc. Nor is there even an approximate law regarding the number of inches the club ought to be drawn back in order to propel the ball an equivalent distance in yards. All that can be done is to give a few general hints as to how to do it, and how not to do it. The sense of weight must be exercised and cultivated by each player for himself.

One rule, without exception, is that no ball, however near the hole, should be played weakly. Even the shortest of all approaches—styme lofting —can only succeed if the ball is swept away, the grip tight, the muscles taut. A weak tap, however long or short the distance, will prove uncertain and disappointing. The length of swing, not the firmness of sweep, should regulate the carry.

The attempt to play an easy full shot is generally recognised as a mistake, and most men consider it wiser to cover the distance with a drive from a weaker club, or an approach shot from a stronger. When it comes to these last, however, the folly of attempting to 'spare' is not equally acknowledged.

Longish approaches are sometimes attempted to be made by means of a half shot. That is to say, the player addresses the ball as in driving; but shortens his swing by getting his hands more under the club than usual, and by keeping all the joints above the diaphragm rigid. This mode of play is scarcely worth cultivating. I do not mean that those who always drive in this way and in no other, or those who, being bad at full shots with irons, have adopted this style with them, ought to reform; but it is difficult to acquire as an occasional means for limiting the length of a drive. The muscles are apt to assert themselves in their usual routine, and a miss to result from the conflict

PART II - CH. 8 – OF APPROACHING

of intention and habit. Nevertheless, half shots of this sort are frequently attempted with a cleek or an iron; but it is an indirect proof of their unsoundness, that no one ever seriously tries to play them with a driver.

Unless under exceptional circumstances, to be considered presently, there are thus only two proper modes of approaching—by full drives from short clubs, and by what are called wrist shots. It will be found that the best players have no styles between these two. According to length of swing for various distances, they speak of quarter, half, three-quarter, or full approach; but these terms are used for their own convenience, and refer merely to longer or shorter shots played in the same style. A half to them means a half wrist, not the half spoken of in the last paragraph. Beginners and others ought clearly to understand that whilst they ought to have one style for driving, whether with wood or iron, successful wrist play is a new departure, and that effective approaches cannot be manufactured out of fragments of a full swing.

What, then, is a wrist shot? For one thing, it is a shot which ought not to be played with the wrists. Their usual name misleads many a beginner, and causes him to flounder hopelessly for years. To use the wrists alone is so neat, comprehensible, and compact an idea that he grasps it at once. He is conscious that using one set of muscles and joints alone, his sense of weight is more delicate. It will not take him long to learn, although it may be years before he is convinced, that this is not the way to do it. It would be less confusing if approaches were called ankle shots *(Note.—Since the above was in type, I have been informed that anciently they were called 'knee' shots, a name for them not misguiding—indeed tutorial, I should like to hear it re-used.)* Properly these joints are brought more into play than the wrists.

Without wishing to direct attention too emphatically to one point, it is nevertheless true that in good approach play the left wrist is absolutely rigid throughout the shot. Men who are masters of the iron may say this is nonsense, and of course they would spoil their play by keeping that or any other point too much in view; but it may easily be noticed that such persons do keep that joint rigid, even although many of them give a preliminary flourish. I say many; but also it may be noticed that, contrary to what is the case in driving, most do not. The rule is to put the club undemonstratively behind the ball, and at once to strike. To the tyro, then, if he is getting on well, I would say nothing; but if he is not, a perfectly stiff wrist will do much to reveal the secrets of approaching. Of course, too much attention to and misapprehension of this point (as of most golf secrets) may lead to faults. The player may make wrist-bending impossible by getting his hand under the club, or by laying the spare end of the shaft along his arm. He is also apt to tuck his elbows into his sides, and play as if they were strapped to his body, or, going to the other extreme in order to give his left arm free play, stick it out so far that the swing must be a slice. The proper position is easy—the left hand well over the club, so that the player may be over his work without stooping over it.

As a rule, players talk and think more about the position of the right than of the left hand in approaching. They discuss whether the thumb ought to be down the shaft or over it, tight or loose. So long as the elbow is close to the body, these things do not seem to be matters of the slightest importance. Approachers of equal skill indulge in all the variations. Indeed, some are not constant to their own fancy, sometimes having the thumb over, sometimes down the shaft. As in driving, the position of the right hand is a point too much attended to, that of the left too little.

Whilst, as we have seen, in driving a good deal of licence is allowable in the matter of stance—some players placing their feet parallel to the line of fire, some with their back a little to it, some with their face —the last is the only proper position for approaching. One has but to take a club in hand, and the necessity for this will make itself evident. Let the experimenter actually pause after swinging back (say) two feet. Standing in the proper way, there will be no tendency on the part of the club to waver from its line. But let him stand square, or in front, and swing back the same distance: the position is stiff, and it is difficult to avoid describing a loop at the beginning of the return journey.

Assuming that the player has accepted the principle that the length of his approaches is to be regulated by distance of swing, he ought soon to become pretty accurate for distances from twenty-five to one hundred yards, one would think. Why men remain so uncertain is due to many causes. For one

PART II - CH. 8 – OF APPROACHING

thing, they do not adhere to the principle. At short distances they are inclined to swing easily, which really means flabbily, and with a loose grip, or else to swing too little, and apply more force. At long distances they hit extra hard. Now, to acquire accuracy, it must be realised that at all distances the grip must be firm and the muscles taut; and that the ball will be reached with more impetus, and therefore hit harder for every inch the club is drawn back. The temptation to over-stiffen one's-self, and force for a long approach, can only be resisted by careful watching. There is a natural tendency to cover a little more distance by an ounce more of exertion—by quickening of the swing, rather than by an inch more of it—leading, if not checked, to a habit of jerking, which renders the regulation of distance impossible. This is a real difficulty; others are either self-made or due to ignorance. One of the latter, almost universal with tyros, is to attempt to scoop the ball up into the air. Nothing is more common than to see the face of the iron, after the shot, held up as if for alms, whilst the ball is trundling along the ground. Let the golfer ever remember that it is the lie of the club, not a turn of the wrist, which is responsible for the loft. Some men can never make up their minds whether they intend to take the ball clean, or to shave off a little turf with it. Having made a good shot with turf, they regulate the swing accordingly, till (a foozle must happen sometimes, however one plays) they take too much, or make a good shot clean. It matters very little whether a player takes ground with him or not; but it becomes serious if he is hazy as to his intentions. Again, the custom of using sometimes a heavy iron, sometimes a light one, sometimes a cleek, sometimes trying to run the ball, sometimes to loft it very high, postpones the day when comparative certainty may be attained. What the player ought to do is to decide what club he will habitually use; whether he will take turf or not; note the height of his loft when he hits as he means to, and stick to this as his standard. This done, there ought to be nothing to think of, in nine shots out of ten, except the length of swing necessary to cover the distance, and accurate hitting.

The player who can make lofts from normal lies to within a yard or so of where he means, even although he foozles in complicated situations, overruns ticklishly-placed holes, or strikes the tops of hills which are between him and the hole, is more effective than he who has as many styles, and as many irons, as there are holes in the green. A showy shot which comes off should be

BOOK I - **THE ART OF GOLF**

hailed as 'good fluke,' and its player ought to thank Providence instead of smiling round complacently. Do I mean that one ought merely to thwack at the ball despairingly whenever it is in a difficulty? Certainly not. But if it seems feasible to play a fairish shot in a normal way, that is better than to attempt anything gaudy. If something exceptional must be tried, let it be as slight a modification as possible of orthodox play—let it be a deduction from it. Out of a cup one's natural inclination is to try to spoon the ball, from long grass to mow it, against wind to force it. The golfer ought to ignore cups, grass, or wind as natural features, reducing each to terms of yards. There are very few lies which it is not the best policy to treat in this way. So long as there is an even chance of getting the ball to within twenty yards of the hole by ordinary means, fancy shots ought not to be undertaken, for there is little doubt that the latter oftener fail than succeed. I do not mean that proficiency in the showier kinds of approaches is impossible. Many a player makes himself the talk of the green for a season by his marvellous power of lofting a ball so as to lie where it alights; but invariably the iron with which this is done breaks; or, in some other way, the proud owner of it loses his abnormal skill, and the last state of that man is worse than the first. His practice of approaching in the simplest way has been abandoned for this more fickle masterliness, and you see him topping, puffing, missing, with cleeks, irons, mashies, in the vain effort to strike out a new road to glory.

It may seem unnecessary to insist so much upon anything so self-evident as the necessity of adhering to one simple mode of approaching; but it is requisite, unless preaching is vain. The temptation to indulge in variations is almost irresistible. The devil seems to hover over the golfer, and ever to whisper In his ear, 'Try this,' or 'Try that.' He listens to the tempter. It would be so nice if he did chop it up in the air out of that hole, and lay it dead. 'It may rise,' he thinks, 'whilst it will only look like a fluke if it scuffles up within holing, played in the ordinary way.' He yields, tries, and odds are it goes but a few yards, eliciting the well-known cry of repentance, 'I ought not to have tried it.'

Take another case. The hole is just beyond a bunker. Playing properly, you must run past. The temptation to lay the iron back, or to put a spin on from the heel, or to deaden the fall by hitting off the point, or to employ some new

PART II - CH. 8 – OF APPROACHING

system lately patented, is very great. That it is not the game is proved by the secret joy experienced when an adversary announces his intention of making one of these showy attempts. Even in a score game, six shots behind and three holes from home, the flames of hope begin to flicker in your sulky bosom.

Although rarer than golfers make them, there are occasions when fancy shots are worth trying. For instance, if a bunker is between us and the hole, danger beyond it, and no chance of even a half unless we are in in two, the ball must be lofted high or else spun. Some players, in these circumstances, use a lofted iron in the usual way, others try to lay back an ordinary one. Both shots are difficult, but, to my thinking, that with the specially made club is the riskier. It must strike the ball with absolute precision. If taken too thick, the shape of the club makes it dive into the ground, and puff the ball a yard; too clean, it will skim it a hundred yards with the force that would have lofted it fifty. Laying back the iron is not so uncertain if properly done. One way not to do it is to play an ordinary approach shot, the face of the club pointing upwards. A top is as certain as if, in driving off the tee, you pose the lead instead of the sole of the play-club on the ground. Properly, the laying back is not done by rolling the club over on its heel, but by putting it on the ground in advance of the hands, and (this is the important point) drawing it back almost along the ground. So low must the swing be that if made full (which it never is for this shot), it would be round the waist instead of over the shoulder. In this shot the ball must be swept away, not cut or nipped. There will be a spin on the ball, but woe to the player who attempts to increase this spin with a turn of the wrist. There is no reason why great certainty in this shot should not be attained. Indeed, it is a favourite with many at from fifty to twenty yards, but its application is limited to clean lies, and lies in soft grass, as is the use of the lofted iron. It is useless to try it on a hard green, still more so from a bad lie. However tightly the club be grasped, the attitude is not adapted for forcing a ball. Attempted in a bunker, the result is almost invariably disastrous. A table-spoonful of sand is too much for the strongest arms.

There is another fancy shot which differs utterly from the last except in respect of results. It may be played at all times instead of the other, whilst from a bad lie it is the only way I know of to loft a ball. In this shot the club is lifted more nearly straight up than in a normal one, crashing into the turf behind the ball. But there is more to attend to. Why many fail at this blow is that, when mother earth interferes with the completion of the segment of their circle, they submit. To succeed, the player must follow the ball, not in the same curve that he swept down on it, which is impossible, but as best he can. This best will be an ellipse. (See this shot illustrated, Plates XIV. and XV.) It is wonderful how beautifully the enemy will spout into the air. Among all these shots, which are loosely described as wrist-shots, this is the only one in which the wrists legitimately come into play. To get the club, as it were, round the corner, after the ground is reached, there must be a twist from them. The disadvantage of the shot is that, even from good lies, the distance is extremely difficult to regulate. It will fail altogether if anything but a strong blow be struck. Still many will remember the wonderful accuracy Jamie Anderson acquired in it some years ago, hitting a full blow at all distances, and regulating the length of his loft by the inches of turf he took behind the ball. In a bunker this shot is also useful (a niblick, or mashy, of course, being the weapon employed), better perhaps than the ordinary dig. By it a ball may, if necessary, be lofted higher, and, what is still more to the point, it will often be got out of a deep cup, in which the common thud would merely bury it.

When the ball is close to a straight face, a shot somewhat like this last may, in desperation, be attempted. The club is lifted nearly straight up, and brought down with a crash an inch or so behind it, as if the only intention were to split open the ground. There should be no attempt to follow. Sometimes (I say emphatically sometimes) the ball will spout up into the air in a marvellous manner. This shot cannot come off except out of loose sand.

A style of approach often employed is running the ball with the iron, either along the ground, or very little above it. When this is attempted, it is customary to turn in the club face. By so doing, the player gets the sentiment of his intention; but that is all. The turning of the iron alone will not run a ball. The essential thing is that the player be well over the ball, and his hands slightly in advance of it—in fact, just as far from the '*juste milieu*' at one side, as they are at the other when he attempts to ' lay back ' the iron. (See Plate XVI.) It is necessary to point out that the position of the hands, not the turning in

PART II - CH. 8 – OF APPROACHING

of the club, is the essential thing in this shot, because, although doing the latter inclines one to the former, the one is quite possible without the other. (Let me observe parenthetically that merely turning the toe of a club, in or out, is of no effect in any shot, except to convert a properly made tool into a bad one. Placing the club out of its proper position is simple folly, unless it be part of the result of the mode of address, not an isolated contortion.) Our player, then, has taken his position for a skimming approach. His hands are well in front, the club face turned in—not to keep the ball low, but partly because it now naturally lies that way, partly because that way of resting it makes it a more upright club for the nonce—and uprightness, we have seen, is conducive to low trajectory. A common mistake is now to jerk—the thing, of all others, which ought not to be done. Jerking raises a ball. The club should rather be dragged, the wrists rigid, the grip excessively firm. From rough ground near the hole, or on a bad putting-green, this shot is very useful. Many prefer it to an ordinary loft at shortish distances, the latter being more difficult within, say, thirty yards than when the player has further to carry. There are some who employ it for all approaches, and with good effect too. These you may recognise by their stance, which is often square or even in front.

There are four clubs used for ordinary approach work— the putter, the cleek, the iron, and the mashy.

The first, of course, can only be used on very flat ground. Long putts, and the putters thereof, are much despised. A putt of sixty yards laid dead causes anger or laughter, according to the temper of the adversary. But I am bound to say that those who are well practised in 'skelping' often call forth the exhibition of one or other of these forms of emotion. The worst of this mode of approaching is that, sooner or later, it undermines the constitution of the most delicate and valuable club in the set; whilst to carry two putters—one as a whipping-boy—is unwise. They cannot be made exactly alike, and, even if they are nearly so, hesitating between the two at intermediate distances is apt to put a player's putting powers out of gear.

Cleek approaches do not lay your respectability open to doubt like long putts, which have the same odour of meanness as the 'sneak' of boys' cricket.

BOOK I - THE ART OF GOLF

Although for the most part low, they are not absolutely crawling things. They have one distinct advantage over iron approaches. The cleek, lofting low, can be used at greater distances than the iron, thus bridging over that rather wild country which lies between a full cleek or spoon shot and the approach proper. But the cleek has little else to recommend it as against the iron, which, played with equal skill, is in most circumstances more effective. The least hillock will catch and kill a cleek approach, whilst, even in the absence of such obstructions, the run at the finish is necessarily so long, that the chances of stopping or turning bumps are greatly increased. Some people will object that there is as much chance of a lucky as of an unlucky fall. This is not so. Nature does not smile upon golf. Being inanimate, she is more apt to oppose obstruction than to further motion. The cleek approacher is consequently proverbial for grumbling at his luck. When the worm cast turns his ball, he is the worm that turns. Moreover, the trajectory of a cleek shot is so low, that the least shade of top will prevent the ball from rising at all, and then it will cling to the ground and go halfway. From an iron, a shot one degree too low is still in the element it was meant to traverse, not in grass, which has double as much resistance. 'But my cleek is as much lofted as an iron,' is what one often hears. No doubt it is. Most cleeks are. It is not the difference of lay, but of shape, which governs their respective lofting powers. A cleek, to loft as high as an iron of the same lay, would require to be thicker on the sole than they usually are, and as sharp as a knife on its upper edge. Even then its height of loft would be very uncertain. The change in thickness of metal from below upwards being so sudden, a microscopic variation in the height of impact would materially alter the amount of loft. In short, it is the depth of face, not the lay, which causes the difference in execution between a cleek and an iron. Certainly a more lofted cleek might be used. But such a weapon would in no respect be better than an iron, and would have the drawback of all laid-back clubs, a subject already noticed.

For approaching, the iron is on the whole the best club yet devised, and the one most in favour with players. It is supposed to be a very difficult thing to get a good iron. This is not the case, although it is very common to see men owners of, and proud of, very bad ones, which vastly increase their difficulties in approaching. This is because they set their affections on a wrong style of club. It is usual to carry two irons—a heavy for driving, a light

PART II - CH. 8 – OF APPROACHING

for approaching. This nomenclature sets men on the wrong scent from the beginning. The two ought to be called the driving and the approaching iron, without this (as I hold erroneous) dogmatic reference to their comparative weights. Whether a driving iron ought to be heavy or light, or whether it ought to be carried at all, is a matter for individual taste to decide. But there is no greater mistake than to have a light 'light iron.' To say what weight it should be is impossible, so much depends upon the player's style and build. Roughly, it may be stated, however, that an iron lighter than a driving cleek is simply a useless toy. Error in the direction of heaviness, whilst less common, would be less fatal.

The lay of an approaching iron, as well as the weight, is a matter of importance. If too straight in the face, it either will not carry over bunkers and hazards, or else its owner will be led into a habit of jerking, in order to make it do so. On the other hand, a much lofted iron is very difficult to use. Unless the ball be struck with absolute precision, it either digs into the ground, or hits with its edge. A medium amount of loft is best. By merely looking at the club, it is impossible to decide whether its lay is right or not. An upright club for the same work requires more pitch than a flat one, experience proving that (as already insisted on) the more upright a club is the lower its trajectory. Again, the thicker the sole is in proportion to the top, the higher it will send the ball. The proper way to decide whether an iron has the right lay or not is to try it. If a half-topped shot travels further than a lofted one over ordinary turf, the club has too much pitch; if the opposite happens, it has too little. However pretty an instrument, to whatsoever great man it may have belonged, reject it, and pick a new one out of a shop.

BOOK I - **THE ART OF GOLF**

PLATE IX. ADDRESSING FOR AN APPROACH SHOT

PART II - CH. 8 – OF APPROACHING

PLATE X. 'JUST WITHIN A WRIST' (1)

BOOK I - **THE ART OF GOLF**

PLATE XI. 'JUST WITHIN A WRIST' (2)

PART II - CH. 8 – OF APPROACHING

PLATE XII. SIXTY YARDS FROM THE HOLE (1)

BOOK I - **THE ART OF GOLF**

PLATE XIII. SIXTY YARDS FROM THE HOLE (2)

PART II - CH. 8 – OF APPROACHING

PLATE XIV. LOFTING HIGH (1)

PLATE XV. LOFTING HIGH (2)

PART II - CH. 8 – OF APPROACHING

PLATE XVI. RUNNING IT WITH AN IRON (1)

BOOK I - **THE ART OF GOLF**

PLATE XVII. RUNNING IT WITH AN IRON (2)

PART II - CH. 8 – OF APPROACHING

PLATE XVIII. RUNNING IT WITH AN IRON (3)

BOOK I - **THE ART OF GOLF**

PART II - CH. 9 – OF PUTTING

9
OF PUTTING

To the beginner putting seems the least interesting part of the game. It feels mean to go dribbling and creeping up to a little hole, whilst a teeing-ground, from which you may drive the ball unknown distances into space, is ready close by. The rabbits in the bents mock at it, rushing into holes of about the same size at headlong speed, and with perfect ease. Like other things, essentially foolish in themselves, such as preaching, pleading, feeling pulses, etc., putting becomes attractive in proportion to the skill acquired in it. The young player will tell you that he cannot putt a bit, as complacently as mankind in general compliment themselves on having bad memories. Not so the experienced golfer. His putting is a feather with which to tickle his lug.

That putters, like poets, are born not made, is a common fallacy which prevents many from becoming masters of the art. It is also a general opinion that to putt you only require to putt, and that there is nothing easier than to do so with the middle of the club. If you heel, toe, top, or draw a putt, you are accused of gross, wilful carelessness. The miserable man whose driving has gone wrong sets to work to amend his style. The putter at fault blames himself for not using his eyes more carefully, or else he gives up for the day, on the ground that his liver is out of order. There is here a fallacy. I do not say that one ought not to consider a semi-miss with a putter wicked, but it is not worse than the same crime with a play-club—any more than failing to thread a needle is clumsier than missing a nail with a hammer. Nay, in my

BOOK I - THE ART OF GOLF

opinion, it is not so bad. Of the two, to hit clean with a driver is the easier operation. With the latter the main thing is to lay on. There are fifty styles in which this can be done, whilst, with the former, there are at most two or three.

Besides, for putting, a well-balanced club is absolutely essential. I am inclined to go further, and add that it must be made of wood. It is true that some hole out wonderfully with cleeks, others even with irons. But, by the shade of many a lost match, they are bad when they go off! Many men always putt with wood; few, never. The user of iron admits the inferiority of his weapon by carrying a putter to fall back upon when his fancy club fails him.

I have just said there are, at most, two or three attitudes in which good putting is possible. I am inclined to be more dogmatic, and to assert that there is but one. The player must stand open, half facing the hole, the weight on the right leg, the right arm close to the side, the ball nearly opposite the right foot. To putt standing square, the arms reached out, is as difficult as to write without laying a finger on the desk.

The idea that a putt is merely a shorter approach shot is one which must be got rid of. Approaches are played with a swing, longer or shorter, according to distance. A putter is not swung, but passed over the ground. It is a common thing for a professional caddy, under special circumstances, to put an iron into your hand near the hole, and to say, 'Play as if you were playing with a putter.' Those who apprehend the shot know that they are to give the ball a sort of push. Many players, however, putt with a swing. It is necessarily a very short one, and they are popularly described as 'nipping their putts.' From start to finish of a properly played putt there must be no free play of muscle. The putter must be guided all the time it is in motion, as much as the artist's pencil in drawing a straight line. In time, and by practice, driving may become partly mechanical, and balls be clean hit almost unconsciously. You may become a driving but not a putting machine. Matter can be fashioned into a clock, but not into a portrait painter. It is because holing-out is a human act that none ever become infallible for even the shortest distances.

PART II - CH. 9 – OF PUTTING

Within narrow limits there is a choice of styles of good putting. It may be done entirely from the wrist, from the shoulder, or by a combined use of all the arm joints. It matters little which of these manners be adopted, so long as it is adhered to and persevered with in prosperity and adversity. But, however old a player you are, however good in other respects, if you are putting with a jerk or swing, a fresh start would be worth while.

A great secret of steady putting is to make a point of always 'sclaffing' along the ground. The best putters do this, although it is not evident to an onlooker, the noise of the scrape being inaudible. To be sure of the exact spot on the putter face which is invariably to come in contact with the ball, is, of course, essential to the acquirement of accuracy. If you play to hit clean, your putter must pass above the ground at varying heights, as it is impossible to note how much air there is between it and the turf. In the other way you feel your road. But the greatest gain from treating putting as a sclaffing process is the less delicate manipulation required when short putts are in question. At a foot and a half from the hole the clean putter often fails, from incapacity to graduate inches of weakness, whilst the sclaffer succeeds because he is dealing with coarser weight sensitiveness.

Although every golfer theoretically accepts it as politic to play for the back of the hole, yet few putt as if they thought it was. The majority treat the hole as a place more difficult to get into than it really is. They seem practically to believe that a putt one ounce too strong, or one hair's-breadth off the line, must be out. Consequently many short putts are played so timidly that they are six inches off the line, or within six inches of the goal. Now the fact is, that (from short distances) the hole is pretty big, and from all distances it is capable of catching a ball going at a fair pace. I admit that more putts of over two yards must be missed than are held, because a putting-green is not a billiard-table; but many more would go in than do if players credited holes with a little of that catching power which they really possess. Some one says I mean nothing more than that a putt should be played 'for a foot past,' as the caddies advise. I do mean more. I object to that phrase. It should stand 'Play

BOOK I - THE ART OF GOLF

to be in and at the proper pace—namely, so hard that, if straight, you are in; if not straight, that you will be, not one, but two feet past.' With this faith in the hole, putts of a yard or under are very easy. Any pace between what will take the ball the exact distance, or two feet past, will do. Practically, in other words, the player does not require to think of the pace, and can give all his attention to direction. The putter who plays thus boldly has much to endure in the way of persecution and ridicule. If, from a distance, he strike the hole and fall in, it is called a fluke. His short putts are laughed at as gobbles. He is assured that had they missed they would have been out of holing. There are two answers; first, they do not miss the hole; second, if they did, they would only be out of holing for the dribbler who sneers at them. It is the inveterate practice of dropping putts over the edge of the hole which makes it necessary to discuss and study the line so carefully, and causes the power of calculating the effect of the minutest undulation or obstruction to be highly necessary. A man whose habit it is to play for the back of the hole at all times will seldom have any difficulty about his line. He will not require to crouch down and take note of obstructions which are scarcely visible. Anything that will turn his ball aside, and compel him to play with bias, will be visible to the naked eye. There will be no need to settle whether he is to take his caddy's line or his own—whether he must start an inch to the right, playing weak, or two inches to the left, playing weaker, or off the heel, or off the toe. Of course, it is very pretty to see a ball meandering into a hole; but, in most cases, it is quite an unnecessary treat, given gratis to the onlookers. Consulting with caddies has much to do with each putt being treated as if it were a thing by itself. If their advice as to the line and strength be followed, and the putt comes off, it is supposed (and they like it to be supposed) that there was no other way of doing it. Naturally, too, they do not advise the easiest way. A roundabout road is more interesting to them, and adds, moreover, to their importance. The simple-minded caddy, who always sticks down a pointer in the direct line between the ball and the hole, is credited with doing so from lack of understanding of lines altogether. But his advice is nearly always the soundest.

Many players acquire faith enough to play for the back of the hole by using a cleek or an iron for short putts, and they then maintain that these

PART II - CH. 9 – OF PUTTING

clubs have the quality of keeping the ball true to its line. The putter will do the same thing if used with equal confidence, and that without the risks of either lofting or of those due to using an awkward, ill-balanced club, which an iron or cleek with its face turned in undoubtedly is.

If there are few who play for the back of the hole in ordinary circumstances, there are fewer still who do so when the only line is curved. If there is a moundlet which will cause the ball to diverge to the left, few go to the right just enough to make up for this. They set themselves to dribble the putt very far to the right, giving the unevenness of the ground as much say in the matter as they can. Anybody will play boldly along the top of a ridge when the hole is at the end of it, but most men prefer, to the detriment of their putting when it is on the side of one, to climb high up and drop down, to running quickly along the lower slopes.

In putting there is much to think about, and much more not to be thought of with long putts, the great stumbling-block is the strength. Before taking his stance the player knows his distance from the hole and the nature of the ground. One glance more after he has done so is sufficient to assure him that he is aiming in the right direction. Looking back and forward between the ball and the hole will tell no more about the distance, but will only distract him from applying the force proportionate to it. For short putts which ought to be holed, the same holds good, except that starting the ball in the exact line is, or ought to be, now more a difficulty than the strength. Some fix upon a spot to play over before addressing the ball, others after; the most diffident get their caddy to point it out when they are about to play. But, however it is come at, there should be no hesitation. There is the line now for strength and accuracy. To take another look at the hole, to think 'Perhaps I am not aiming quite straight,' will certainly prove fatal. You will give an involuntary pull or push, or dribble hesitatingly up to the lip. But with faith in your line, your stroke delivered, you will look up and likely see the ball disappear down the middle—like a rabbit, perhaps, on account of the determined energy of your faith—perhaps by the side (a hole is very large if played at boldly), on account

BOOK I - THE ART OF GOLF

of some bias in the ground not noticed, and best unnoticed, but down all the same.

When a putter is waiting his turn to hole-out a putt of one or two feet in length, on which the match hangs at the last hole, it is of vital importance that he think of nothing. At this supreme moment he ought studiously to fill his mind with vacancy. He must not even allow himself the consolations of religion. He must not prepare himself to accept the gloomy face of his partner and the derisive delight of his adversaries with Christian resignation should he miss. He must not think that it is a putt he would not dream of missing at the beginning of the match, or, worse still, that he missed one like it in the middle. He ought to wait calm and stupid till it is his turn to play, wave back the inevitable boy who is sure to be standing behind his arm, and putt as I have told him how—neither with undue haste nor with exaggerated care. When the ball is down, and the putter handed to the caddy, it is not well to say, 'I couldn't have missed it.' Silence is best. The pallid cheek and trembling lip belie such braggadocio.

CH. 9 – OF PUTTING

PLATE XIX. PUTTING (1)

BOOK I - **THE ART OF GOLF**

PLATE XX. PUTTING (2)

10
OF MATCH AND MEDAL PLAY

Having examined in detail the different kinds of shots which the golfer is called upon to make, a few remarks on combining them into a game may fittingly conclude this little treatise.

There is no such thing for the properly balanced mind as an uninteresting match at golf. Some greedy and ill-conditioned persons will not play in what they call 'duffers' foursomes '—matches in which the real flukes are the clean-hit shots, and the winning side that which has the luck to make the greatest number of these. On the other hand, there are dull fellows who will not stake their reputation on a serious match in which defeat means sorrow and victory joy, which classifies them as golfers, or decides the ownership of a five pound note. The wise golfer who wishes his game to flourish will supply it with a judicious mixture of the two kinds—the friendly and the big match.

A friendly match is the earnest golfer's holiday, and his opportunity for practising as well. It gives him time to listen to the singing of birds, and to observe the natural non-golfing beauties of the links. It is also his time for trying new clubs, modifications of style, or fancy shots which have been clamouring for recognition, more pleasantly, than in an hour's solitary practice. It enables him to set at rest questions about his thumb, the possibility of lengthening his driving, the advisability of taking to a cleek for putting, a mashy for approaching, etc., etc.; all this, of course, without his partner knowing that his half-crown is being trifled with. But to play too many friendly matches is a great mistake. It is the direct road to a bad style

BOOK I - THE ART OF GOLF

and careless putting. The tone of mind during most games one plays ought to be an earnest, oathful desire for victory, which alone will fix a man down to the great monotonous essential of hitting the ball true, and distract him from the will-o'-the-wisp of style.

Games at golf ought not to be played for nothing, more particularly where adversaries are in the habit of meeting often. Glory may be a sufficient spur when trying conclusions with a stranger; but between friends there must be something more. If there is not, the worse player will not take odds, and the better, from having nothing to do, will fall back to his level. This trades-union, communistic plan of offering no incentive to skill, slowly undermines it. But with a stake, the worse player will demand his odds, the better give them grudgingly, and both strive to win. 'What!' exclaim those who consider there is some mysterious wickedness in exchanging money for anything but perishables, such as food, drink, clothing, and shares in bubble companies —'What! degrade golf to a gambling game!' Gambling! what nonsense! Is dinner a gluttonous and drunken thing because at it there is eating and drinking? 'I see,' says the tolerant moralist, 'small stakes. You would limit the betting to the 'statutory ball' or equally 'statutory half-crown.' Why should I? Are there many cases of golfers crippling their resources by betting? Even if there were, who made us these people's grandmothers? Nevertheless the statutory half-crown has its merits. By adding up your collection of them at the end of the year, you can judge of your qualities as a match-maker. It is a fair criterion of your progress, or retrogression too. It has the advantage of being a uniform stake, which to wrest from your friend may be greedy, but is not cruel. From some people one might feel conscience-stricken when taking gold. It is unfeeling to crow when dormy three and the stake is large; but it is a fair game to jangle even half a dozen of a man's 'statutories' below his nose, or to invite him into a shop to see you spend them. Before we can do this, however, the money must be won. Attention to several little matters will help players to win it.

It has already been remarked that excessive golfing dwarfs the intellect. Nor is this to be wondered at when we consider that the more fatuously vacant the mind is, the better for play. It has been observed that absolute idiots, ignorant whether they are playing two more or one off two, play

PART II - CH. 10 – OF MATCH AND MEDAL PLAY

steadiest. An uphill game does not make them press, nor victory within their grasp render them careless. Alas! we cannot all be idiots. Next to the idiotic, the dull unimaginative mind is the best for golf. In a professional competition I would prefer to back the sallow, dull-eyed fellow with a 'quid' in his cheek, rather than any more eager-looking champion. The poetic temperament is the worst for golf. It dreams of brilliant drives, iron shots laid dead, and long putts held, whilst in real golf success waits for him who takes care of the foozles and leaves the fine shots to take care of themselves.

If you have started with no other idea but to hit, in a short time it will appear that you are driving far. Take no notice of the fact. Regard the extra distance covered as anybody's business but yours. The greedy, grovelling spirit of the true golfer, anxious to win holes, is not to be beguiled from its purpose by the soul-satisfying, pocket-emptying glories of brilliant shots. During a match there is usually a great deal said about the state of the game, or the adversary's position in regard to the hole, and one is very apt to attempt to play accordingly. By doing so, many holes are lost which would not otherwise fall to the opponents. For instance, how often does it not happen that you are playing two more, and think it necessary to hole in less than the perfect number to secure a half? You make an effort, fail, lose a shot more; which shot, not the two more. It turns out, costs you the hole. Everybody knows that to press a drive will not add to its length; but it is not equally acknowledged that extra mental pressure for an approach or a putt is worse than useless. The supposed necessity for pressing is born of too much respect for the enemy. Because they have got the best of you for the moment, and played the hole perfectly up to a certain point they are credited with being infallible, and you see no chance of their going into a bunker or taking four to hole off an iron. It is scarcely ever politic to count the enemy's chickens before they are hatched. Cases constantly occur of holes being lost because it seems absolutely necessary in order to save them to get home from a bad lie. Your forcing shot sends the ball from bad to worse, and what might have been won in five is lost in seven. A secret disbelief in the enemy's play is very useful for match play.

This contempt must, however, be largely seasoned with respect. It does not do lightly to lose the first two holes, or any hole. When one is down it is

BOOK I - THE ART OF GOLF

natural to hunger for holes, but even with five up play greedily for more—play a yard putt as if the match depended on it. Likely enough it will turn out that it did. With five up express, as is polite, regret at laying a stimy, but rejoice in your heart.

It is a great thing in a match to be one or two up, and to keep the lead. An advantage maintained for seven or eight holes almost certainly breaks down the enemy and wins the match. Yet every one is inclined to be carelessly confident when they are ahead, and when they have lost their lead and some more, partly by their own fault, to apply themselves with undue and fatal earnestness. If golfers would but humbly acknowledge to themselves (which is true) that they lose heart and have bad luck when they are down, they would be more careful to husband their advantages. How men 'funk' is comically noticeable at the close finish of a big match. With all even and three to play, the side which can finish in fair figures is almost certain to win. But in these circumstances even first-class players generally give an exhibition of lamentable bungling all round.

Some particularly tender-hearted golfers play better in foursomes than in singles, because in the latter they are apt to have their bowels of compassion moved and their game made loose by the grumblings and lamentation of the adversary whom they have got well in hand. Playing a foursome will not lessen his dread of the other side when down, but it will prevent the merciful man from being moved by pity. The wailing, the discontent about the odds, the deprecation of stymies, the harping on the flukiness of long putts held, his good luck, their bad luck, will not melt his heart and soften his muscle. Between him and them is one nearer and dearer—his partner. It is not selfish to crush the enemy; it is duty—duty to the partner. What are the tears of two enemies to the joy of one friend?

The choice of, and conduct towards, a partner are matters of considerable importance. If we get beaten, no matter who he is, or how he has played, or how we have played, it will, as a matter of course, be entirely his fault. During the match, however, it is politic to mask our disgust and contempt; for it is not the scolder, but the scolded, who is apt to go to pieces. No man who takes a partner ever questions for a moment that he himself is the amiable

PART II - CH. 10 – OF MATCH AND MEDAL PLAY

factor in the combination. This is all very well; but this belief in our own imperturbability often leads us to challenge along with some notorious grumbler, to play badly in consequence, and to lose. If we thus break down, we blame him, and unjustly. The fact is, our temper is proved to be such as to unfit us to play with a quick man. He has roared like a lion indeed, but played like one, whilst we have trembled at his roaring, been put out when he showed us our putts, sulked when he interfered with our shots or advised how to swing. It is we who have bad tempers, and should therefore chose perfect partners. He is qualified to play with either angels or devils, and win.

What is the ideal partner? He should be of a Laodicean disposition—neither too hot nor too cold, ready to utter one hearty groan over any gross mistake he happens to make, and then to say no more about it. At yours, he should show disappointment in so far as they affect the game, letting you believe at the same time that they were simply failures, not the results of vainglorious attempts—of selfish attempts—to do something brilliant. When you have bad luck he should sympathise; but fulsome falsehoods about the badness of the lie are loathsome to an upright-minded man. Gross hypocrisy on his part is only politic when you miss a short putt. This he ought to try over again, and miss. There are grave circumstances in life which make lies moral. This is one of them. A short putt missed may bring on a holing-out paralysis unless it is promptly treated.

The perfect partner, without letting you know it, looks upon himself as the backbone of the game, on you as the flesh which may err. He plods on whilst you miss—plods on still when you are brilliant. If you are efficient, he lauds you; if variable, he says nothing; If hopeless, he smiles and says, 'It can't be helped.' To him you are the chances of the game.

The perfect partner is not awed if you are exacting, nor sorry for you if amiable to his mistakes. If he is playing ill, he does not think of what you will say afterwards. He tries to recover for the sake of the match. If he be leader, he does not try to pull you through by extra brilliancy of play. If you are in a class above him, still more careful is he to attempt nothing beyond himself. Glory for the leader, duty for the subaltern. And if, perchance, it is he who is

BOOK I - **THE ART OF GOLF**

fighting the best fight, he is careful to hide his consciousness of this from his superior.

The perfect partner never volunteers information as to why you are playing badly, never suggests that you are taking the wrong club, although certain you cannot get up with it. He knows that although you accept a correction civilly, or even with hypocritical gratitude, you would not be human if you were careful to prove yourself wrong by making a good shot.

There *are* partners to be found possessing these and other virtues; but it is useless to look for one who, in recounting a lost match afterwards, will either forget your mistakes or remember his own.

A perfect partner is what one desires. A perfect adversary on the other hand is to be avoided. To be regularly beaten is—Well! it is not golf, and it is politic to avoid or watch carefully those adversaries who have a knack of getting the best of it in every match they make. The two most dangerous types are the grumbler and the flatterer. The former begins by huckstering for more odds than he ultimately intends to accept, asserts that he is best in a foursome if a single is proposed, reminds you that you outdrive him, speaks about his liver, has a sore hand, or a sprained wrist—can't play in wind if it is blowing, in hot weather if it is fine, in bad weather if it rains. If you are wise, make a match irrespective of these things, or let him go home to bed. But the wariest are apt to be caught after winning the first match and lunching. They are apt to lose the next two by carelessness, believing what he says about being out of form. It is so difficult to judge of an adversary's play. Unless one is getting beaten off the green, there is a predisposition to believe that the grumbling enemy is not as good as ourselves, and that (if he is winning) he is winning by luck. If we are some up, and he harps on his bad shots, walks with his head bowed, only raising it to wail, there is a risk of his being treated as nought, and perhaps pulling off the match in consequence.

Flattery is still more dangerous than grumbling. Under its influence a level match for shillings may be followed by a round for pounds, giving odds. Out of the hundred shots more or less you have made in the round, the flatterer easily finds five good ones with which to turn your head. With putts

PART II - CH. 10 – OF MATCH AND MEDAL PLAY

especially, he will succeed. A very straight or a very long drive may be used against you; but a few good putts are still more dangerous in the mouth of a match-maker. The drives—unless utterly given over to vanity—you know to be exceptional. But putts! who doubts that on his day his putting is remarkable?

The adversary who outdrives us is not difficult to deal with. If he does so on the average, he naturally gives odds, a man's driving being the usual standard by which his game is measured. If it is only when he hits them that he drives far, he is still easier to deal with. Those who hit occasional screamers, over-estimate their own game even more than the rest of golfers. Judged by his apparent merits, the most dangerous man is he who is exceptionally good within the hundred yard radius. To estimate the comparative efficiency of men's driving is easy, but near the hole casual observation is quite deceptive. The faculty for occasionally sending the ball high in air to land dead causes a man to be overestimated. He who, time after time, holes from a yard and a half is not necessarily a permanently dangerous adversary. It may be his own bad putting which so often renders these efforts necessary. If you are puzzled at So-and-so constantly winning, the key to the enigma will probably be found in the inconspicuous regularity with which he performs the apparently simple duty of holing in three, off his iron. His approaches are not brilliant perhaps. It may even be that many of them are scuffled along the ground; but a close observation will show that they are invariably straight. Nobody is oftener past the hole than short, but the deadly player will have a good average of approaches finishing on the far side. In short, an adversary who does not seem to be playing his short game at all well, may be winning every hole because each approach is laid within fifteen yards and each long putt within fifteen inches—a very simple matter, which rouses no astonishment, but is perfect play nevertheless.

In match play, as a rule, it is the finish, in medal play the start, which is most exciting. In the latter, one feels how dismal it would be to drag round the links with an incubus of ten or twelve strokes too many for the first three holes. After one has warmed to the work it is not so crushing, slowly, surely, imperceptibly to tail off. Successful medal play, however, calls for more nerve and patience than match play. So long as our card remains good, each shot is

BOOK I - THE ART OF GOLF

as important as the first, and as we near home with a good record the excitement becomes intense. Even from the last tee a carefully compiled and creditable card may be driven to the winds.

Some men give a very good account of themselves on medal days by playing a bold, gambling game, which either comes off, or requires three figures to record it. For him who is always there or thereabout, the medal round is too trying to be pleasant. Each shot is a solemn and difficult interview, on which depends momentous issues. After each there is a moment for thanksgiving, a moment of relaxation, a short walk, and to business again —to the business in hand. There should be no thought of anything else. The good medal player is no Lot's wife, ever adding up his card to see what is behind him. When he has to drive, he drives. Approaching, he does not see himself in the bottom of the hole in three; he only sees the ball which has to be struck. Visions of the calamities of missing do not flicker along the line of his putt. His round is dismal business, without reflection or anticipation.

Some golfers advise great caution in medal play. They advise to drive gently, to play round bunkers, to play putts for dead. It is not likely that the cautious medal player will have to tear up his card, or that there will be any double figures on it, but he may easily have a worse total than if there were one or two, whilst anything better than a moderate score is improbable. An easy shot is as uncertain as a pressed one.. A flabby muscle is as little under control as an over-strained one. To play round a bunker is to give yourself leave to top—a permission likely to be taken advantage of, for the golfer's body hates to hit and loves to foozle; whilst his game is easily insulted by being made to go round, or play short of, a bunker, it ought to be allowed to try to carry. Besides, a bunker is not necessarily a very terrible place when you are in it. The player in one is as likely to win the hole as his adversary thirty yards further back on grass. Especially when the bunker is within forty yards of the hole is caution folly. A cupped ball on the grass is as likely a contingency as a very bad one in the bunker. The bunkered ball will likely be got out, whilst the same pusillanimous spirit which played the other short may likely put it in. Besides, why should the bold player get in? To hit clean with a driver is not more difficult than to do so with an iron. In short, the bold game saves a shot if successful, and does not necessarily lose one if too daring. That

PART II - CH. 10 – OF MATCH AND MEDAL PLAY

timid play is a mistake will be made apparent on a moment's reflection to any one who has ever entered for a scoring competition. He will remember having thought, 'If I go in there I am done for,'—how he has gone in, got out, and only at most lost a shot. Of course this argument only applies to ordinary bunkers. On every green there are some terrible ones—unfair ones, in which the punishment does not fit the crime. These must be avoided.

It is in putting, more than in any other part of the game, that the would-be medal winners, and those who enter to see what they will do, are apt to fail on medal days. Bad driving, with a turn of luck, may lose you little or nothing; but bad putting runs up a score that you will only reveal to inquiring friends after one or two askings and some explanation as to what bad luck you had. Every one starts for a medal a little shaky, needing something to picket his mind to, so that it may not wander away into realms of dread. In driving, one can prevent stray thoughts by employing the mind in keeping the eye on the ball; in approaching, one can deafen himself with 'Be up;' in putting, all formulae but make us more erratic. Any kind of reflection or moral resolve seems to put the delicate machinery out of gear. Resolve to be up, and you are too far past; to be dead, and you are short; to be in, and you are out of holing. Good putting grows like the lilies. In match play it is vigorous when the sun is shining, and fades a little as the prospect grows dark. But the atmosphere of medal play is either too hot for it or too cold. One wants it to save shots for the future at one time, at another to retrieve the faults of previous play. To putt well on a medal day, one must be careless;—advice easily given, but difficult to follow until our card is hopelessly beyond the reach of human aid.

BOOK I - **THE ART OF GOLF**

'We may outrun
By violent swiftness that which we run at,
And lose by over-running.'

HENRY VIII. I. I.—(*Shakespeare on Golf.*)

BOOK II

THE GOLF SWING

DARYN HAMMOND

ERNEST JONES

BOOK II - **THE GOLF SWING**

The Golf Swing
(illustrated)

The Ernest Jones Method

by

DARYN HAMMOND

ERNEST JONES

Reproduction 2012 by **dutchygolf.com**

In the public domain due to copyright expiration

(original date of publication before 1923)

BOOK II - **THE GOLF SWING**

CLASSIC REPRODUCTION

[The view of the golf swing expressed in this book forms the subject of a series of articles contributed by Mr. Daryn Hammond to *Golf Illustrated* of America.]

First Published, April, 29, 1920

Second Impression, July, 30, 1920

Reproduced by dutchygolf.com 2012

This book may have occasional imperfections such as a couple of missing pictures that were part of the original artifact, but we have taken the trouble to make this book readable, by reformatting the content and re-screening for typographical errors and including most of the referenced figures.

The Earnest Jones method is fantastic and we need more instructional manuals on it.

Fig 1. Ernest Jones before the War

BOOK II - **THE GOLF SWING**

CONTENTS

	LIST OF ILLUSTRATIONS	
	FOREWORD	165
1	THE MENTAL PICTURE	173
2	THE GRIP	179
3	THE SWING	193
4	THE ACTION OF THE WRIST	211
5	THE BALANCE OF THE BODY	227
6	STANCE	235
7	OVERSWINGING	243
8	SOCKETING	253
9	SOME OTHER ENORMETIES	267
10	RECAPITULATORY	271
	ABOUT ERNEST JONES	279

LIST OF ILLUSTRATIONS

FIG.

1. Ernest Jones before the War
2. During the War
3. To-day
4. Down-swing. The body has turned on its own initiative
5. The body has followed the lead of the hands
6. The hands have started the club-head moving but the shoulders have not responded
7. How not to grip the shaft
8. Top of up-swing. The extension of the fingers has been overdone. Control has been sacrificed
9. Top of up-swing. The fingers have not been allowed to extend. The "dead hand" position
10. Top of up-swing. The second, third, and fourth fingers have extended, so giving elasticity to the swing
11. The ideal finish of the shot. The second, third, and fourth fingers are extended to the same extent as in Fig. 10
12. How the club is gripped
13. Another view
14. Note position of forefinger and thumb
15. The line of the shaft across the left hand when the hand is opened after gripping the club as in Fig. 16
16. A proper hold of the shaft
17. The ideal grip
18. The ideal grip
19. Wrong position : left wrist bent outward
20. Wrong position : left hand over-turned
21. Correct position
22. Left hand has not forced club-head back
23. Proper action of left hand
24. Quarter shot
25. Half shot
26. Full iron shot
27. Corollary to Fig. 24
28. Corollary to Fig. 25

BOOK II - **THE GOLF SWING**

29. Corollary to Fig. 26
30. Finish of short push shot
31. Finish of socketed approach
32. Perfect finish of short iron shot. Contrast with Figs. 30 and 31, and note how the club-head has been forced through
33. How the blade of the iron should normally come on to the ball
34. Another view of the type of shot shown in Fig. 32
35. Straight position of wrist
36. Movement of the wrist joint
37. Movement of the wrist joint
38. Straight position
39. Other movements of the wrist joint
40. Other movements of the wrist joint
41. Action of right wrist beginning up-swing
42. The right wrist has bent as far as it will go
43. Straight position of right wrist in follow through
44. Left wrist bending in follow through
45. Shows "give" of fingers in any flexible movement
46. Figs. 46 and 47 exemplify again the essential "give" of the fingers
47. Compare with Fig. 46 where the fingers have not "given"
48. An ideally balanced position at the top of the up-swing
49. An ideally balanced position at the finish of the shot
50. The old-fashioned up-swing : exuberent, yet controlled. A slashing and powerful movement
51. Clumsiness and lack of control
52. Good as far as it goes
53. A frequent sight on the links
54. A trifle too careful
55. Compare with Fig. 50
56. The socketing position par excellence
57. An ideal finish
58. The push shot
59. Note the delicacy and freedom of the finish of this iron shot
60. The finish of a firm iron shot
61. Two perfect iron shots. Note the essential similarity of the positions
62. No suspicion of stiffness or rigidity
63. Finis

FOREWORD

"What is wrong with the teaching of golf?" asks a writer in the *Daily Express*.

"That there is something wrong with it," he goes on, "is realized by all people who attempt to play golf, and by all those who watch them doing it.

"Undoubtedly golf is a difficult game, and undoubtedly it attracts a large proportion of devotees whose only qualification for playing it is their devotion. But it is not on these grounds alone that one can explain the pathetic failure of the average golfer's life, or the tragicomedy that is always being enacted by golfing contortionists over the links of the world. One must seek other causes. One must consider, not only the subject and the pupil, but the teacher.

"Broadly speaking, the teachers of golf are either professional golfers or enthusiastic amateurs. In the main, the professional golfer knows how to play golf, but not how to teach it; and in the main the enthusiastic amateur knows neither how to teach it nor how to play it.

"It is one of the characteristics of golf that every exponent of it, no matter how immature his knowledge, no matter how spurious his methods, has moments of exaltation in which he is convinced that he has discovered the true secret of the golf swing, and that he must at once proclaim his discovery to the world at large. Probably what he has discovered is some bad trick which, combined with certain other bad tricks (constituting what he is pleased to call his swing), succeeds in giving him greater length or greater steadiness - for a while. Thereupon he rushes into print. Whereupon some other golfer, whose own box of tricks has gone unutterably to pieces, ingeniously works the new artifice into his golfing system, and emerges temporarily triumphant -

BOOK II - **THE GOLF SWING**

not, however, because of the thing which he has taken pains to acquire, but because of the confidence (ill-founded though it may be) with which that thing has for the time being endowed him. And so the process goes on, in an ever-widening circle. Then the original prophet discovers that what he fondly imagined to be illumination is really hallucination; but even now his impulse to kick himself is arrested by some fresh flash of inspiration, obviously, unmistakably the real thing this time, and off he goes again. . . . He is a dear, human, lovable fellow, but he is a deadly foe to good golf.

"It is another of the characteristics of golf that the ability to teach it does not necessarily flow from the ability to play it; the champion golfer has probably enunciated at least as much false doctrine as the enthusiastic amateur. It should be borne in mind that the professional golfer has always lived in an atmosphere of golf; to him, indeed, golf is ' second nature' - a matter of instinct. He has a trained hand, but he has not a trained mind. What happens? He is asked to explain how he executes a particular shot; in a word, he is asked to explain how he does a thing which to him is instinctive, a problem which might well harass even the most highly trained mind; and it is not surprising that the professional should flounder. It would, indeed, be surprising if he did not flounder.

"The floundering is naturally worst when he attempts the explanation in writing; for in the first place he has not the art of writing, and in the second place he is unable to help out the explanation by an actual demonstration of the shot. The accidental is mistaken for the essential, the responsive for the initiatory, coexistence for causation, the sign for the thing signified. The results are seen in a bewildering mass of print, both in magazine articles and in book form; and they are reflected in the grotesque performances of countless golfers over the face of the earth. The writer is himself a sufferer, and this is his *cri de coeur*"

* * * * *

The present writer took up golf about ten years ago, when he was thirty. He had not been a cricketer, nor, in fact, had he indulged in any game in which a ball has to be hit, except lawn-tennis; and at lawn-tennis he had achieved but little success, because it was not until he took up golf that he grasped the only two ideas that matter in lawn-tennis: following; the ball on to the racquet and "hitting through." For a few months he played golf "in the light of nature" and derived - and gave to others- considerable enjoyment. It was then borne into him that golf was a game that he was likely to continue to play until old age, or something not less drastic, intervened, and that consequently it would be sane to try to acquire a sound method. He consulted the nearest professional.

This professional was a good fellow, and he played a fine game. He was animated, however, by an overwhelming passion for analyzing the swing, and it had never occurred to him that his powers of observation and deduction were unequal to the task. Nor did it occur to the writer until he had lived through six months of tribulation, during which he had heroically endeavoured to play golf by turning over the left wrist as far as it would go at the beginning of the swing, by squeezing his right elbow into his side, by tucking his left knee into his right knee, and his right knee into his left knee, and, above all, by straining every nerve to get into a statuesque position somehow or other at the finish of the swing, whether the ball had been toed, heeled, sliced, pulled, or topped.

The writer then took advice from another professional. This excellent fellow was not at all of the analytical turn of mind. He had but few theories, but he enunciated certain propositions which, though they appeared somewhat crude at the time, are now seen to be full of elemental truth. The writer now cordially subscribes to such dicta as, "The golf swing ain't a trick"; "You don't have to wriggle about like an eel: you just stand up to the ball and hit it"; "There's only one thing to remember - you've just got to put the club round your neck both ways"; "Not so much foot-work, sir; golf ain't a sparring match."

On the whole the writer emerged a better man for this cold-douche treatment, and he was given a handicap of 18.

He then began to read every article and book on golf in the English language, and so great was his thirst for knowledge that he deplored that golf had not become part of the literature of Germany and France. He coquetted with many notions and ideas, and one of these, "the straight left arm," stood him in such good stead for a while that his handicap came down to 12. (He

BOOK II - THE GOLF SWING

now knows why the notion of the straight left arm subsequently played him false.)

This experience was followed by strange lapses from golfing sanity, but the writer was patched up from time to time by various professionals, and his handicap was reduced to 10. He had now got rid of many false ideas with regard to the swing, and had adopted certain useful ideas, with the result that his game showed an all-round improvement, which brought his handicap down, first to 8, and then to 5.

It is easier, however, to get rid of false ideas than to get rid of bad habits, and the even tenor of his game was liable to be gravely disturbed by recurrences of tricks picked up or accentuated in the early days of his training under the pseudo-scientific professional.

The most persistent and the most demoralizing of these tricks was that common phenomenon of the swing - "body in too soon." In the periods of impotence produced by this scourge, every remedy known to the literature of the game and the Solons of the links was tried; and the writer, discarding one after another, came to place faith in the doctrine enunciated in a small book on golf bearing the engaging title, "The Simplicity of the Golf Swing." In a nutshell, the principle on which that doctrine is based is that at the beginning of both the up-swing and the down-swing it is the shoulders that move first, and that one should, therefore, leave it to the shoulders, in turning, to suggest the proper relative movement to arms and hands. This principle has the merit of extreme simplicity - it presents one concept, one mental picture, instead of a dozen; and in the writer's case it had for a time the effect of facilitating the timing of the full swing. It was not long, however, before first the short game and then the long game went utterly to pieces. The shot became a ponderous, lumbering affair, as unlike the quick, crisp movement of the professional as it was possible to be.

The writer now applied himself to the discovery of some other simple mental picture of the swing. He was convinced that, whether the shoulders moved first or last, good results would not be obtained by consciously trying to move them first. What the golfer has to do is to get into the best hitting position at the top of the up-swing. It may be that in doing this his shoulders will move first. It may be, on the other hand, that if he *tries* to move his shoulders first he will *not* get into that position. The instinct to turn the shoulders may be so strong that the shoulders will do their full part in the swing if the mind ignores them altogether, and concentrates itself on, say, moving the club with the hands. Indeed, after much thought, observation, and trial, the writer came to the conclusion that this was so, and that unless the shoulders were left to look after themselves, their part in the shot was likely to be over-emphasized and the shot impaired.

About this time (July, 1916) it was stated in the newspapers that Ernest Jones, the Chislehurst professional, who had had a leg shot off in France in March, had played round the Royal Norwich links (standing on one leg for each shot) in 83, and a little later, playing with David Ayton, he (still on one leg) had holed out the Clacton course - a long course - in 72. It was at once clear to the writer that Ernest Jones at all events must have thoroughly acquired the art of obtaining his results with the minimum exertion, and the writer lost no time in getting once more into touch with a player whose game he had always admired.

Before the war Ernest Jones had been one of the most promising golfers in the metropolitan district, and the Chislehurst Golf Club, the late home of the Empress Eugenie, had come to be known as the home of Ernest Jones.... . Though he had not headed the list at any of the most important meetings, Ernest Jones had always been "there or thereabouts." He never failed to qualify for the Open Championship, he generally appeared well toward the top of the final lists, and his scores were uniformly sound. In the *News of the World* competitions he was wont to qualify, and to give a good account of himself in the subsequent rounds; and he did excellent work in the French Championship. In the Kent Championship he adopted the role of runner-up, and in three consecutive finals he lowered the record of three links - Eltham, Hythe, and Herne Bay. There can be no doubt that in the normal course of events Ernest Jones would have attained front rank among his fellow-professionals well before he was thirty. Then came the war....

Jones was ready to respond to the call of King and Country, and in January, 1915, he - along with many other golfers - joined the Army. In November he was out in France, near to Loos; he went through the winter unscathed, but was badly wounded in March, 1916, by rifle grenade. Some sixteen pieces of metal were removed from his head, his right forearm, and

BOOK II - **THE GOLF SWING**

his right leg, and this leg was subsequently amputated close below the knee. Nevertheless, the enemy had so far failed to destroy the golfer in him that four months later he was performing the incredible feat of holing out a long and testing course in an average of fours, handing his crutches to the caddy precisely seventy-two times in the round.

The achievement becomes the more startling when it is considered that Jones is a slightly built man on the short side - his height is under five feet six inches and his weight less than 10 stone: he was therefore unable to rely on any reserve of brute force.

His method of hitting the ball had always been conspicuously easy and decisive. In his use of the hands and the fingers he resembled Vardon, but his swing was flatter and rather more compact than Vardon's, and it was accompanied by less suggestion of power, but perhaps even greater suggestion of speed. It was a method which *primâ facie* would stand well the ruthless test that was to be applied to it.

Ernest Jones, moreover, was known to his fellow-professionals, and to some fortunate amateurs, as a golfer who had brought an uncommonly penetrating mind to bear on an uncommonly perplexing subject. He was known as a player of original views, a player who had satisfied himself about the mechanics of the swing, and who played the game fully concious of what he was doing and why he was doing it.

When the writer first saw Jones after his convalescence he had just got his artificial leg, and though obviously embarrassed by it, he played noteworthy golf in an exhibition game with Vardon, Taylor, and Braid. One saw that he experienced difficulty in finishing the shot freely - the right leg came lumbering forward after the ball had been hit - but there was the same clean, crisp hitting as before. At the time of writing, however, he is on better terms with the artificial leg, and though it still complicates the question of balance, especially when the stance is uneven - as it frequently is at Chislehurst - it does not succeed in helping Jones's opponents to anything like the extent they would naturally expect it to do. Sequences of fours interrupted by threes continue to be the order of Jones's day.

The writer found that Jones was convinced that the golf swing could be readily taught and consistently performed only if it were conceived as one movement, that various members of the body (including the shoulders) were normally anxious to get busy too strenuously and too soon, and that the only way of insuring their working in due co-ordination with the other members of the body, notably the hands and the fingers, was to treat them as disastrous leaders, but as wholly admirable followers. The basis of the swing, as Jones had worked it out before the war, was the proper action of the hands and fingers.

His accident had put his theory of golf to the touch, and had intensified his faith in it; and it was not long before the present writer was swinging a golf club with a decisiveness which had previously seemed beyond his range of accomplishment.

More than ever Ernest Jones felt the artist's itch for asserting his point of view before the largest possible audience; but though at the very forefront of *vivâ voce* teachers, he was not a practised writer; nor would he resort to the device of commissioning a golfing journalist to produce a book purporting to be written by himself. It was in these circumstances that the present writer came to essay the task of explaining the principle and the method which Ernest Jones had made so vividly clear to him on the links.

The writer is fully aware of the danger of conveying impressions other than those intended to be conveyed, and he earnestly asks the reader to check the impressions formed by him by immediately trying them out on the links with club and ball.

In this book one lesson only is taught, and that one lesson is taught all the time. Each chapter is but a re-statement - from a different angle - of the principle enunciated in every other chapter. The risk of wearying the reader by reiteration has been preferred to the risk of leaving him in doubt.

"Surely," says the writer in the *Daily Express*, "among the thousands of golfers in the two hemispheres there is some one person who can make this plague of a game intelligible?"

BOOK II - **THE GOLF SWING**

There is. He is Ernest Jones. And if there is anything unintelligible in the following pages, it is the writer, and not Ernest Jones, who is at fault.

Fig 2. During the War

Fig 3. Today

CH. 1 – THE MENTAL PICTURE

1 THE MENTAL PICTURE

It will have been gathered from the preceding chapter that in this exposition of the golf swing the writer's aim is not to decide such points as whether in the up-swing the shoulders move before, at the same time as, or later than, the hands, but to suggest to the reader that mental picture of the physical processes involved which will help him to obtain the result he seeks.

In the long game the golfer wants the utmost length that he can get without sacrificing control. It is of little use to him to hit a ball "to blazes"; for almost invariably it is difficult to get back from that locality to the green. It will not even serve his purpose to hit one long straight ball at every second shot. Obviously what he requires most of all, if he is sane, is control. In the short game indeed, control is everything. Nothing else matters.

The primary question, then, for the golfer is how to control the behaviour of the ball - that is, how to gain control over the club head.

Control over the club head connotes two things - power and "touch/' Power can be gained by gripping the club in the palms of the hands, but it is given only to few people to obtain "touch" in that way. "Touch" can be obtained by gripping the club lightly in the fingers, but power cannot be gained in that way. Something between the two methods of gripping is required.

There are, perhaps, two natural methods of holding any implement with which one intends to strike. If one were about to break stones or fell a tree, one would instinctively take hold of the hammer or the hatchet deep in the palm of the hand. The grip would adapt itself to the notion of power. If, on the other hand, one were nonchalantly decapitating daisy-heads in the course of a country walk, one would instinctively hold one's cane lightly in the fingers: the grip would adapt itself to the notion of flexibility and speed.

The golf ball is a light thing compared with the stone, a heavy thing compared with the daisy-head; and the golf club is a light thing compared with the stone-breaker's hammer, a heavy thing compared with a cane.

Jointly, then, the golf club and golf ball should suggest to the mind a compromise between power and speed, between "hefti-ness" and flexibility.

It is the blending of these two qualities which baffles the average golfer. He is apt to attach by far too much importance to power, and the result is that he manipulates his club ponderously and ineffectively, never for one moment realizing the idea of speed or "touch/ and usually failing to achieve his one objective - power. His mental picture is ill-conceived, and therefore his action goes astray. His hands and fingers have failed to do their full share of the work, and consequently his body comes into the shot at the wrong time and in the wrong positions.

In the revolutions of a wheel the speed of the hub bears a fixed ratio to the speed of the rim, but the golfer who mistimes his shot suggests the analogy of a wheel in which the hub and the rim are at variance, the hub being determined to increase the ratio of its speed to the speed of the rim. The result, in the example of the wheel, would be broken spokes and a buckled rim. In the case of the golfer, the arms are too flexible to break (though the club is not), but the result is a jerky and retarded, not a quickened, movement of the club-head; moreover, the course of the club-head is out of truth: the shot is a failure.

The fingers bear to the other members of the body involved in the golf swing a somewhat similar relationship to that which subsists between the toes and the other members of the body involved in walking. If one walks, thinking only of the action of the hips, one will instinctively take long strides, and the gait will suggest considerable power but little "life." If in walking one thinks only of the action of the knees, the effect produced will be one of feebleness and ineffectiveness. If, however, one walks concentrating on the action of the toes and the ankles, the stride will be short and quick, and great

CH. 1 – THE MENTAL PICTURE

flexibility and vitality will be felt and suggested. The reader is invited to make the experiment and enjoy the sensation of the toes gripping the ground and promoting a rapid forward movement of the legs. The type of gait, it will be observed, is the outcome of the mental picture.

It is so with golf. The swing is the outcome of the mental picture. Let the reader visualize clearly a swing in which the motive force is applied by and through the hands and particularly the fingers; let him cease to care what other physical processes are involved; and let him rest assured that if his brain prompts the hands and fingers to do their work, the other members of the body will probably do theirs. If he does this, he will be well on the way to achieving that crisp, decisive method of hitting a golf ball which makes the professional's game the despair of the ordinary amateur player.

The golfer should fix it firmly in his mind that his object is not to pit his strength against the inertia of the golf ball, but to lash a responsive ball away by flinging the club-head at it at the highest possible speed. Speed is the *sine qua non*.

Much learning has been devoted to the question whether the golfer's action is a swing or a hit. Most good golfers say it is a swing, but what most good golfers have in mind when they make a shot is to hit. This kind of bewildering inconsistency is rampant in golf. The mental picture suggested by the idea of sweeping the ball away may be instinct with rhythm, but it does not suggest that dash, that speed, that crispness, that "pinch," that "nip," which is of the essence of the modern professional's action.

The golfer should picture to himself that he has to hit the ball away with the club-head, and that in order to do this most effectively he must set the club-head moving and keep it moving all the time by hand and finger work. He must not give a moment's thought to the action of the legs, or the feet, or the hips, or the shoulders, or even to keeping his eye on the ball. He must be preoccupied, he must be obsessed, by the one idea of bringing the clubhead on to the ball by means of a persistent movement of the hands and fingers. He must not think of keeping his left arm and the club-shaft in one line as long as possible (this idea shows a complete lack of appreciation of the functions of hands and fingers); he must not think of keeping his left arm stiff (this, in so far as it happens, is an effect, not a cause); he must think of nothing other than the one idea of making the club-head move all the time with the hands and fingers, and of letting arms, shoulders, hips, legs, and feet respond unhampered to the call made upon them. As a fact, if he goes on taking the club back by finger pressure as far as it will go, he will find that his left knee will automatically turn toward his right, that the left side of his left foot and the left heel will slightly leave the ground, that the left shoulder will turn underneath the chin, that the left arm will be moderately extended (certainly not fully extended or rigid), that at the top of the swing the hands and wrists will be underneath the shaft of the club, that the sole of the club-head will be facing upward, and so on. If any of these effects are not produced, it will not help him consciously to insert them into the up-swing. He must get back to the basic notion of persistent finger work, and he will find that in so far as the traditional symptoms are not exhibited in his swing, he has failed somewhere in that finger work. Somewhere in the upswing the finger work has been relaxed and has failed to give the necessary impetus to the other, the subordinate processes. Similarly, if the down-swing betrays any lack of rhythm, if the body moves too soon or too late or in the wrong curve, if the weight does not follow the club-head - if, in short, anything goes wrong with the swing, let the player try to discover where he has failed in his hand and finger action. He is almost sure to find that at some point or other the finger action has ceased to assert itself, so allowing processes which should be subsidiary and accommodating processes, to take the initiative. If the mind is concentrated on manipulating the club-head by means of hand and finger work, the body can hardly get into the shot too soon, and if the player is determined to let everything respond which wants to respond to the impulse suggested by the hands and fingers, the body is not likely to lag behind. The hands and fingers must so control the club-head that at the vital moment they are ready to make the club-head (which up to that point in the down-swing has been behind the hands) lash through the ball, pulling hands, arms, shoulders, and legs after it.

If one considers for a moment the movements which take place in an ordinary Indian club exercise, one will realize that the performer's mind is concentrated on the work of the hands and fingers. The arms, the shoulders, the body, the legs and the feet respond sympathetically to the movements suggested and set up by the work of the hands and fingers. They do not initiate, but on the other hand, they do not retard. Their province is to be ready and willing to move in order to allow the manipulation of the clubs to proceed with the utmost freedom, precision, and rhythm. It may be that the shoulders and other members of the body do in fact move at the same time as the hands, but the essential thing for the mind to dwell upon is not what movements take place, but how and where to apply power. For if power is

CH. 1 – THE MENTAL PICTURE

properly applied the accessory or accommodating movements are not likely to give trouble.

Fig 4. Down swing. The body has turned on its own initiative

Fig 5. The body has followed the lead of the hands

Fig 6. The hands have started the club-head moving, but the shoulders have not responded

BOOK II - **THE GOLF SWING**

2 THE GRIP

The view that the execution of the golf swing depends on hand and finger action brings out emphatically the immense importance of the grip. The grip is seen to be at the root of the matter; for clearly the player's control over the club depends primarily upon it. His hold of the shaft must be firm yet it must be flexible. Here are two qualities which appear to be incompatible with each other, and it is the golfer's first duty to acquire that method of gripping the club which will allow him to bring these apparently incompatible qualities together in sweet accord.

The old-fashioned palm grip gave power, but not flexibility or "touch" (the writer speaks always of the normal case, and takes no account of what long practice or genius may accomplish with any method under the sun.) The double V grip gives both power and touch, but not unity of action to the two hands. The interlocking grip conduces to that unity of action, but only at the expense of both power and touch (for it puts the powerful forefinger of the left hand almost out of action). The overlapping grip, however, has all the qualities and none of the defects of the other varieties. Its superiority might, indeed, be inferred from the fact that it is the grip of almost every professional golfer and of nine first-class amateurs out of ten.

It is unfortunately the fact, however, that the majority of golfers who use an overlapping grip entirely miss one of the essential features of this form of grip. They realize that the little finger of the right hand is to be allowed to ride over the forefinger of the left hand, so that the hands may have some chance of acting as one, and they realize that the overlapping grip is a finger grip. What they do not realize is that the very essence of the grip is the dominating part played by the forefinger and thumb of each hand.

The advice usually given - though never practised by the expert - is that the first step in gripping the club is to lay the shaft along (that is, parallel with the joints of) the fingers of the left hand. The position indicated is shown in Fig. 7 and the consequent positions of the hands at the top of the up-swing are as shown in Figs. 8 and 9. The position in Fig. 8 is unusual, because the player instinctively realizes that such a position would give him no control of the club, and allows the shaft to move into the palm of his hand as the up-swing proceeds. The result is that that which set out to be a finger grip becomes a palm grip, a grip lacking in flexibility and the capacity to produce high speed in the club-head.

The true finger grip is to be achieved, not by laying the club along the fingers of the hand, but by the following method:

1. Lay the face of the club-head against the ball, allowing the club to take its natural lie.

2. Take hold of the shaft with the thumb and forefinger of the left hand, pressing them together (Figs. 12 and 13). Note that the V made by them on the top of the shaft is a short one, the crook of the forefinger being pronounced and slightly lower than the tip of the thumb.

3. Wrap the other fingers round the shaft (Figs. 14 and 16).

Note. -

(a) The back of the hand is not on the top of the shaft, but at the side of it - that is, facing toward the hole. As the player looks down, he should see the knuckles of the first and second fingers, but not more than a suggestion of the knuckle of the third finger. If the back of the hand is further on the top of the shaft, the wrist and forearm will be stiffened, and the swing will consequently be cramped. If the back of the hand is further to the side (that is, more toward the hole), then the left wrist will tend at the beginning of the up-swing to bend outward (a movement known to anatomy as the "extension of the wrist-joint," and utterly out of place in the golf swing: Fig. 20). If, however, the club is gripped as shown in Figs, 17 and 18, and the proper mental picture of the processes involved in the up-swing has been conceived, the fingers in initiating the movement of the club-head will automatically bring the wrist and forearm into the ideal position. There will be no "extension of the wrist-joint," and the hand and forearm will turn as shown in Fig. 21.

(b) Though the back of the hand is not on the top of the shaft, or facing the sky, the V between the thumb and forefinger *is* on the top of the shaft. It will probably require some little practice in order to get the V into this position without bringing the back of the hand too far over the shaft.

(c) The grip is dominated by the pressure of the forefinger and thumb, the second, third, and fourth fingers contributing in decreasing order to the control of the club so obtained.

(d) If the fingers and thumb are opened out, the shaft will be found to lie, not along the finger joints (Fig. 7), but along a line from the tip of the forefinger, across the lower part of the second finger, the root of the third finger, and the cushion of the palm (known in palmistry as the Mount of the Moon). See Fig. 15.

4. Having mastered the grip of the left hand, place the right hand about the shaft so that the little finger rides easily over the forefinger of the left hand, and the thumb and forefinger grip the shaft in similar formation to that of the thumb and forefinger of the left hand. The knuckles of the first and second fingers are visible to the player, the V between the thumb and forefinger is on the top, or almost on the top of the shaft, and the grip is secured mainly between the crook of the forefinger and the thumb, though the second, third, and fourth fingers, in descending order, play their part.

To sum up, the grip (Figs. 17 and 18) is dominated by the forefingers and thumbs of both hands, the other fingers fulfilling a necessary but ancillary function.

BOOK II - **THE GOLF SWING**

The reader will be able to satisfy himself by experiment, without a club, that if he closes all the fingers of his hand as tightly as possible, he will stiffen the wrist and forearm and even the upper arm, whereas if he grips as firmly as possible with the forefinger and thumb he can retain a completely free wrist, forearm, and upper arm. Such freedom of action, coupled with control of the club, means the playing of good golf, whereas a conscious tension at any point in the mechanism other than the grip of forefinger and thumb is an obstacle to good golf. It is on these grounds that so much importance is attached to the question of gripping the club.

Figs, 10 and 11 indicate the respective positions of the hands and fingers at the top of the up-swing and at the end of the follow-through. They show that the grip is preeminently a finger grip, and they make clear the nature of the work done by the second, third, and fourth fingers. From this point of view Fig. 10 should be compared with Figs. 8 and 9.

CH. 2 – THE GRIP

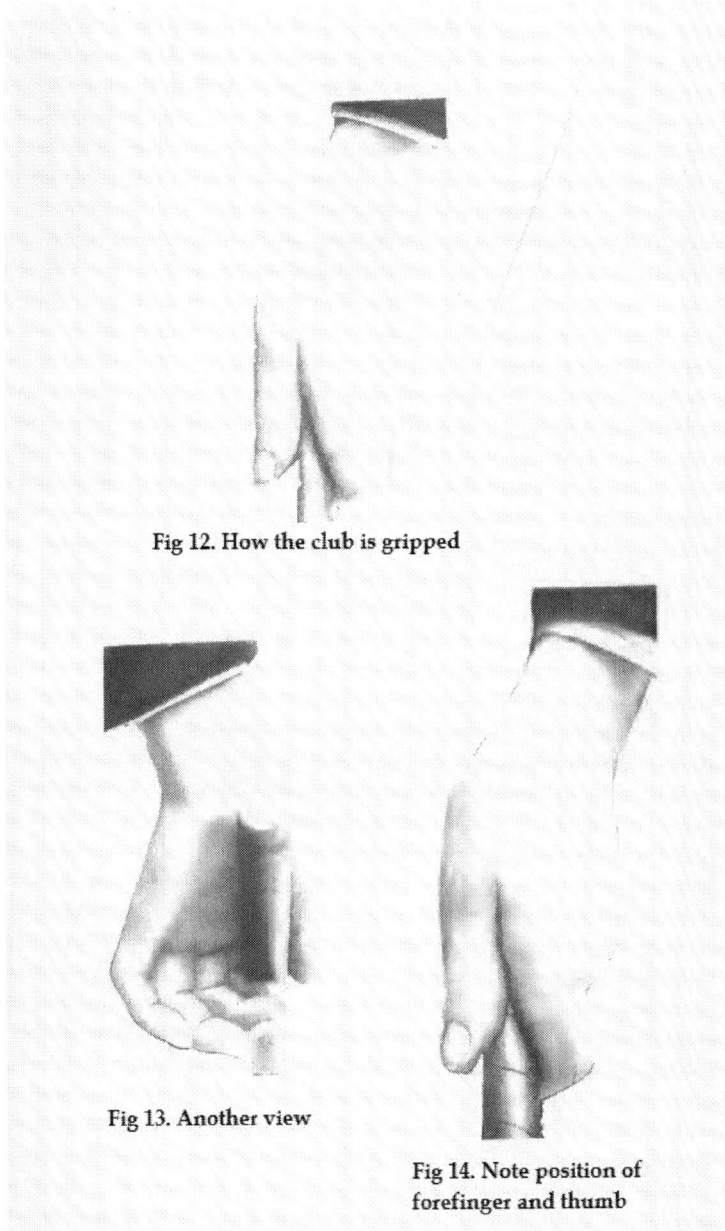

Fig 12. How the club is gripped

Fig 13. Another view

Fig 14. Note position of forefinger and thumb

BOOK II - **THE GOLF SWING**

Fig 11. The ideal finish of the shot. The second, third and fourth fingers are extended to the same extent as in fig. 1

CH. 2 – THE GRIP

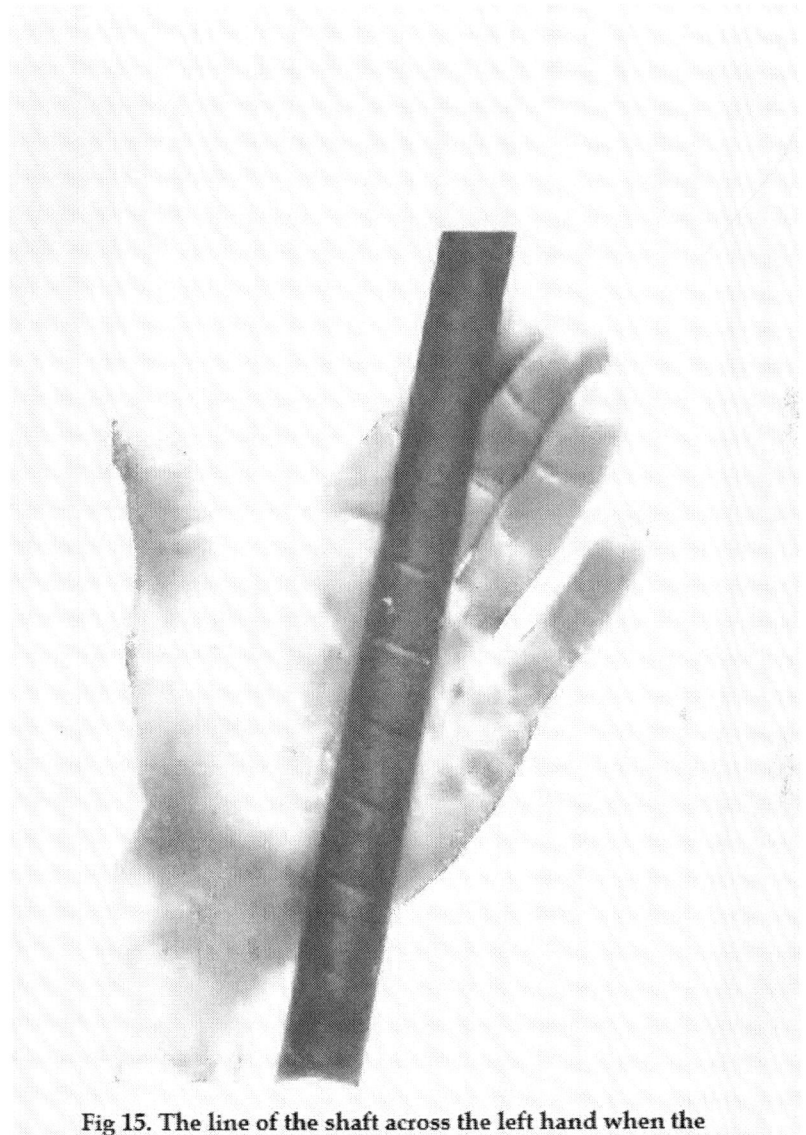

Fig 15. The line of the shaft across the left hand when the hand is opened after gripping the club as in fig 16

BOOK II - **THE GOLF SWING**

Fig 16. A proper hold of the shaft

CH. 2 – THE GRIP

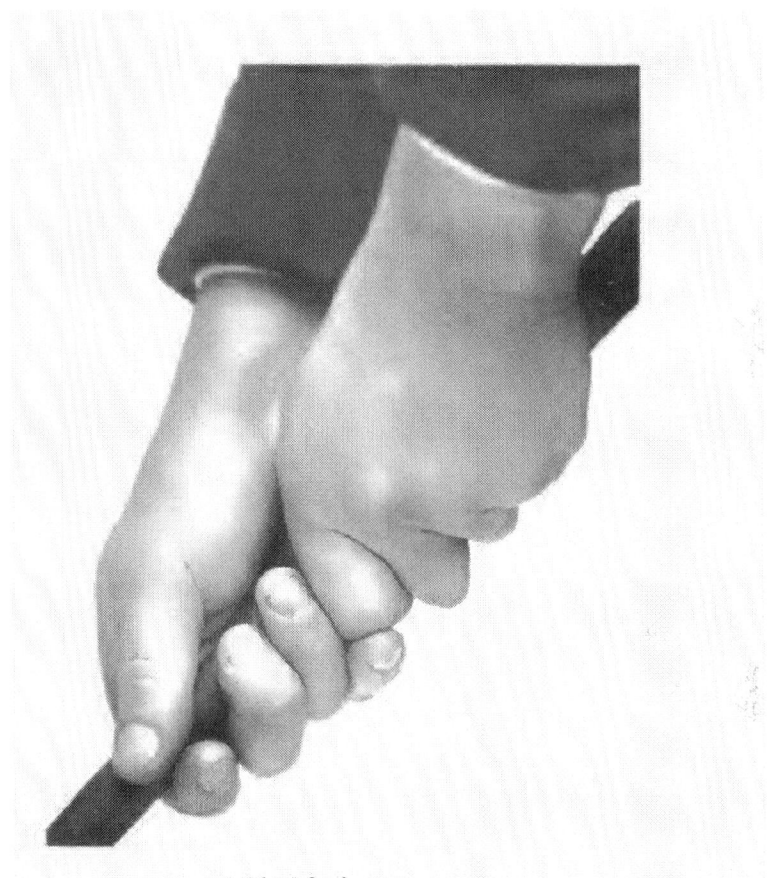

Fig 17. The ideal grip

BOOK II - **THE GOLF SWING**

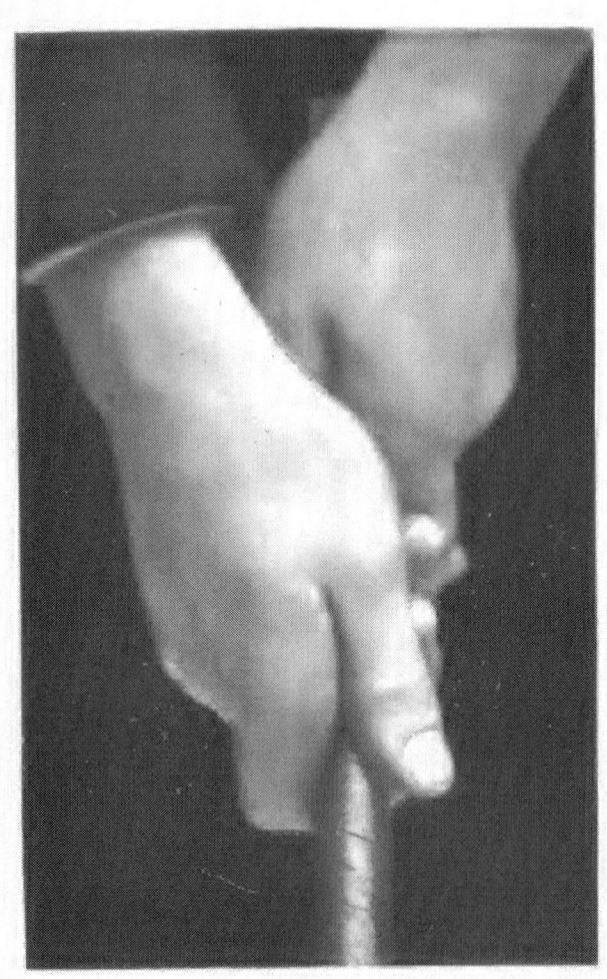

Fig 18. The ideal grip

CH. 2 – THE GRIP

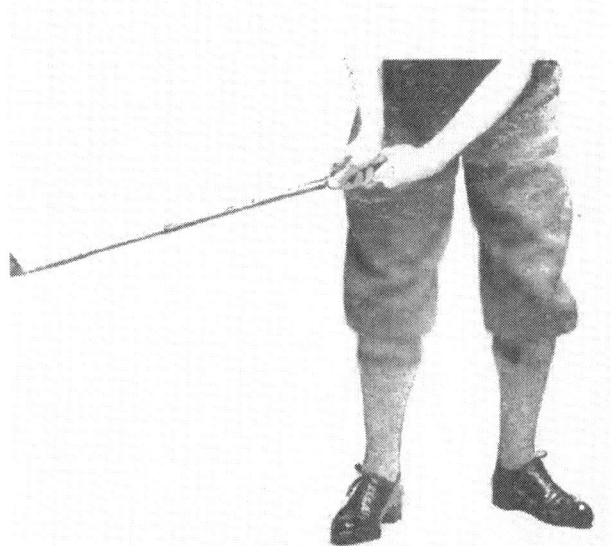

Fig 19. Wrong position - left wrist bent outward

Fig 20. Wrong position - left hand over-turned

BOOK II - **THE GOLF SWING**

Fig 21. Correct position

CH. 2 – THE GRIP

Fig 22. Left hand has not forced club-head back

Fig 23. Proper action of left hand

BOOK II - **THE GOLF SWING**

3 THE SWING

THE WAGGLE.

Having satisfied himself that he knows exactly how the club should be gripped, the player should practise the movement, preliminary to the swing, inelegantly described as the "waggle." Much is to be gained from the waggle treated as an exercise. The waggle should be performed, not aimlessly, but by the conscious application of power by the ringers. The golfer should move the club-head backward, and then move it forward, thinking only of producing the movement by finger work. He will soon become at ease with his grip and on good terms with his club; he will get the "feel" of the club, and become conscious of an increasing command over its movements. In doing this exercise he must determine -

(1) to grip the club firmly in the forefingers and thumbs.

(2) to keep every other part of the body relaxed, notably the wrists, arms, and shoulders.

(3) to apply the motive power continuously, persistently, by the fingers.

If these three points are observed, then:

(a) the body can never lead; and

(b) the body will always follow.

The player will quickly become an expert waggler, and he can then extend the waggle until it becomes a complete backward and forward swing. If the same principles be always borne in mind, the shoulders will turn and the knees will bend in due time and place.

This backward and forward swinging (which incidentally is an excellent physical drill) rapidly promotes that sense of balance and that feeling of control over the club which hundreds of rounds of golf often fail to give; and no matter how expert the golfer may be, no matter how much he may be "on his game," he cannot fail to derive advantage from the exercise, provided that it is performed, never perfunctorily or carelessly, but always with the resolve that the three fundamental principles of grip, relaxation, and finger work shall be consciously and conscientiously carried out. The exercise so practised will produce not only freedom and certainty of movement, but that habit of mental concentration which golf demands as much as anything else in life, whether work or play.

If the body and mind are constantly trained in this manner, the actual hitting of the ball is not likely to present any grave difficulty. Naturally, the very presence of the ball will tempt the golfer to forget one or more of the three articles of faith, and he will often fall before the temptation; but so long as he realizes that the failure of the shot must be due to the failure to observe one or more of the three articles of faith, and to nothing else, and is to be cured by due observation of those articles and by nothing else, his progress in the game will not be long delayed.

The Quarter-Swing

It is best to begin by making quite short shots with an iron club - a mid-iron or a mashie: what is known as a quarter-swing or a half-swing (Figs. 24, 25, 27, and 28). It is this movement which forms the essential part of the full swing, and it is because this movement is so often absent from the full swing that the ball is not really hit away, but is merely pushed away by the club (Fig. 30). When this relatively slow and powerless movement is performed, the fingers and hands have failed to dominate the movement as the hands come toward their lowest point in the down-swing. Instead of forcing the club-head from its position behind them to a position in front of them in order that the ball may be hit away in the most definite manner, the hands and fingers have failed to exert themselves at the vital moment; they have exercised no leverage over the club, and the shaft and arms have moved through the lower sector of the swing practically in a straight line. In other words, the action of the hands and fingers, obviously essential in the quarter-swing or half-swing, has been absent, and the hands have performed no function other than that of a strap fastening the club to the arms. The control, the power, and the "touch," which should have been in the hands and fingers, have been lost. The shot at the best can only be second-rate. At the worst . . .

It is the omission from the full swing of the fundamental action in the short swing that causes the normal driving of the amateur to lack that unmistakable quality of definiteness which distinguishes professional play. The full swing is therefore to be conceived as an enlarged quarter-swing - enlarged solely in order that greater impetus may be imparted to the club-head.

Slow-Back

The principle of slow-back which is dinned into the ears of every beginner is practised by no first-class golfer. The beginner is led to believe that some subtle magic resides in the process, and he performs the laborious operation as though he were anxious to get the club over his right shoulder without any profane onlooker seeing or hearing what he has accomplished. He is like a thief in the night, or a housemaid circumventing a meat-fly. It is, of course, possible to hit a good shot after treating a golf club in this ridiculous manner. It may be less difficult to hit a good shot in that manner than after snatching the club-head away from the ball as though the golfer had suddenly gone mad or suddenly imagined that the club-head was burning the new half-crown ball away. But the up-swing is neither a funeral rite nor a music-hall trick. It should be just a light, easy, free, flexible movement, pleasing to execute, pleasing to observe. The slow-back doctrine is a clumsy statement of the principle of control. The golfer must obtain and retain control of the club. It is seen that he almost necessarily loses control when he jerks the club away from the ball, and instead of the root principle of control being intelligently explained to him, he is told without ceasing to go "slow-back." He begins to regard "slow-back" as an end in itself instead of a bad means to that end, and he plods on, for ever missing the whole significance of the golf swing.

It may be objected that the person who makes the up-swing at a snail's pace does in fact possess control of the club. This, however, is untrue. In the first place, the movement he makes is not an up-swing at all - it is merely an upward movement, or rather a series of upward movements. There is no swing in it, and it cannot conduce to the development of swing in the downward movement. The phrase "control of the club" means control of the club *qua* golf club, not *qua* sledge-hammer; it connotes the ability to set up speed in the club-head, from the utmost speed that it may be capable of achieving, as in the drive, down to the lowest speed at which it can be induced to move effectively, as in the short putt Such control is not to be obtained by the observance of any shibboleth, least of all the shibboleth of slow-back. The up-swing must be a *swing*, and its only function is that of the best possible pre liminary to the down-swing. It is not an end in itself: it is only a means to an end. It is not a means to that end unless it is light, easy, free, flexible. If it has those qualities, and is controlled, its speed is a matter of no importance. The best golfer is the golfer who has greatest control of the club, and it may well be that he is the golfer who has the quickest up-swing - this being an effect, not, of course, a cause, of supreme control. The beginner should therefore always keep in mind the great question of control, and he must steadily refuse to be side-tracked, whether he is considering, or practising, either the up-swing or the down-swing. As a matter of fact, he would do well never at all to think of the swing in separate parts. The waggle, the up-swing, the down-swing, the follow-through, and all the rest of it, are in reality one thing - the movement by which the golfer obtains, and expresses, his mastery over the club-head. This mastery is to be achieved by the cultivation of proper hand and finger action, by relying on the hands and fingers to provide the initiating motive power - in other words, by setting the machinery going at the fingers.

The Down-Swing

One of the most vital moments in the golf swing occurs just before the up-swing is completed. Even the player who has begun to realize the importance of persistently moving the club-head with the hands, is tempted at this point to forget to carry this action out and to let the body go on twisting on its own account. When this tendency is yielded to, it becomes extremely difficult to give the proper start to the club-head at the beginning of the down-swing; for if the hands fail at any moment they are all the more likely to fail at the next moment. And the right shoulder, instead of being pulled round as a result of an impetus set up and kept up by the hands, will turn on its own account (Fig. 4). Consequently, when the club-head strikes the ball, the shoulders will not be in anything like the position they occupied when the ball was addressed, but will be turned toward the hole - they will, in fact, be already more or less in the position they should take at the finish of the shot. This is the normal case of "body in too soon." The player will be told by his caddy that he has cut across the ball or pulled his arms in, and he will be urged to throw his arms out after hitting the ball. Such advice is on a par with the recommendation to lock the door after the horse has gone. The player has not pulled his arms in. His body has turned prematurely and on its own impulse. The arms cannot help coming across the line of intended flight as the ball is struck, and nothing that the player can do as he strikes the ball, or after he has struck it, can be of the least avail. One must get back to the source of the trouble - that point in the swing, possibly in the up-swing, possibly at the beginning of the down-swing, at which the hands and fingers have failed to do their work. (Compare Figs. 22 and 23.)

In most of the books on golf, that vital moment in the swing, the beginning of the down-swing, is passed by in silence, but in one or two of the books greater or less attention is devoted to it. In the Harry Vardon book it is dealt with at some length, and the player is recommended to aim, at the beginning of the down-swing, at an imaginary person behind him. This kind of teaching may conceivably do some good, but it is, in principle, unsound. It does not go to the root of the matter. If in the true swing the club-head passes through certain points, it does not follow that the true swing can be produced by guiding the club-head through those points. In the true swing, the fingers, hands, arms, etc., perform coordinate movements, and if those movements are properly produced, the club-head cannot help following the proper path. To guide the club-head along that path in the hope that the anatomical movements will be sound is to put the cart before the horse, effect before cause. One must begin at the beginning and endeavour to secure the effect desired by mastering the processes of which that effect is the inevitable outcome.

BOOK II - **THE GOLF SWING**

In "Golf Faults Illustrated," Taylor, in speaking of the down-swing, admonishes the reader not to "put on leverage too soon." The meaning here is not too clear, but it may be the same as that conveyed by that golfing commonplace "Don't hit from the top." If it is, then it is diametrically opposed to the injunction of Braid in "Advanced Golf," who directs the player to hit from the top as hard as he can, Taylor is apparently anxious that the player should not force the shot with his body; Braid is apparently anxious that he should take the risk. And so long as the player always applies his power with his hands, letting everything else freely respond to the action so initiated, there can be no doubt that he who hits most vigorously will hit best.

In several other books it is stated that the down-swing is begun by a pull of the left arm. This, at best, is a half-truth, and is misleading. The initiation of the movement is in the hands, and the pull of the left arm is a responsive - an immediately responsive - movement. The operation is simply the operation of hitting - it is instinctive when once the principles of the movement have been mastered; and it is significant that no good golfer who is on his game has ever anything in mind when making a shot other than hitting the ball. He is not trying to hit an imaginary person behind him; he is not trying not to put on leverage too soon, or not to hit from the top; he is not trying to initiate the downswing with a pull of the left arm - he is merely moving the club-head - hitting the ball.

Head-Lifting

Even the resolution to glue the eyes to the ball is an irrelevance. If the player has the hitting idea immovably in his mind, he is sure to look at the ball; the player only fails to look at the ball when that one dominating idea is momentarily absent. If the mind for one instant leaves that idea and concerns itself with anything else, as, for example, the result of the shot, the head will, as likely as not, go up. Moreover, if the mind flits for one moment from the one idea of hitting the ball, the rhythm of the movement will be disturbed, the swing will probably go wrong, and the player's head will inevitably go up - it will be jerked up. Every indifferent player is a victim from time to time to fits of head-lifting. All sorts of "tips" have been devised for the treatment of this malady, but it is common experience that no matter what specific is applied the head-lifting continues. It is, indeed, not to be cured by nostrums, not even by a fixed determination to keep the head down. For head-lifting is usually an effect of a bad swing, not a cause of one. The only real cure for head-lifting or any other golfing malady lies in concentrating the mind on forcing the club-head into action by proper hand and finger work.

Letting The Club-Head Do It

The idea so often put forward of letting the club do the work is misconceived and misleading. The club-head will certainly not do the work if the golfer is anything like so passive towards it. The golfer must learn to make the club-head do the work.

The illustration of the beginning of the upswing (Fig. 23) bears directly upon this principle. This is a posed as distinguished from an action photograph, and it undoubtedly differs to some extent from what would be revealed by an action photograph. The latter would show a fuller development of the accessory or accommodating movements. At the same time, if the golfer tried to make his movements correspond with those indicated by an action photograph, he would be tempted to give undue attention to the accommodating movements. The posed photograph emphasizes the importance of hand and finger work at the very outset of the swing, and if this idea is allowed to dominate the mind of the golfer (coupled always with the complementary idea of *not interfering* with the full and free development of the accessory or accommodating movements of the other members of the body) the golfer will often achieve something closely akin to golf.

Approach Shots

The significance of the clear mental picture is perhaps most apparent in the approach shot. Where the exact length of the shot can be measured, and where the character of the shot is determined by the hazards and other features of the course, every golfer who has obtained some command over his clubs addresses his ball with confidence. His environment forces the correct mental picture upon him. He cannot escape from it. There is no doubt, no vagueness as to what is required. But in the opposed type of shot, as, for example, an open approach to an unprotected green, with nothing to indicate clearly the length of shot which is called for, the golfer has himself to make up his mind as to the type of shot to be played. Probably half a dozen shots are open to him, and he has to select one of them. He may find difficulty in deciding which is the best, and he may change his mind whilst executing the shot. A large percentage of foozled approaches are due to this cause, as every golfer knows only too well. It is obviously of first importance that the player should never proceed to execute any shot, no matter how short or how easy it may appear, until he has definitely outlined in his mind the type of shot he intends to produce.

The Run-Up

In order to produce this shot the golfer is usually instructed to turn over the right hand on, or immediately after, hitting the ball. If, however, the player concentrates on this turning over of the right hand as a thing in itself, he is not likely to obtain good results. He will probably turn the hand over too soon, too late, or too much, and his action will probably be stiff and artificial. The proper shot can be consistently produced only when the shot is made from the proper point of view; and in the run-up, as in every other shot, the player must get down to the essence of the matter. What is the essence of the run-up? What are the characteristics that leap to the eye when the shot is played by an expert? First, consider the flight of the ball. The ball rises but little from the turf, and the inference is that it has been struck by a club with little loft or by a club whose loft has been to some extent neutralized by the stance, the address, and the action of the player. It runs a long distance after striking the turf, and the inference is that it has been hit without any suspicion of "jabbing" or "stabbing." This inference, moreover, is strengthened by the fact that the ball travels very evenly and steadily and goes further than it appears to have the power to do. Now, observe carefully the action and stance of the player. His weight is forward on the left leg, the ball is toward his right foot, and consequently his hands, when he addresses the ball, are in front of it. This is exactly the position one would expect after watching the flight and run of the ball. The up-swing is short, slow, and deliberate, and the down-swing is short, slow, and deliberate - the movement is even and delicately controlled from beginning to end. The club-head almost caresses the ball; if it is slow to reach the ball, it is loth to leave it.

It is by drawing attention to these points that Ernest Jones teaches the run-up. Clearly visualize the shot, gain control of the club in the fingers, then play the shot. It is the fact that the right hand turns over to some extent, but that turning over is only an incident in the shot. It is not the essence of the matter. The essence of the matter is a clear conception of the nature of the shot, and that sense of "touch" which can only be obtained by means of finger control. It is quite easy to turn over the right hand without having any real control of the club whatsoever - one has only to observe the game of the average amateur to realize that this is so. The golfer must, if he is to do any good, learn to differentiate between symptoms and causes, and he must always be on the alert against the teacher who directs him to try to reproduce symptoms.

The Pitch, Pitch And Run, Push Shot, Etc

What has been said of the run-up is equally applicable, with the necessary changes, to all the other shots. The player should first closely observe the behaviour of the ball, then the attitude and action of the expert as he makes the shot - always correlating the two things, effect and cause. Then, if he has acquired control of the club in his fingers, he will have no difficulty in expressing what he has in his mind. And that is the essence of golf.

BOOK II - **THE GOLF SWING**

Fig 24. Quarter shot

Fig 25. Half shot

Fig 26. Full iron shot

CH. 3 – THE SWING

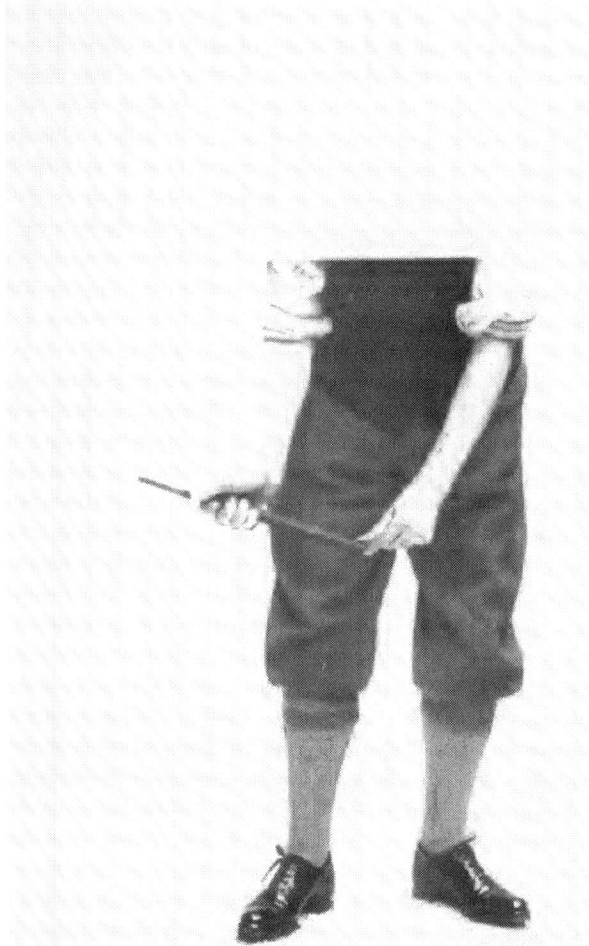

Fig 45. Shows "give" of fingers in any flexible movement

BOOK II - THE GOLF SWING

Fig 46. Figs 46 and 47 exemplify again the essential "give" of the fingers

CH. 3 – THE SWING

Fig 27. Corollary to fig 24

BOOK II - **THE GOLF SWING**

Fig 28. Corollary to fig 25

Fig 29. Corollary to fig 26

206

CH. 3 – THE SWING

Fig 32. Perfect finish of short iron shot. Contrast with figs 30 and 31, and note how the club-head has been forced through

BOOK II - **THE GOLF SWING**

Fig 33. How the blade of the iron should normally come onto the ball

Fig 34. Another view of the type of shot shown in fig 32

CH. 3 – THE SWING

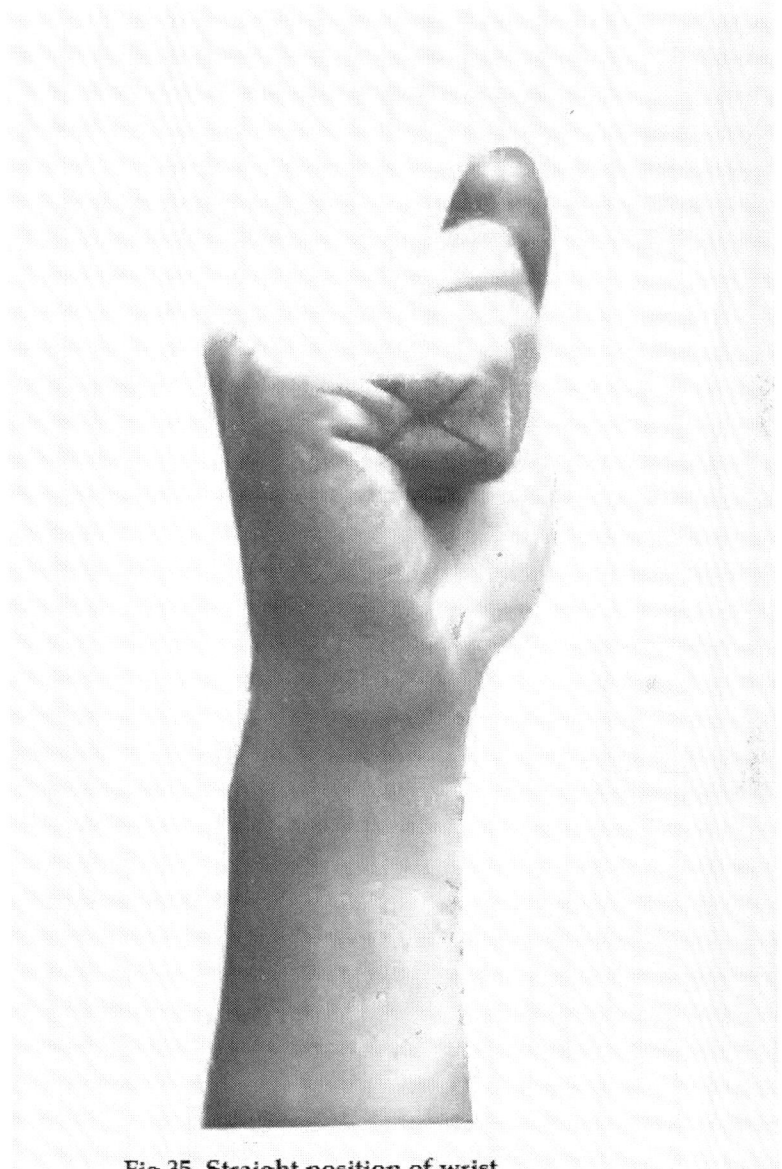

Fig 35. Straight position of wrist

BOOK II - THE GOLF SWING

Fig 44. Left wrist bending in follow through

CH. 4 – THE ACTION OF THE WRIST

4 THE ACTION OF THE WRIST

I

"I draw it (the club) back close to the ground with my wrists. ... I turn the face away from the ball with my wrists. This turning of the wrists (any "turning" is, or course, a turning of the forearm, not of the wrists) imparts greater speed to the club-head, and is the great secret of long driving. To master this turn of the wrists is to add many yards to the long game. . . . After my arms have been allowed to follow through a reasonable distance I turn my wrists and finish the stroke over the left shoulder." - Jerome D. Travers.

*   *   *

"Now we have seen the operation as it should be - the inward turn of the left wrist. . . .

The left wrist has not turned sufficiently."- Vardon.

*   *   *

BOOK II - **THE GOLF SWING**

"The first movement must come from the wrists. They and they alone start the head of the club moving back from the ball.

"The initiative in bringing down the club is taken by the left wrist. ... At this point - about a couple of feet from the ball - there should be some tightening up of the wrists. . . . I am certainly one of those who believe that the work done by the wrists at this point has a lot to do with the making of the drive. . . ."- Braid.

*   *   *

"The movement of the upward swing must be begun entirely with the wrists . . . the majority of beginners, instead of letting their wrists do the work ... It is the left wrist begins the downward swing. ... At that moment (when the head of the club is separated from the ball by a space of twenty inches or thereabouts) the two wrists come into play." - Arnaud Massy.

*   *   *

"Bring it (the club-head) behind the ball with a fairly flat swing, and give it a little flick with the wrists so as to introduce plenty of vim.

"When the club is about eighteen inches from the ball I hit with the back of the left hand, and at the same time put in that right wrist flick which counts for so much." - Herd.

*   *   *

"The most notable changes with regard to the swing are . . . the wrists come much more into the stroke, the body much less. . . . We note the strong flexion (here used in its popular sense) of the wrists. ... It is very nice to be able to drive a ball two hundred yards with this power of fingers and this turning of the wrists. . . . Taylor, though he uses his wrists freely, has not the

CH. 4 – THE ACTION OF THE WRIST

Vardon flex or flick, but he gets there just as well with his forearm work. . . ."
- John L. Low.

* * *

"The left wrist takes the club back ... If the left wrist is not turned as it should be . . . This turn of the left wrist is a gradual movement. The club-head should meet the ball, the wrists having, in bringing the club down, accelerated the speed at the moment of contact. ... If control of the club is not lost, leverage from the wrists is so much more easily acquired." - J. H. Taylor.

II

"The object of this book is to show that the mechanism of the golf swing depends on forearm rather than wrist action. Indeed, apart from putting, it will be contended that there is no such thing as a pure wrist shot in the whole domain of golf.

* * *

"The exposition, as well as the performance, of the golf swing is a comparatively simple matter, provided the action of the wrist-joints can be excluded from the movement.

"The wrist-joint, so far from coming into play, is passively rotated backwards and forwards *en bloc* with the hand and forearms.

* * *

"The pace and power of the club-head at the moment of impact are greatly increased by the incipient pronation of the right hand which contributes the whip-like snap to the movement . . . it is a pure forearm action which takes command of the wrist and hand together.

BOOK II - THE GOLF SWING

*   *   *

"At the moment of impact the sudden tightening up of the muscles of the forearm brings the right hand and forearm from the position of slight supination to the position midway between pronation and supination; and this movement, in conjunction with the straightening out and extension of the right elbow, imparts the characteristic flick to the club-head.', - Burnham Hare *in "The Golfing Swing."*

III

"First and foremost, and one might almost say simply and solely, there is in proper manipulation the *feeling* that one is hitting the ball by means of the wrists.

"Take thought only of smiting the ball as with the wrist, and the proper twist or roll, the turn of the right hand over the left at the impact, follows automatically.

"Let everything be contributory to what is *called* and *felt* to be wrist action . . . *forearm action though it be in reality.*

"Let the gentle reader be warned against any conscious effort to twist or roll his forearms.

"It is very hard (quite so. It is very hard, because the feeling which should be the central feature of good golf action is not wrist action, but hand and finger action) for the average man to believe that the feeling of wrist action which produces forearm action is a central feature of good golf action." - R. S. Weir, *Golf Illustrated*, March, 1918.

IV

CH. 4 – THE ACTION OF THE WRIST

It will thus be seen that according to Messrs. Braid, Taylor, Vardon, Travers, and Low, and, indeed, ninety-nine first-class golfers out of a hundred, the essence of the shot is to get the wrists into it; that according to "Burnham Hare" (who may be taken as fairly representing the anatomical school) the essence of the shot is to keep the wrists out of it; and that according to Mr. R. S. Weir, an engaging exponent of the humanistic compromise, the essence of the shot is to get the forearms into it by aiming at getting the wrists into it. In a word, Messrs. Braid and Co. say the action is a wrist action, so work the wrists; Messrs. Hare and Co. say the action is a forearm action, so work anything but the wrists; while Messrs. Weir and Co. say the action is a forearm action, so work the wrists.

V

Messrs. Weir and Co. appear to proceed on ' two reasonable hypotheses. The first is that it is almost inconceivable that such accomplished players as Messrs. Braid and Co. can be wrong in their *feeling* for the shot. The second is that it is almost inconceivable that such erudite anatomists as Messrs. Hare and Co. can be wrong in their analysis of the shot. What, then, is the explanation of these seemingly contradictory propositions? If A is right in what he says, and B is right in what he does, B must, all unconsciously, achieve what A says; and may not B's method be the best practical way of producing the effect noted and defined by A? After all, the only thing B really has in view is to hit a good shot. After making many good shots and many bad ones, he becomes conscious of certain differences of feeling as between the good shots and the bad ones. It seems to him that when he is hitting good shots he is using his wrists freely, and that when he is hitting bad shots he is failing to use his wrists freely. That is enough for B. And nothing that A can demonstrate will affect him.

But there is C to consider. Is C to follow B and think of his wrists, whilst admitting that the essential action is forearm action as stated by A? Or can C be given some surer guide to success? Is it certain that Messrs. Hare and Co. are entirely correct in their theory that the action is purely forearm action? Or may it be that the wrist-joint plays a real part in the movement? In other words, may there be something in the wrist theory even from the anatomical point of view?

In order to answer this question, one must first determine whether the much-discussed action of the wrist is entirely forearm action, entirely wrist action, or both forearm and wrist action; and one must also determine whether the action, whatsoever it may be, is an initiatory or merely a resultant action, whether it is a cause or an effect.

VI

The wrist joint in itself is capable of four different movements, and four only. These are shown in Figs. 36, 37, 39, and 40.

With a view to determining to what extent, if any, these movements take place in the course of the golf swing, the reader is invited to take hold of a club in each hand successively, and then in both hands together, and to make the complete swing, slowly observing the wrists all the time.

He will observe the following points:

Right Hand

Up-swing: (a) The wrist-joint moves as shown in Fig. 41, and is extended to the full by the time the arm has reached the position shown in Fig. 42 ("extension" is complete - This movement is accompanied by a slight responsive turning of the forearm.)

(b) The remainder of the upward movement is achieved mainly by the arm, but at the last moment the wrist-joint gives, allowing the hand to incline towards the shoulder (abduction), and at the same time the fingers give.

Down-swing: The movements involved in the up-swing are reversed.

CH. 4 – THE ACTION OF THE WRIST

Follow-through: There is no movement of the right wrist-joint after the club-head has passed the ball, except for the almost negligible abduction of that joint at the end of the swing; what happens is that the forearm turns

Left Hand

Up-swing and down-swing: There is no movement of the wrist-joint except for the almost negligible abduction of that joint. The forearm turns (Fig. 21).

Follow-through: The wrist-joint bends, as shown in Fig. 44.

Both Hands

To recapitulate (ignoring for practical purposes the feeble movements called abduction and adduction):

1. ***From Address to Impact:*** First part of upswing and last part of downswing: a vigorous movement of the right wrist-joint ("extension"); no movement of the left wrist-joint, but a turning movement of left hand and forearm (note: The beginner often finds difficulty in moving his hands in the correct manner at the beginning of the upswing. He is prone either to bend outward the left wrist-joint (flexion), as in Fig. 19, or to go to the opposite extreme and overturn the left hand, as in Fig. 20, loosely known as overturning the wrist. He can, however, always arrive at the proper movement of the hands by noting the position which the left hand will automatically take if it is allowed to accommodate itself to the extension of the right wrist-joint (see Fig. 21). He should not, of course, allow his left hand to be passive when he is making the up-swing of an actual shot; the left hand should be at least as active as the right, but the complete extension of the right wrist-joint will always give the true position of both hands and arms, and consequently the true course of the club-head.)

BOOK II - THE GOLF SWING

2. ***From Impact to Finish.*** - First part of follow-through: a vigorous movement of the left wrist-joint ("extension"); no movement of the right wrist-joint, but a turning movement of the right hand and forearm.

3. The movement technically called flexion (Fig. 19) does not take place at any part of the swing.

VII

In these circumstances the writer puts forward the following propositions:

1. The expression "the turning of the wrists' (*vide* Messrs. Braid and Co.) is misleading. In so far as the wrist turns, it turns *en bloc* with the forearm, as maintained by Messrs. Hare and Co.; the movement is really a hand and forearm movement.

2. Though the "turning of the wrists "is a misleading expression, the wrist-joints do play a vital part in the swing, Messrs. Hare and Co. notwithstanding; and when Braid says, "the first movement must come from the wrists," he is not so far from the truth as Mr. Hare suggests. At all events, an essential and a pronounced part of that movement does come from the extension of the *right* wrist-joint.

3. As regards the whip-like snap which occurs at the moment of impact in a well-hit shot, the popular view that the snap is produced by a "wrist flick," though not quite correct, is preferable to Mr. Hare's "incipient pronation of the right hand."

4. Mr. Hare's statement that the movement is "a pure forearm action which takes command of the wrist and hand together" is unsound in theory, and full of trouble if followed in practice.

5. Mr. Weir concedes too much to Messrs. Hare and Co. as theorists, and too much to Messrs. Braid and Co. as practical teachers. It has been shown

CH. 4 – THE ACTION OF THE WRIST

that the right wrist-joint before impact, and the left wrist-joint after impact, do play a most important part in the movement, quite distinct from the turning or twisting of the forearm. But it is to be noted that this movement of the wrist-joint should not be produced by executing the movement as a thing in itself. In the golf swing it is not an initiating movement at all; it is a responsive and contributory movement. The golfer holds the club in his hands, largely in his ringers. Everything that he does with his club is done by means of the hands and fingers. The "feel" of the club, and the power to use the club, come to him through the hands and fingers. "Touch" is entirely a matter of hands and fingers. If the hands are used without finger work, the swing is the clumsy, lumbering movement known as the dead-hand swing. Vitality goes into the swing at the fingers. It is communicated by their controlled extension and contraction (see Figs. 42, 45, 46, and 47). The wrist is a remoter and duller part of the mechanism than even the dead-hand. The player may bring the most practised concentration to bear on the working of the wrists without ever realizing what finger action means, and the fact that, in spite of this concentration on the wrists, many players are so apt at hitting a ball that they also develop perfect finger action is not a good argument for concentrating on the wrists. The average player will doubtless suffer less if he thinks of his wrists than if he thinks of his forearms or his biceps, or his shoulders, or his hips, or his feet; but in nine cases out of ten he will suffer; for though he is nearer to the truth than he might be, he is further from it than he need be. If the rules of golf made it necessary to strap the club to the wrists and not to hold it in the hands, it would doubtless be a good plan to think of using the wrists. But as the golfer does as a fact take hold of the club in his hands and fingers, the writer cannot for the life of him see why he should not try to hit with them.

BOOK II - **THE GOLF SWING**

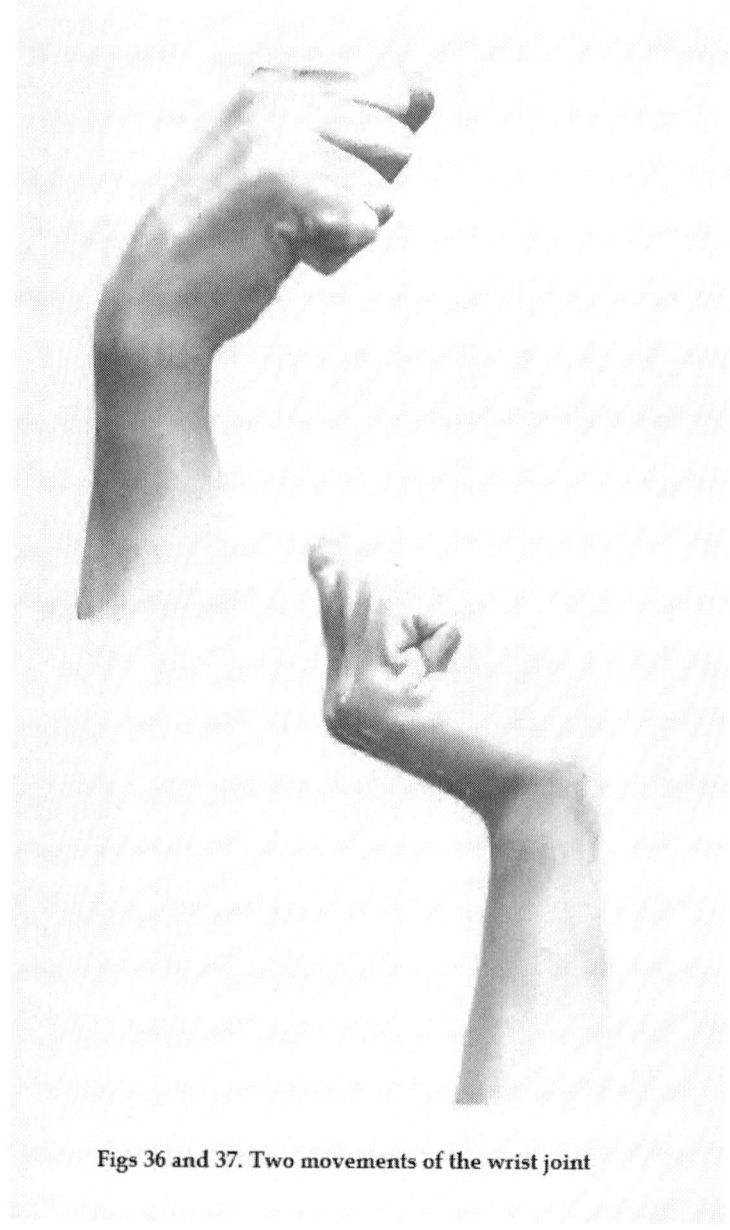

Figs 36 and 37. Two movements of the wrist joint

CH. 4 – THE ACTION OF THE WRIST

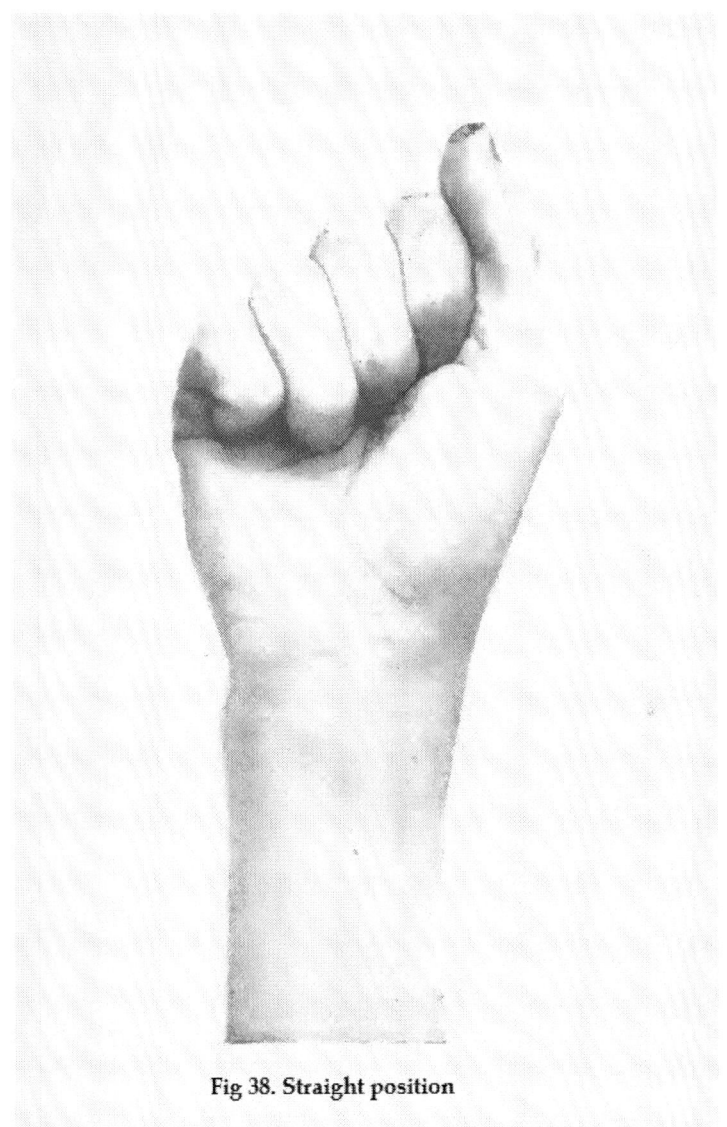

Fig 38. Straight position

BOOK II - **THE GOLF SWING**

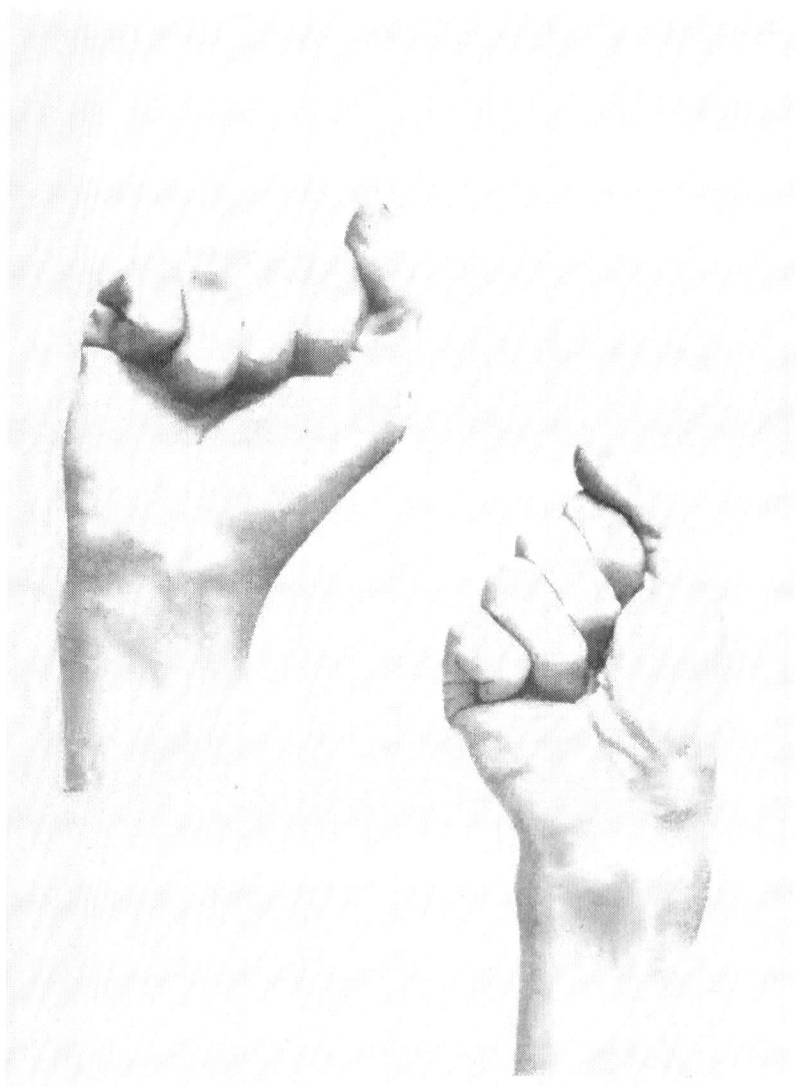

Figs 39 and 40. Two other movements of the wrist joint

CH. 4 – THE ACTION OF THE WRIST

Fig 41. Action of right wrist beginning up-swing

BOOK II - **THE GOLF SWING**

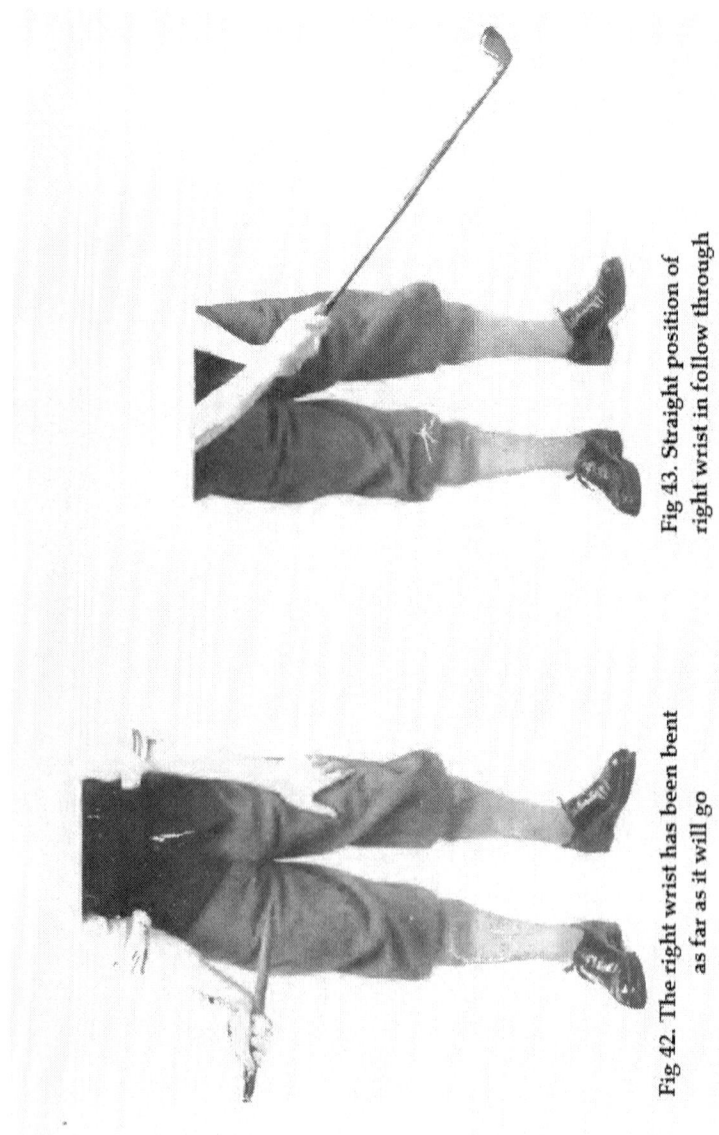

Fig 42. The right wrist has been bent as far as it will go

Fig 43. Straight position of right wrist in follow through

CH. 4 – THE ACTION OF THE WRIST

Fig 47. Compare with fig 46 where
the fingers have not "given"

BOOK II - **THE GOLF SWING**

5 THE BALANCE OF THE BODY

In the composition of the golfer the two elements, balance of body and balance of mind are intimately correlated, and from observation one would conclude that neither is easy to maintain. To some extent each may be either a cause or an effect of the other, and whilst it is possible for the one to exist without the other, the two are usually found together - either present or absent.

It is for the reader himself (or herself) to determine whether, and, if so, to what extent, his (or her) faulty balance of body is the cause or the effect of his (or her) faulty balance of mind, and whether treatment should be applied to the one element or to the other, or to both elements.

The writer will not treat specifically of the balance of the mind; for on this point he is ready to receive rather than to give advice; but he will treat specifically of the balance of the body, and it will be agreed that any improvement in the balance of the golfer's body is likely to yield an improvement in the balance of his mind, as a natural consequence.

The type of golfer who regards golf as a game that can be played by anybody, anyhow, finds satisfaction in pointing to differences in the method and style of first-class players. It is not, however, the differences, but the samenesses, that are of real significance. Broadly speaking, indeed, all first-

BOOK II - **THE GOLF SWING**

class golfers swing alike. The differences are differences of detail - tricks of personality; the samenesses are fundamental.

Not the least important of the samenesses is the perfection of body balance, the quality of the even keel. And, conversely, not the least important of the samenesses in the action of bad golfers is the absence of that quality.

The average golfer does not appear to realize the close relationship which exists between the general method of swinging the club and the balance of the body. He thinks of the swinging of the club as one thing, and of the balancing of the body as another thing, and he aims at securing balance by setting his feet wide apart and grimly trying to keep them flat on the turf throughout the swing. This, on the face of it, may not seem to be a wholly bad method. If the player keeps flat on both feet, it would appear to follow that he cannot get on to his toes, that he cannot jump, that he cannot fall away from the ball. But the reasoning is false. Anything and everything may happen to the golfer who tries to root himself to earth in this manner - anything and everything but good golf. For balance is not to be achieved by any short cut; and the effort to do anything with the body or the legs or the feet, beyond allowing them to respond to the movement set up by the hands and fingers, is foredoomed to failure.

There may, of course, be some first-class golfer, unknown to the writer, whose feet throughout the swing remain flat on the ground; but if there is, he proves nothing except that genius, or perseverance, or both, can accomplish most things. Subject to this reservation.

all first-class golfers allow the left knee and foot to give in the up-swing, and the right knee and foot to give in the follow-through, and all first-class golfers preserve an even keel. It is true that Sandy Herd and Edward Ray both sway appreciably in making their shots; but a certain amount of sway is not incompatible with a sustained balance of the body. Both Herd and Ray visualize a certain path for the club-head which the club-head could not follow unless the body were allowed to move outward to the right; but in both cases this movement of the body is just as much a response to the movement set up by the hand and fingers as is the movement of the body in the case of the most perfect corkscrew twister. There is no golfer who conveys more emphatically than Ray the idea that the mastery of the club

CH. 5 – THE BALANCE OF THE BODY

remains in the player's hands and fingers. At the same time, the writer does not agree with Ray when he says that his sway is the crowning ornament of a finished golfer's style. Fine golfer as Ray is, the writer always feels that he would have been a stroke or two a round still better had he not made his golf a slightly more difficult, a slightly more uncertain, game than even golf need be.

In the orthodox swing the hands and fingers initiate the action of winding the club-head round the body. When the club-head has been got under way a certain tension is felt in the body and legs, and unless this tension is relieved by the giving of the left knee and the left foot, the fingers will cease to control the club-head, the stiffness of the knee-joint will set up an obstacle to their proper functioning, and the balance of the body will be lost. Similarly, if the left knee gives before it receives impetus from the movement set up by the fingers, the mechanism will be put out of joint, and the balance of the body will again be lost.

In the orthodox up-swing, the hips and shoulders must turn so that the left shoulder comes underneath the chin. How can anyone who is not an elastic man or a music-hall artist get into that position unless he allows a certain amount of pivoting to take place? Could this turning movement possibly be made more difficult than by resolutely endeavouring to keep the left foot flat and firm? It is quite clear that something must go - either the ribs or the spinal column, or the balance. Fortunately from the point of view of the death-roll, unfortunately from the point of view of golf, it is the balance that goes in most cases.

The writer had a dear friend whose golfing life had been one long effort to acquire what it pleased him to call a firm stance; but he could be guaranteed to lose his balance every time he essayed anything beyond a quarter-swing. Just before the war broke out he announced confidentially that he had discovered that the secret of a good balance was to plant the right foot firmly on the ground and then to stiffen the right leg so as to form a buttress which should support the whole body. He made an effort to put this great idea into practice, the buttress proved unequal to the strain, and the result was that there was one more cripple in this country and one less soldier than there would otherwise have been. (The number of *golfers* was not, however, affected.)

BOOK II - **THE GOLF SWING**

It is true that in most treatises on golf the golfer is admonished to stand firm on his heels when he is addressing the ball; but in the writer's opinion that advice, having regard to the interpretation normally placed upon it, is bad. In the address the golfer should stand firm, not on his heels, but on his feet. It is with the ball of the foot and the big-toe, as well as the heel, that the good golfer feels himself gripping the turf. Any tendency to get the weight chiefly on to the toes must, of course, be checked; but it should not be checked by going to the opposite extreme of keeping as much weight as possible on the heels. The pedagogy of golf is full of the pernicious plan of endeavouring to get rid of one fault by substituting another fault for it, and the golfer should ever be on his guard against it. To give the feet and legs liberty to move at the dictation of the fingers, is not to invite them to dance a tango or to pirouette in airy independence of the action of fingers, hands, and arms. There is a *via media* between an uncompromising rigidity and a fatuous freedom.

A certain type of golfer habitually keeps an even keel till somewhere about the moment of impact of club-head and ball. At that moment he appears to explode, and the onlooker is surprised that a straight ball of good length is often the result. The explanation of this phenomenon of the links appears to be this: the player regards his duty as done when the ball has been hit - his conception of the golf swing does not take him beyond that point - and he ceases to apply power with the hands and fingers. The result is that the body, which is still under considerable momentum, continues its mad career without the sustained guidance and impetus of its natural leaders, and the swing ends in a sharp sequence of contortions instead of a statuesque repose.

A perfect sense of balance, whether at the top of the up-swing or the finish of the downswing, is only to be acquired by the free action of body, legs, and feet moving in response to the assertive action of hands and fingers. It is to be noted, however, that the specific object of continuous action of hands and fingers after the ball has been hit is not to secure a balanced finish, but to get the last fraction of speed out of the club-head; for the player who aims at continuously developing speed in the club-head after the ball has gone will find it easier to move the club-head at its maximum speed at the moment of impact than he who has no thought of applying power after the ball has

CH. 5 – THE BALANCE OF THE BODY

gone. The elements in the question are not only mechanical, but psychological.

To resume. The balance of the body is an effect rather than a cause of good swinging; if there is any fault of balance the cause is likely to be found in some fault of swinging (at some point or points in the swing, either the hands and fingers have been lazy, or the legs and body have interfered and not co-operated with them), and the cure is to be found in perfecting the swing.

It may usefully be borne in mind that Ernest Jones, on coming out of a military hospital with one leg, played a round of golf, and found himself still on the one leg after every shot he played. One leg, then, is sufficient for balancing purpose if the swing is sound, yet one knows long handicap men who find two legs wholly inadequate for the purpose, and who must surely envy the centipede.

The sure guide to the feet is the fingers.

BOOK II - **THE GOLF SWING**

Fig 48. An ideally balanced position at
the top of the up-swing

Fig 49. An ideally balanced position at the finish of the shot

BOOK II - **THE GOLF SWING**

6 STANCE

The text-books on golf all devote considerable space to the subject of stance. Most of them give a dissertation on the rival types of stance, the "square" and the "open," and adjudicate on their merits and defects; they describe the stance which is considered best adapted for each of the various shots of the game; the straight shot, the slice, the pull, the low ball, the high ball, and so on; and they proceed to give measurements whereby, they allege, the correct stance for any shot in particular may be acquired.

The basic principle underlying the bulk of this literature is that the swing is determined by the stance; witness the following dicta:

"*The stance being carefully chosen and analyzed*, all that is left is to hold the club correctly...." - Massy.

" To gain this result ... *place your left foot* more in line with the ball...." - Massy.

"The swing is, *from the position I have assumed,* naturally a more upright one." - J. H. Taylor.

BOOK II - THE GOLF SWING

"[The diagram] may serve a most useful purpose in helping him (the reader) to grasp quickly the principle that *the swing must adjust itself to the stance.* . . . I prefer to stand open, and my swing has, *in consequence,* adjusted itself in the manner described." - J. H. Taylor.

The italicizing is the writer's, but the quotations are taken almost at random, and they fairly represent the doctrine which is to be found, explicit or implicit, in almost everything that is written on the subject - the doctrine that the natural order of events is first stance, then swing; that the stance is a set position consciously taken up by the player in order to produce a certain type of shot. But is this doctrine sound?

After all, what is the player's object when he stands up to the ball? His object is simply to get into that position which will best give him (a) the direction he requires, and (6) the distance he requires.

As regards direction, it is axiomatic that the ball will follow the direction in which the club-head is moving as it meets and "goes through" the ball. The player's position, then, must be such that when he makes his normal swing the club-head will meet the ball and "go through" it in the line of intended direction.

How is the player to arrive at that position? Should he take up his stance by placing his teet and shoulders, according to some method of measurement, in a certain relationship with the ball, and then make his swing, or should he allow his stance to adjust itself to the swing?

According to the authorities, he should adopt the former course; witness the following quotations, which are typical:

"The true position the ball should occupy relatively to the feet, or, in other words, that which the feet should occupy in relation to the ball, is that in which the ball lies on an imaginary line drawn six or seven inches or so to the

CH. 6 – STANCE

right of the left heel. . . . The toes should be turned slightly outwards." - Massy.

"If you look at the photograph . . . you will observe that the toe of the left foot is on line b, that is level with the ball, while the right foot is (say) twenty-five inches from the same line, whereas in an ordinary shot it is only nineteen inches." - Massy.

"Refer to the diagram, and you will observe that the ball should lie exactly between your feet, each of which is at twelve inches from the line b, and something less than an inch nearer the ball than in the ordinary drive." - Massy.

"The right foot should be moved in a parallel direction with the line of flight until it is just touching the next white line. In other words, the foot should be just over six inches behind the ball." - J. H. Taylor.

"Place the feet so that the ball is in a line about six inches to the right of the left heel." - Braid.

The reader is asked to consider whether this sort of thing seems right; whether, on the face of it, it is likely that the fine, free, slashing movement known as the golf swing can be arrived at in this way; whether the professionals who preach this doctrine practise it; whether an analysis of their play suggests that they have anything of the kind in view when they stand up to the ball. . . .

Let the reader now examine the alternative method, the method of deriving stance from swing. It has been seen that the player's position must be such that when he makes his normal swing the club-head will meet and "go through" the ball in the line of desired direction. If he is not to take up a position in the manner laid down by the pundits, how is he to proceed?

It is suggested that he should make trial swings over the ball until he finds the position in which the club-head is moving along the line of desired

BOOK II - **THE GOLF SWING**

direction as it passes over the ball. That position is his stance. As he advances in experience he will be able to dispense with the trial swing over the ball; he will be able to make the necessary adjustments of his feet and shoulders as he waggles the club; and in time he will take up the appropriate position instinctively.

What is true, moreover, for the normal straight shot is equally true of the "advanced" shots, the intentional slice and pull, the low ball against the wind, the high ball down wind, and so on. In setting out to make any kind of shot, the first thing to do is to visualize the shot required, and the path which the club-head must take if the shot is to be achieved; the second thing to do is to find the position which allows the club-head to take that path.

If a slice is required, then the golfer knows that as the club-head comes on to the ball it must be crossing the line of direction, that is to say, it must be coming in toward the player. He must therefore stand so that in making his *ordinary* (the player is not called upon to juggle with the club) swing the club-head passes naturally in that direction.

If a pull is required, then the golfer knows that, as the club-head "goes through" the ball, it must be crossing slightly the line of direction in an outward sense - that is, away from the player. He must stand therefore so that in making his *ordinary swing* the club-head passes *naturally* in that direction.

In the case of the low shot against the wind, it is clear that, as the club-head "goes through ' the ball, it must be descending and tending to keep to the turf as long as possible. In swinging the club with that behaviour of the club-head in view, the player will naturally tend to keep his weight forward on his left foot.

In the case of the high shot down wind the mental picture will be the opposite one: the club-head must be tending to rise sharply as it "goes through" the ball, and the players weight will naturally be kept well back on the right foot, in order that the club-head may take that path.

CH. 6 – STANCE

Such, it is submitted, is the proper view of stance in so far as the direction is concerned. It now remains to consider stance in relation to the length of the shot. The text books are again prolific in suggestions for the use of the inch-tape and for the use of the club-shaft as a stance guide. Thus Braid: "As a general rule, the player should stand just so far from the ball that when the face of the club is laid against it, the end of the shaft just reaches to his left knee when the latter has got just a suspicion of a bend in it."

This kind of advice may be well meant, but it is ill-conceived. It is not only bad in itself, it is bad because it suggests an entirely wrong attitude to the shot and the game. There is no spectacle on the links more pathetic than that of the player whose mind is atrophied and whose bones are stiff with this kind of doctrine. Uric acid is not more insidious or more deadly. It is~ one of the pleasures, and part of the pride, of Ernest Jones that his pupils never look as though they had been taught golf. They proceed from cause to effect and stand up to the ball as though they were going to hit it, and to enjoy hitting it - not as though they were doing a medieval penance, or entering a torture-chamber, or bracing themselves for the crack of doom, or performing a religious rite, or setting a theodolite. . . . All that the player has to do is to stand up to the ball so that he can swing freely, forcefully, and accurately - that is really all that can usefully be said about it. Obviously, if he stands beyond a certain distance away from the ball he will lose his balance and, with it, accuracy, and he will stretch out his arms and stiffen his shoulders so that he must lose freedom and power. And, obviously, if he approaches beyond a certain distance towards the ball, his swing will be cramped and ineffective. A few experiments and a little thought will teach him all that can be learned.

The writer passes to the question of the square and the open stance, a question magnilo-quently described by one of golfs journalists as "The Battle of the Stances" - a thing ranking in importance, apparently, with Marathon and the Battle of the Marne.

The impression of the open stance normally conveyed in the textbooks is that the player's body is so turned that a line across the player's shoulders is approximately parallel with a line across his toes - that the player is, in fact, turned more or less toward the hole. Thus Webb: "The player should slightly face the hole." But this is not so. *The difference between the open and the square stances is essentially a difference in the position of the feet, the difference in the position of the shoulders and hips being slight - almost negligible.* The failure to realize these facts leads to endless confusion.

"Slicing," says Braid, "is commonly due to a faulty stance . . . the right foot too far forward." Again: "The most elementary direction for obtaining a sliced ball is to take your stance with your right *foot* advanced." And Vardon: "In playing for the slice, the stance should be open." The books are, indeed, practically unanimous on the point. They speak continually of the feet, and if they refer, directly or indirectly to the shoulders or hips, they usually mislead. They suggest that the open stance and the slicing stance are one and the same thing; they do not point out that it is the forward position of the right *shoulder* that gives slice, and they do not warn the player that in the ordinary open stance - the stance which gives the straight ball equally with the square stance - the right shoulder must be kept back, and in no circumstances allowed to come forward to the extent suggested by the advanced position of the right foot.

If it were the fact that in the open stance the shoulders did follow the line of the feet, then the open stance would properly be called the slicing stance, as the player can readily prove to his own satisfaction. Let him stand up to the ball in the position just indicated and make an experimental swing over the ball, observing the path of the club-head as the ball is passed. He will find that as the club-head passes over the ball it is swinging, not in the line of intended direction, but across that line. The stance he has taken up is, in fact, the position in which he would have found himself had he stood up to the ball with a view to the club-head crossing the line of direction - that is, with a view to slicing.

The player is now asked to stand up to the ball (without thinking for a moment about the position of his feet) so that when he makes his

CH. 6 – STANCE

experimental swing the club-head shall pass over the ball in the line of intended direction. That is to say, he is asked to stand up to the ball as though he were about to make an ordinary straight shot. Let him now notice the position of his feet. They may be set either "open" or "square." If they are open, let them be placed square. If they are square, let them be placed open. It will be found that this operation can be done with only a very slight adjustment of the line of the shoulders or the line of the hips, and that if the experimental swing over the ball is repeated, the course of the club-head will not be changed. The moment, however, that the line of the shoulders or the line ot the hips, is materially interfered with, that moment a fresh direction will be determined for the club-head, with corresponding results in the shot.

It will thus be seen that in analyzing a player's stance the essential characteristic to be noted is the line of the shoulders (and the hips), and not the position of the feet; for the position of the feet may be varied, within limits, at the caprice of the player. In the slicing stance the line of the shoulders is turned towards the hole. And, of course, the converse holds good, the line of the shoulders in the pulling stance being turned away from the hole.

The vital point to observe in the stance for the straight shot is that whether the feet be open or square, the right shoulder is well back. It is the position which that shoulder must take if the player sets about finding the stance by reference to his swing. The player who has this mental attitude to the stance will instinctively adopt a position in which his head will be turned slightly away from the line of direction; he will have in mind a type of swing based on a back-handed "swipe" at the ball with the left hand and arm. Observation of any expert golfer, whether he stand open or square, will show that his head in the address is turned away from the line of direction, and if the backward position of the right shoulder is less noticeable, the player will tell you that *the feeling he has is that the right shoulder is back*. This feeling is one of the fundamentals of golf. This does not mean, of course, that the beginner must place his right shoulder back when he is addressing the ball, for the position is an effect, not a cause. His right shoulder will automatically take its proper position if he has a proper mental picture of the shot.

BOOK II - **THE GOLF SWING**

To recapitulate. The writer submits that it is no part of the player's business to think of the shot in terms of stance. To do that is to put the cart before the horse, to confuse effect and cause. The stance is determined absolutely and entirely by the swing. It is the swing, and the swing alone, which conditions the stance. When the player has learned to swing the club, he will have nothing to learn about stance. Until he has learned to swing the club, he can learn nothing about stance. It is for these reasons that the writer believes that the teaching of the text-books is unsound - the more, not the less unsound, because that teaching is aimed at the beginner. It is quite true that a beginner who has not acquired the art of swinging the club may perform less egregiously if he measures out his stance with the help of his club-shaft and an inch-tape. The player who tries to hit the ball when the club-head is the length of the shaft from the left knee will, *ceteris paribus*, fail less miserably than the man who can only reach the ball by adroitly springing forward at a well-chosen moment in the down-swing; and similarly the chances of hitting the ball are undoubtedly increased when the feet are out of the way. But, after all, even the person who takes up golf should be presumed to have some intelligence, and it is only fair to him to ask him to use it. It is obviously not good for the beginner to get hold of the right end of the club if he gets hold of the wrong end of the stick.

7 OVERSWINGING

It is the custom to speak of any movement which allows the club-shaft in the up-swing to pass appreciably beyond the horizontal position as over-swinging. It does not matter how this position is achieved, whether by relaxing the grip or by carrying the club high over the shoulders, or by both processes combined - it is glibly called over-swinging.

Observation shows that the few players who really control the club usually have an up-swing in which the horizontal position is not appreciably passed, and that the many players who fail to control the club usually have an up-swing (or rather an upward movement) in which that position is left far behind; and these coincidences invite the inference that the test of over-swinging is to be found in the length of up-swing.

In the days of the gutty ball, however, no golfer worthy of the name was content with an up-swing which failed to give the club-head a close view of the left heel - witness illustration of such famous players as Douglas Rolland and Lady Margaret Scott; and it would be absurd to suggest that this fulness of movement was mere rhetoric - something flowing out of the exuberant egotism of the player rather than the stern necessities involved by the stolidity of the ball and the length of the club. It would also be absurd to suggest that the good player of those days failed in complete control of the club.

BOOK II - **THE GOLF SWING**

It must therefore be admitted that there is no essential incompatibility between complete control of the club and a luxuriantly prolonged upswing, and that, inasmuch as controlled swinging can never be over-swinging - the two terms are contradictory - the test of over-swinging is to be found elsewhere than in the length of the up-swing alone.

Lady Margaret Scott threatening her left heel in the up-swing and her right heel in the follow-through, yet controlled her club. Mrs. X., whilst falling far short of the former achievement, falls still further short of the latter. What is the difference between the swing of Lady Margaret Scott and the swing of Mrs. X.? The difference lies in the fact that the swing of Lady Margaret Scott was a swing, and that the swing of Mrs. X. is not a swing at all. One proceeds inevitably to the generalization that the person who can swing a club will never over-swing it, and that what is called over-swinging is simply not swinging at all. The logical conclusion is that the cure for what is called over-swinging is to be found in learning to swing, and not, as is popularly supposed, in shortening the swing.

Though Lady Margaret Scott might choose to allow the club-head to coquet with her heels, she never permitted the club-shaft to toy with her shoulders. On the other hand, no such restraint on the club-shaft is imposed by Mrs. X.

What happens in the "swing" of Mrs. X. is this: (1) Instead of being set in motion by hand and finger work, the club is pulled away from the ball by the premature turning of the shoulders. (2) Instead of being incessantly moved round the body by hand and finger work, the club is lifted more or less vertically upward, and the shoulders having expended their energy too soon, now find themselves without stimulus to further action; they therefore cease to turn. (3) The whole mechanism is by this time out of gear - the movement is obviously incomplete; the player's position is cramped and feeble: she must free herself somehow; but the body is rigid and the arms have gone as far as they will go. Something has to give way - the fingers oblige, the grip is relaxed, the club-shaft strikes the shoulder and rebounds. (And this rebound is the beginning of the down-swing !) Instead of an up-swing, there are three movements - a drag, a lift, and a flop - and the down-swing is inaugurated with a jerk !

CH. 7 – OVERSWINGING

Now, what is the attitude of Mrs. X. to her incompetence? As a rule she resigns herself to what she deems to be the inevitable - it is not, she argues, given to everyone to play like a professional, and it is evidently in the nature of things that she should drag, lift, flop, and jerk the club rather than swing it. . . . But Mrs. X. may be of different texture. She may be determined to rid herself of the scourge at all costs. How does she set about it - in the normal case?

In the first place she makes a wrong diagnosis. She commits the cardinal error of confusing symptom with disease. She regards the flop as the disease; she ignores the drag and the lift which precede it. To her mind the movement goes wrong at the moment she relaxes her grip, and not before. Alternative methods of treatment promptly suggest themselves to her. The first is to maintain at all costs a fiercely tight grip throughout the movement. The second is to stop the movement before the temptation to relax the grip becomes pronounced. The effects of the first method need not be dwelt upon. It is enough to say that golf can never be amongst them. The second method may usefully be analyzed.

What is Mrs. X. left with when she has eliminated the "flop" from the upward movement of her club? Is it anything more nearly resembling a swing than it was before? It is not. She has made no material alteration in her action. She has left the root and the stalk of the weed and merely cut off the flower. Instead of drag, lift, and flop, her action is now drag and lift. That is all. Mrs. X. doubtless regards herself as a short swinger. But she is not. She is merely a caricature of a short swinger. Even the short swinger must be given his due. . . .

What, then, is the typical action of the short swinger?

The short swing properly so called is a swing which is quite sound as far as it goes (Fig. 52). It is the ordinary up-swing stopped short of its maturity. It is, in fact, the swing normally adopted for an iron shot. It is the ideal swing for an iron shot because it lends itself to the exact placing of the ball. It is not the ideal swing for a wooden club shot (in ordinary circumstances) because a longer swing will give greater distance and as much accuracy of direction as is normally required in a shot with a wooden club. The question, it will be observed, is, like most other questions, one of compromise. Every shot in the

BOOK II - THE GOLF SWING

game must have two qualities - a certain length and a certain degree of accuracy. The proportion between these two qualities varies in different shots, and the type of swing varies with it. Normally the full shot with a wooden club is the one in which the element of accuracy is most subordinated to the element of length. But even in this shot only a small degree of variation is possible, and the swing must therefore always be thoroughly controlled - whatever its length.

It has been seen that the players of a past generation were able to control a longer swing (see Fig. 50) than the swing now favoured. But experiment will show that the difficulty of control is increased when the swing is lengthened beyond a certain point.

The problem presents itself in this way. The gutty ball is an unresponsive thing compared with the rubber-cored ball. It requires a greater effort to drive it a given distance, but its behaviour on being miss-hit is less erratic. In these circumstances the golfer was preoccupied in getting the utmost length of which he was capable, knowing that if he did not hit the ball quite accurately - so long as he hit it freely - it would not behave in the eccentric manner of the modern rubber-core. In other words, of the two qualities of accuracy and length, he could afford to think more of the latter than the former. He chose, therefore, a club with a long shaft, and adopted - largely as a consequence of using a long-shafted club - a long and exuberant swing.

With the modern ball, however, it is found that no greater distance is obtained by using a long-shafted club and prolonging the up-swing beyond a certain point, whilst accuracy is endangered; and the expert wisely contents himself with an up-swing finishing in the region of the horizontal position. But this up-swing, though short in comparison with the up-swing of twenty years ago, is a complete up-swing. The club is taken back as far as it will go on the basis adopted. The hands and arms have described a spiral round the body and the body has twisted in response, and the club comes to rest at the top of the up-swing, not because the player actively stops it at that point, but because fingers, hands, arms, body, legs and feet have completed their work (Fig. 48). If the club went further, the player would fare worse - he would be a surgical case.

CH. 7 – OVERSWINGING

It is of the very essence of the golf swing that the club-head should be kept moving all the time. "Keep the club-head moving ' might well be substituted for "Keep the home fires burning." And the shoulder hitter who thinks to cure himself of his disease by stopping the club at a chosen point in the up-swing is "flying in the face of Providence." He wantonly stops the movement of the club at the very moment when the hands and fingers should be forcing it into a position of precision and power. Let him take his courage as well as the club in both hands, and at the point when he imagines the fatal flop is about to begin, let him force the club-head resolutely further behind his head by persistent hand and ringer action. He will then find that the shaft will not strike his shoulder, and that the up-swing will stop when the hands and fingers have accomplished the fullest natural movement of which they are capable.

Under-swinging is not less of a vice than over-swinging, and the golfer should always be on his guard against it. For under-swinging is neither more nor less than the failure to make full use of the hands and fingers. It is just as easy to under-swing in a short mashie chip as in a full swing; for even in a short mashie chip the hands and fingers should function to the fullest extent possible having regard to the type of the shot.

It is this determination to move the club-head as far as possible with the hands and fingers at every point in the swing which is at the root of all good golf. It precludes the possibility of relaxing the grip, of shoulder-hitting, and other pathetic symptoms of incompetence (see Figs. 51 and 53); and it allows the player to get the utmost speed and the finest precision out of that good servant, but bad master, that faithful friend, but bitter enemy - the club-head.

BOOK II - **THE GOLF SWING**

Fig 50. The old-fashioned up-swing: exuberant, yet controlled. A slashing and powerful movement.

Fig 51. Clumsiness and lack of control

CH. 7 – OVERSWINGING

Fig 52. Good as far as it goes

BOOK II - **THE GOLF SWING**

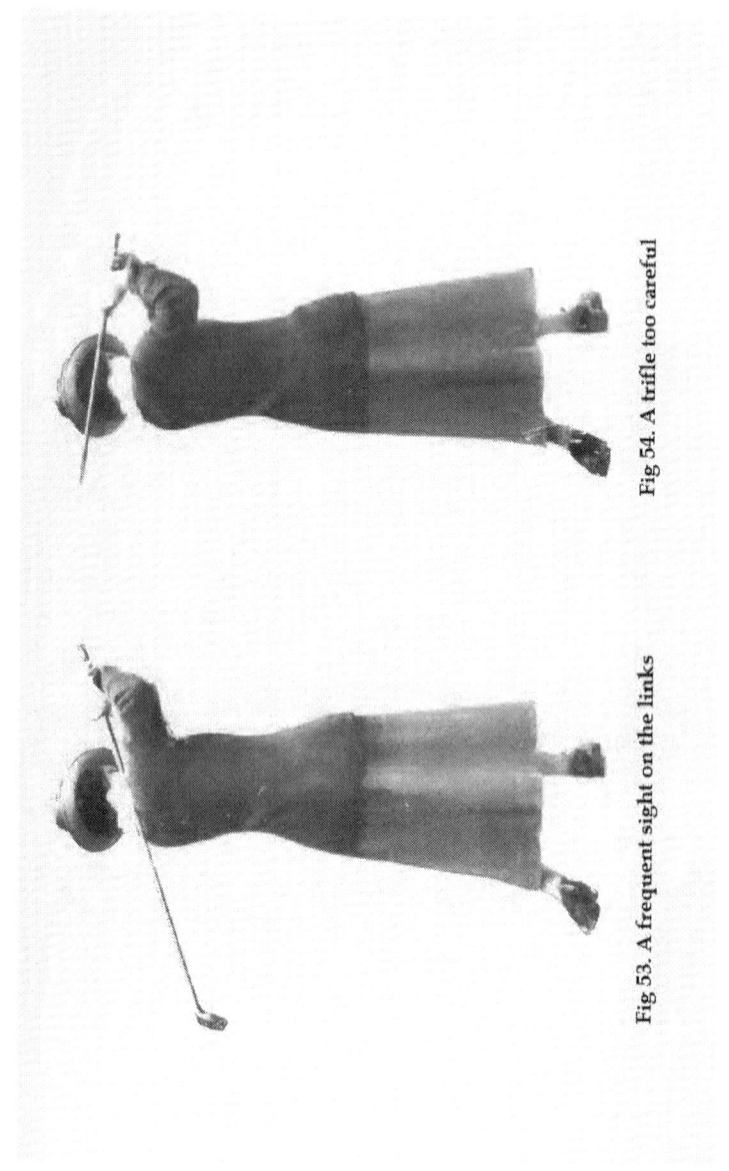

Fig 53. A frequent sight on the links

Fig 54. A trifle too careful

CH. 7 – OVERSWINGING

Fig 55. Compare with fig 50

BOOK II - **THE GOLF SWING**

8 SOCKETING

It is one of the many ironies of golf that some of its maladies beset the mature player almost equally with the novice; and of these maladies socketing is perhaps the chief. Not even players of the first flight are immune from it. The writer knows many scratch and plus players whom it victimizes from time to time - occasionally over long periods. One of these is an English international of golf-wide reputation who distinguished himself in an international match by an orgy of socketing, resulting (so far as international matches are concerned) in a record round for the number of holes lost. Another is an open champion who for months failed to hit a mashie shot off the middle of the club-face except by accident. It is, of course, to be expected that the novice should be capable of any golfing enormity - he may give at the knees, he may fall forward whilst trying to hit the ball, he may refuse to work his elbow-joints, he may do a score of things he ought not to do - and socketed shots may be the result of any one of them. For him there is but one method of treatment: he must learn to swing properly; and there is nothing more to be said. But the case of the mature golfer who falls a victim to socketing may be analyzed usefully; for his knowledge of the game is such that he is able to appreciate points which could but befog the beginner.

As first sight it seems that there must be something in socketing which even in golf is unusually mysterious. The writer is, however,, of the opinion

BOOK II - THE GOLF SWING

that the mysterious element is rather apparent than real, and that the practised eye can always trace the germ of the disease in the normal action of any mature player who is capable of periods of socketing.

The player is recommended to analyze the normal socketed shot on the following lines:

(1) To note the position in which he finds himself, and the position in which he finds the club-head, at the finish of the faulty shot.

(2) To compare these positions with the corresponding positions in the correct movement.

(3) To discover what method he would adopt if he wished to commit the fault he is trying to cure.

(4) To compare this method with the method of attaining the correct positions.

(5) To locate - by means of the comparison

- the point at which the differentiation begins, and to identify the particular action which distinguishes the correct shot from the faulty shot.

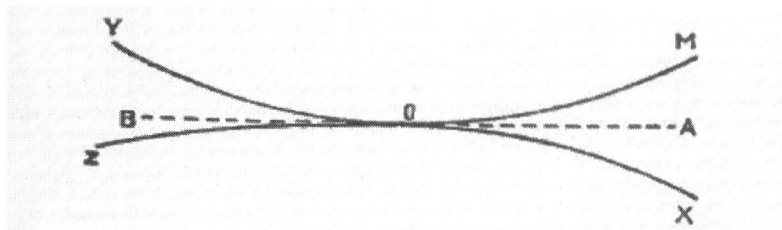

Proceeding on these lines, the writer offers the following observations on the socketed shot:

CH. 8 – SOCKETING

(1) (a) The player's right shoulder has not followed on in its natural curve; its movement has been checked at some point either before or at the moment of impact. (b) The club-head has finished, not to the left, but to the right of the line of desired direction.

(2) In the diagram, AOB represents the line of desired direction, XOT the path of the club-head, XOZ the path the club-head should have taken.

(3) Experiment will at once show that in order to make the club-head take the line XOY, the best plan is -

(i.) to keep the right shoulder from turning;

(ii.) to keep the hands and fingers inactive; and

(iii.) to push the club-head out in the line OY by straightening out the right arm at the elbow-joint, and by preventing the right forearm from turning from right to left.

(4) When the club-head takes the proper line XOZ, it is found -

(i.) that the right shoulder responds to the pull of the club-head;

(ii.) that the hands and fingers assert themselves and make the club-head do its work; and

(iii.) that there is no stiffness anywhere, the right forearm turning freely from right to left in response to the impulse set up by the hands and fingers.

(5) The differentiating movement is really performed by the hands and fingers. If these are made to do their work and the body and arms are allowed to move so as to give them free play, the club-head will take, not the line OT, but the line OZ.

The reader will probably have noticed some similarity in the behaviour of the club-head in the socketing shot and the behaviour of the club-head in the cut-mashie shot. Indeed, socketing is often the outcome of playing the cut-mashie shot with stiff forearms.

The cut-mashie shot can, however, be played with safety if two points are borne in mind:

(i.) The directing energy should be determinedly applied through the hands and fingers; and

(ii.) The club-head should travel, not in the line XOY, but in the line MOZ.

[In the up-swing it should travel outside the line of direction, and in the follow-through inside that line, whereas in the socketing movement it travels, in the up-swing, inside the line of direction, and, in the follow-through, outside that line.]

The push-shot (Fig. 58), even more than the cut-mashie shot, bears certain outward resemblances, and oftener than not, alas ! certain inward resemblances, to the socketed shot (Fig. 56).

In the push-shot there is, of course, considerable firmness of wrist and forearm; the clubhead follows through further on the line of flight than in the ordinary iron shot; and the toe of the club does not get in front of the heel. The margin of error is obviously small. If instead of taking the line XOZ, the club-head goes outward ever so slightly in the line XOYy the shot will be socketed.

Nearly all the textbooks and nearly all the teachers make a fetish of the essential difference between the iron shot (ordinary as well as push) and the swing with the wooden clubs. The player is told that in playing his irons the grip must be firmer, the arms and wrists tauter, the body more rigid, the up-swing shorter, and so on.

The effect of this teaching is to stiffen and cramp the iron play, even of many first-class players: in a word, to implant in it the seed ot socketing, a

CH. 8 – SOCKETING

disease which, it is vital to note, is practically confined to play with iron clubs and has no counterpart in wooden club play. There is no essential difference in the manipulation of iron and wooden clubs, and socketing would be rarer if this fact were recognized and iron shots were made with some of the freedom which distinguishes wooden-club play. The golfer must gain control of the club - whether iron or wood - in his hands and fingers. He must know clearly the manner of the flight of the ball that inevitably results from a certain type of swing, and he must make the club-head perform the desired type of swing by means of appropriate hand and finger action. If he wants to force an iron shot against the wind, he will obviously not flick the ball lightly into the air with a delicate movement of the fingers; he will beat it down and forward by actions at once definite and powerful. But those definite and powerful actions should be the result of hand and finger work consciously applied. They should not be the result - as is so persistently urged by those who mistake symptoms for causes - of holding the body, the forearms, and the wrists rigid or of gripping the club with vice-like pressure.

If the seat of control is in the hands and fingers, the player can produce any one type of shot as readily as any other type of shot. It is just as easy for him to make the club-head finish in front of him, as in the push-shot, as to swing it heroically over his left shoulder. If the club-head stops in front of him he will notice that the forearms and wrists are taut. He has, in fact, produced the shot in such a manner that the wrists and forearms must be taut. This is a totally different matter from trying to produce the shot by means of taut wrists and forearms. The difference is the difference between cause and effect. Thus in the case of the push-shot, if the player aims at producing the shot in the correct manner - that is, by a movement of the club-head dominated by the fingers - he will never be likely to socket. If, however, he aims at producing the shot by stiffening certain limbs and muscles, he will never - despite any success he may achieve - be an entirely sound golfer; he will always be more or less liable to lapses from form, and amongst the lapses socketing will most probably find a place.

The following propositions are offered for the reader's consideration:

BOOK II - **THE GOLF SWING**

The player can never socket who keeps control of the club in his hands and fingers and does not interfere with the responsive movements.

Socketing may occur whenever the stiffening of the arms or wrists or body interferes with the full and free working out of the swing at the instance of the hands and fingers.

The time-honoured doctrine of accentuating the follow-through along the line of flight or throwing the arms out after the ball, is a dangerous one; it tends to devitalize hand and finger work, to stiffen the forearms, and to put the line of the follow-through out of true relation to the line of the up-swing.

The caddy's advice to stand further away from the ball is pernicious; if carried out, it is likely to accentuate the stiffness which is the cause of the disease.

The advice of the club-seller to buy a set of non-socketing irons should be ignored even by millionaires. Non-socketing irons have one grave defect: they socket.

The advice to keep the right elbow close to the side, the right arm close to the body, and the left elbow close to the side, is not good; these positions are symptoms, not causes, of properly hit shots; and if the player concentrates on making his swing conform with a number of fixed points instead of so producing the swing that it must conform with those fixed points, he will inevitably deaden it. The true golf-swing is to be achieved, not by *placing* the body and the limbs into a series of carefully chosen positions, but by learning how to communicate life to the club-head through the fingers. The artist gives life to his line, not by tracing the line through a series of points, but by making one unfettered sweep of the pencil - he communicates life to the line through the fingers. . . .

The socketer will appreciate that alternatives are open to him: one is to learn to swing properly; the other is to give up the game. The writer apprehends that the former course will normally be followed as being the easier of the two.

CH. 8 – SOCKETING

BOOK II - **THE GOLF SWING**

Fig 56. The socketing position *par axcellence*

CH. 8 – SOCKETING

Fig 57. An ideal finish

Fig 58. The push shot

Fig 59. Note the delicacy and freedom of
the finish of this iron shot

BOOK II - **THE GOLF SWING**

Fig 60. The finish of a firm iron shot

CH. 8 – SOCKETING

Mrs. Alan Macbeth
(Miss Muriel Dodd)

Figs 61 and 62. Two perfect iron shots. Note the essential similarity of the positions. No suspicion of stiffness or rigidity.

BOOK II - **THE GOLF SWING**

Fig 63. Finis.

9 SOME OTHER ENORMETIES

Sclaffing and digging

Sclaffing and digging differ from most faults in that the player is conscious of them before the ball is hit away. In both cases the club-head meets the ground before it reaches the ball; but though the two faults have this point in common, they are essentially different. In the sclaffed shot the club-head passes more or less lightly along the turf, the rhythm of the shot is not necessarily lost, and the speed of the club-head may not be seriously reduced. But in the shot known as digging, the club-head digs into the turf, the rhythm of the shot - if it ever had rhythm - is inevitably destroyed, and the movement of the club-head is piteously retarded. Sclaffing is by no means synonymous with foozling; digging is one of the most common forms of foozling.

An analysis of digging will show that in the down-swing the right side of the body has been relaxed, and that the right shoulder and probably the right knee have dropped. In short, the hands and fingers have failed to assert themselves, and the action has been led by the body. The player has really been trying to help the club-head on to the ball with his shoulder, instead of controlling the club-head with the hands and fingers and allowing the body to respond. It will be found that it is difficult to drop the shoulder if the swing is definitely made by means of vigorous hand and finger action; but that the moment that notion is lost sight of, the body will come lumbering in, to the utter ruin of the shot.

As regards *sclaffing*, the player will gain insight into the disease by asking himself how he would produce a sclaff if a sclaff were desired. He would stand in such a position that the club-head would reach its lowest point in the down-swing before it reached the ball. That is to say, he would stand a little farther away from the hole than he would normally do. It is clear, then, that a false stance may be responsible for sclaffing. As pointed out in the chapter on faults of stance, the stance should always be determined by the swing; and if the method of arriving at stance is followed, the player can obviously never suffer from the kind of sclaffing that comes from a wrong stance.

Is there any other easy way of sclaffing? If instead of allowing his body to be pulled through after the club-head, the player keeps his body back so that his weight at the end of the swing remains largely on the right foot, he will find sclaffing quite simple. And such sclaffing may permit of quite useful shots being made. For here the hands and wrists are doing their good work, and it is only the body that lags to some extent. The cure for this type of sclaffing is obvious. The player must let his hands work out his salvation by placing himself unreservedly in their hands, so to speak. His body must be like the child - it must not speak till it is spoken to, but when it is spoken to it must answer cheerfully and not grudgingly.

Killing

The player will find this operation easy if he determines to use his right hand for the purpose of turning the club-face over toward the turf as the club-head strikes the ball; and the operation will be facilitated if in making the shot he allows his body to turn prematurely so bringing his weight prematurely forward. The confirmed "killer" should note carefully, in the correct shot, the angle of the face of the club with the ground, as the club comes on to the ball and in the succeeding two or three inches of its journey. He should get this picture clearly defined in his mind, and keep it vividly before him when he is making a shot. His movements will soon learn to paint the same picture.

Toeing

On the face of it, toeing appears to be the very antithesis of socketing, but the two things have much in common. In the chapter on socketing it has

CH. 9 – SOME OTHER ENORMETIES

been shown that the easiest way to socket is, as the club-head comes on to the ball, to stiffen the elbow-joints and to fail to use the hands and fingers, the effect being that the body, no longer under any impulse to turn, stops, with the shoulders facing the direction of the socketed shot. In the toed shot there is, as a rule, a somewhat similar failure of body action, but the hands at the last moment make a desperate effort to put things right and assert themselves. The club-head duly finishes on the left side of the line to the hole, but, the body being out of position, it is the toe of the club and not the middle of the face that meets the ball. The reader will not find it difficult to "toe" in this manner. He has only to check the natural turning movement of the shoulders and to use his hands at the last moment to find that he can toe nine shots out of ten. If, moreover, he tires of this method, he can achieve the same result by going to the other extreme (how true this is of almost everything in golf!). Instead of arresting the turning of his body, let him encourage it to get always in front of its proper position at every point in the swing, and he will find toeing possible again - not quite so easy as before, but still by no means beyond the average man's powers. Of course, if the player lifts his head as well, the operation will be still further simplified.

Fluffing The Short Approach

There is a strong tendency in making every golf shot to stiffen the wrists and forearms as the club-head comes on to the ball. The tendency is doubtless akin to the tendency to anticipate the kick of the gun in shooting. It takes *' quality" out of any shot and it utterly ruins the short approach, which may be two inches instead of two yards, or two yards instead of twenty. The player should practise these shots with one thing, and one thing only, in view, and that is to make the club-head move "through" the ball by means of persistent hand and finger work unimpeded by any stiffness of wrists or forearms. It will help him in this practice if he will consciously relax all his muscles and his grip except for the first two fingers and the thumb of each hand, and assertively make the club-head travel as far as possible - having regard, of course, to the limitations imposed by the nature of the shot. Let him guard against (i) the tendency to cease to actuate the club-head by means of hand and finger work at some point near to the ball, and (ii) the complementary tendency to stiffen the wrists and forearms at that moment. It is not enough for him to start the club-head down with a certain impetus and then to let it do the work. He must figure out the shot, and work out the shot, on the basis that his hands and fingers are going to keep the club-head moving all the time.

Faults Of Putting

These are (a) faults of direction, and (b) faults of strength.

Faults of Direction. - As regards direction, the player has obviously to stand to the ball so that, in making the normal movement of the club, the club-head passes through the ball along the line of direction, with its face at right angles to that line. The stance matters little, provided it is conditioned by the swing.

Faults of Strength. - The writer suggests that the finest control of the putter is likely to be attained by the player who grips mainly between thumbs and forefingers, and persistently keeps the club-head moving by persistent finger work. In this way he gets the utmost out of the club-head within the limits of any particular swing, and acquires a knowledge of what result to expect from the movement he sets out to make. He is better able to judge his effects than the player who checks the club-head and thereby introduces into an alarmingly uncertain thing still one more element of uncertainty. In this respect approach putting has much in common with mashie approaching. (At the same time the writer's advice to those players who can stab long putts up to the hole, and short putts into the hole, is to go on stabbing!)

* * * *

The faults which have been dealt with do not, of course, exhaust the whole tragedy of the game. Golf is not unlike Cleopatra - age cannot wither her, nor custom stale her infinite variety. It is hoped, however, that the suggestions for diagnosis and treatment that have been given are sufficiently broad in principle and sufficiently precise in method to help the victim, no matter what his malady, to make a man of himself, and a golfer.

10 RECAPITULATORY

GENERAL

THE RESPONSIVE MOVEMENTS

It is one of the misfortunes of golf that the correct playing of the shot should make a pretty picture; the observer - and the player as well - is apt to become too much interested in the pretty picture, that is, in effect, and too little interested in the causes of which that effect is merely an expression. In no other game does the statuesque position occur so regularly. In golf it appears at the finish of almost every properly played shot, from the shortest of short approaches to the longest of long drives. The club, the hands and arms, the shoulders, the legs and feet, are all seen in a more or less stereotyped relationship, all in repose, the repose that is the logical result of well-directed effort, the repose that invites the camera or even the sculptor's chisel. There is nothing comparable with this characteristic in, for example, baseball, football, cricket, tennis, or billiards. In those games the vitally interesting thing is the action by which the result is achieved, not the appearance of the performer when the action is being, or has been, made. And this fact doubtless explains to some extent why in golf the action of the average player looks, and indeed is, so much less spontaneous than in other games.

The footballer kicking a football does not know, or think, or care, where his right knee or his left hip will be at any given moment in the operation of kicking. His mind sends a direction to his feet, and his feet obey if he is a good footballer, or disobey if he is a bad footballer. The billiard player is not at all concerned with the position in which he will be found at the finish of his stroke. He is not at any moment in the game an inspiring subject for the photographer, much less for the sculptor. He consequently gets on with the work. The mind directs the fingers and the fingers direct the cue. The elbows, arms, shoulders, body and legs also move; they move, however, not on their own account, but in response to the impetus in the cue set up by the action of the fingers. The person performing Indian club exercises never thinks for one moment about the position of his elbows or his knees. What he does think about all the time is the movement of the club, and the action of the hands and fingers by means of which that movement is produced. He is pre-eminently a creature of action, not a hero of repose, and he is not in the least degree interested in what his appearance may be at the **end** of any movement or sequence of movements that he may make.

The footballer's mind is directed to the one point of contact - toe and ball; the Indian club performer's mind is directed to the one point of contact - fingers and club; the billiard player's mind is directed to the two points of contact, cue and ball, fingers and cue. And so the golfer's mind should be directed to the two points of contact, club and ball, hands and club.

The golfer's object is to gain command of a golf club just in the same way as the Indian club performer's object is to gain command of an Indian club. True, it is not necessary for the golfer when making his shot to twist his club about as though it were an Indian club. At the same time, the golfer should be able to twist it about in that manner. He should be able to swing the club about in his hands and fingers, freely and fluently in any direction. The pianist learns all sorts of exercises that never come actually into the performance of any piece of pianoforte music. He does so in order to gain command of his fingers. And in the same way, the golfer will do well to make any and every movement with his club that will increase his skill in manipulating it, increase his sense of intimacy with it, his feeling of power over it. When he is swinging the club about in this casual manner, whether with right hand or left hand, or with both hands, he will observe - if it occurs to him to do so - that though he thinks only of communicating movement to the club by means of his hands and fingers, the forearms, the elbow joints, the shoulders, and probably the legs and feet, are also in action - responsive action; responsive in the sense that they move without any specific direction from the mind, but on the impulse created by the action of the hands and fingers in the club. If an attempt were made to swing the club about by using the hands and fingers to the exclusion of the action of other members of the body, that is to say, without the naturally responsive movements, the result would not only be stilted and powerless; it would produce an appreciable strain on the muscles involved.

This is exactly the stilted and powerless movement or series of movements that is known as mistiming the shot. Of the various parts of the body that should act in harmony, some parts act either out of harmony, or not at all. It is good to start the club-head by hand and finger action, but it is useless to do this unless forearms and upper arms and shoulders and hips and legs and feet and head are allowed to follow. Everything must "give" when the call comes - except the grip of the thumb and forefinger of each hand; for with an adequate grip there, control or the club can always be preserved without retarding any responsive movement whatsoever. The responsive movements are just as vital to the proper execution of the shot as the initiatory movements.

One of these responsive movements, as has been suggested, is the movement of the head.

A still tongue may make a wise head, but a still head does not make a wise golfer, no matter what may have been said by the pundits to the contrary. And the pundits have spoken with no uncertain voice. Take a few examples:

Taylor: "[The illustration] shows my head has been kept *immovable* during the back swing, a most important factor in accuracy."

Herd: "Keep that necessary nuisance down as long as you can *as though you had it in a vice*. And keep it down for half a second after you have hit."

Massy: "The player must keep his head *perfectly motionless*."

Vardon is so overwhelmed by the fetish that in his book, "How to Play Golf," he devotes a chapter to it, and recommends the player when practising to tie himself up to a contrivance which tinkles a bell whenever the head moves!

But what is the fact? The fact is that unless the head is allowed to give in the up-swing, in the down-swing, and in the follow-through, the movement will be cramped and ineffective. So long as a movement is purely a responsive movement it must not be interfered with.

There are, of course, many movements of the head that are not responsive movements, just as there are many movements of the arms and shoulders and hips and legs and feet that are not responsive movements. And all such movements are bad and must be cut out.

To what extent, then, are the movements of the head in the swing responsive movements? The answer is - to an extent which varies according to the build of the player and his mental picture of the swing.

Take as an example Edward Ray, whose golf is well known on both sides of the Atlantic. Is Ray's head "immovable," "perfectly motionless," rigid as "in a vice"? On the contrary, it moves emphatically from left to right in the up-swing, and from right to left in the down-swing. It would ring Vardon's little bell all the time. Yet Ray is a champion golfer.

It is customary for pseudo-theorists to say that Ray is a genius and can do these odd things; but Ray's view is that his apparently casual attitude to his head is the "crowning ornament" of his style. It is not, however, because Ray is a genius that he can move his head without fatal consequences; nor is that movement the "crowning" ornament of his style. The swing which Ray visualises in his mind is not a swing made about a fixed vertical axis, but a swing made about an axis which is moved sideways thirty or forty degrees by the pull of the club-head. Ray can move his head without fatal consequences because he allows it to move, not on its own account, but in response to an impulse set up by the action of his hands and fingers.

Whilst Ray is an extreme example of head movement, there is probably no first-class golfer whose head does not move in order to allow of a free and full development of the swing. Let the reader try to swing freely whilst keeping his head as rigid as if it were in a vice.

The very idea of the head in a vice is enough to cramp his style.

In these circumstances it will be seen that the cure for head-lifting is not to try to keep the head down till after the ball has been hit away. To try to do that will inevitably destroy the rhythm of the shot and so jerk the head up! The so-called cure must accentuate the disease. That is why players who experience a patch of head-lifting are so seldom able to get rid of it at will. The head must be allowed to move responsively - and if it moves responsively it will move evenly. If, then, the player concentrate on hitting the ball he will not look up prematurely. In a word, if he can make the club-head obey his hands, his own head will obey the club-head.

Another golfing fetish is the stiff left arm. The golfer is admonished to see to it that his left arm is kept extended throughout the swing. He is urged to do this consciously. But the extension of the left arm is an effect, not a cause. It is an effect of the proper action of the hands and fingers. When one attempts to catch a ball one does not think of extending the arm; one reaches out with the hands and fingers, and in doing so, one inevitably extends the arm. The extension of the arm is a natural result of the action of the hands and fingers. It is precisely so in the golf swing.

Examples could be multiplied almost indefinitely. The golfer will now be able to find them for himself. And the great lesson for all golfers to learn is this: In the making of the swing two kinds of movements are involved, the initiatory and the responsive movements. For practical purposes the hands and fingers may be regarded as giving the initiatory movements, and the arms, shoulders, legs and feet as contributing the responsive movements. The hands and fingers should be assertive, masterful; the other members of the body ever ready to respond - to speak immediately they are spoken to, but not before.

SOME FURTHER NOTES

METHODS

I.

(i) In the ideal swing the hands and fingers force the pace all the time, and other members of the body and the body itself respond: they do no less; they do no more.

(ii) In the normal shot the club-head, at the moment of going through the ball, is moving on the line of intended direction, and the face of the club is at right angles to that line.

(iii) The player stands to the ball so that in making the swing as in (i) the club-head behaves as in (ii).

(iv) The player keeps his balance; he does this by taking up his position as in (iii), by standing on his feet and not on his heels alone, and by swinging as in (i).

II

When a fault creeps in, or smashes in, to a player's game he should proceed as follows: (a) Reflect that something has gone wrong under one or more of the four heads set out above.

(b) Resist the temptation to move ferociously or gloomily away from the scene of the outrage, and, instead, carefully note his position and the position of the club, so that he may know exactly what sort of caper he has cut.

(c) Compare this position with the relative position in the correct shot, noting the points of dissimilarity.

(d) From the comparison ascertain the method by which the faulty shot can be produced.

III

The player who can most readily produce the faulty shot by design is the player who is least likely either to produce the faulty shot by accident or to be worried by it if he does. To know how to commit is to know how to cure.

PRINCIPLES.

Here are a few of the basic ideas recapitulated. Golf is not a trick, and is not to be learned by trickery. Power is applied by and through the hands and fingers. All golfing faults are aspects of one root fault. Faults occur when the fingers have failed to lead or where the other members of the body have failed to follow. The player should have a clear mental picture of each shot. The player must learn to control the club. The club is a good servant, but a bad master. The body should not be kept back - the hands and fingers should make the club-head lead. There must be no stiffness at any point of the swing. All joints and muscles should be free from tension except those concerned in the grip of the forefinger and thumb. Notably, the wrist and forearm and shoulders must be perfectly free. Control in the fingers, and freedom everywhere else - that is the doctrine. The golfer who concentrates on hitting and controlling the ball by the exertion of power through the hands and fingers will not want to look up. Head-lifting is not a disease, it is a symptom of disease: no golfer really impressed with the necessity of controlling the club will be in danger of prematurely lifting his head. The golfer should beware of stiffening the wrist and forearm as the ball is hit - unless it has to be punched out of a bad lie.

The tendency to stiffen the wrist and forearm, and all other evil tendencies, recede when the player concentrates throughout the swing on continuously applying impetus by and through the fingers.

Even though approached from the simplest and the sanest point of view, it is apprehended that golf will still be found to be a sufficiently difficult and elusive game to keep the player's interest alive. Even Ernest Jones nods.

ABOUT ERNEST JONES

BOOK II - **THE GOLF SWING**

ABOUT ERNEST JONES

Ernest Jones (1887–1965) was an English professional golfer. He is renowned for his accomplishments in teaching many famous professional golfers as well as amateurs. He tutored Virginia Van Wie for many years, including during her stretch of three consecutive U.S. Women's Amateur Championships from 1932–34. He also worked with Glenna Collett Vare, Lawson Little, Betty Hicks, Phil Farley, George Schniter, Horton Smith and other top players of the era.

Early history

Jones was born near Manchester, England. He began playing golf as a young boy and by the age of 18 secured employment at Chislehurst Golf Club as an assistant professional. In 1913 at the age of 25 he was made head professional at that club. As a soldier in the First World War, he was in France. There in March 1915 he was serving in the Sportsman's Battalion of the Royal Fusiliers, near Loos. As the result of an exploding grenade, he suffered the loss of his right leg just below the knee. While a severe injury on its own merit, Jones was afraid it would be a handicap and perhaps be the end to his career as a professional golfer. He was sent back to England where he recuperated for four months. Able to walk using crutches, he proceeded to attempt his first round of golf at Royal Norwich in 1916 where he carded an 83 (38/45) on that first outing. He followed shortly thereafter with a 72 on a long and challenging course. While a relief regarding his prospects for continuing the golf profession, these rounds would prove to bring a surprising and revolutionary change to his concept of golf and its instruction. Later, he was fitted with a prosthetic.

In 1936, at the invitation of Marion Hollins, Jones accepted the position of Head Golf Professional at the Women's National Golf and Tennis Club in

ABOUT ERNEST JONES

Long Island, New York. This was the beginning of a life long career of teaching in the U.S. Subsequent to this position, Jones began teaching in New York city. He had an indoor teaching facility in the Spaulding building at 518 Fifth Avenue.

Instructional development

Jones began to ask himself how it could be that he could yet score so effectively, with such a radical change needing to be made to how his body swung the club having only one leg. Jones himself as well as countless others proved to be able to play well with missing body parts or body parts that were limited in their functioned. Despite the prevalence of golf instruction that described these missing or misfunctioning parts as being essential, Jones and others demonstrated that a golfer's brain would devise compensating strategies to yet produce fine golf shots. This success, in conjunction with his reading of Sir Walter Simpson's book, "The Art of Golf", brought him to the fundamental fact that the key to a successful golf shot was not the correct movement of certain body parts, but the correct movement of the club. Instead of the movement of body parts, the real key was the successful movement of the golf club. Jones had happened upon the then-little-understood fact that the human brain need only experience a persons desire to perform a task. On its own the brain devises a means to create the muscular action to achieve the task. The individual is only aware of "what" they want to do. The brain's action in deciding "how" it will accomplish the task is completely unconscious. This explains how very proficient golfers often report that they have little understanding of "how" they swing and only understand that they can do so when they choose.

Thus it was the case that Jones began his now-famous quest to discover, document, and disseminate a description of "how" the club swung and how to most easily teach the club's movements to others. The result was the writing of many articles on this subject and the publishing of two books. Further, Jones took every opportunity to share his insights with fellow professionals. Jones' simple concept is summarized in this classic "The Golf Swing" instruction. Ironically, it is the drastic simplicity of his approach to golf instruction that met with rancor and objection when he was invited by the PGA (Professional Golfers' Association of America) to present his work. Horton Smith, then the incoming president of the association, told Jones his system was "too simple. We wouldn't sell enough lessons." Perhaps much to the PGA's chagrin, whereas an average pro would have give about 600 lessons a year, Jones would give 3,000. Jones often said, "The trouble with the teaching of golf, is that one is taught what a swing produces [body movement], instead of how to produce a swing [club movement]."

Career overview

His career included playing competitively on the European tour, head golf professional at several of America's most esteemed golf clubs, and a career of teaching both tour professional and amateur golfers. In the years after World War II, he conducted his instruction indoors at the Spaulding Building in New York City. He found that the could achieve better success with his students indoors because they would not be distracted by ball flight and instead focused on performing the swing correctly. Along with Harvey Penick, Tommy Armour, and Percy Boomer, he was inducted into the World Golf Teachers Hall of Fame in 1977.

REPRODUCED BY DUTCHYGOLF.COM 2012

BOOK II - **THE GOLF SWING**

BOOK III

THE DUTCHY GOLF SWING TRAINER

DUTCHY GOLF TEAM

The Dutchy Golf Swing Trainer

Illustrated training guide based on The Ernest Jones Method

by

DUTCHY GOLF TEAM

Published 2012 by **dutchygolf.com**

BOOK III - **THE DUTCHY GOLF SWING TRAINER**

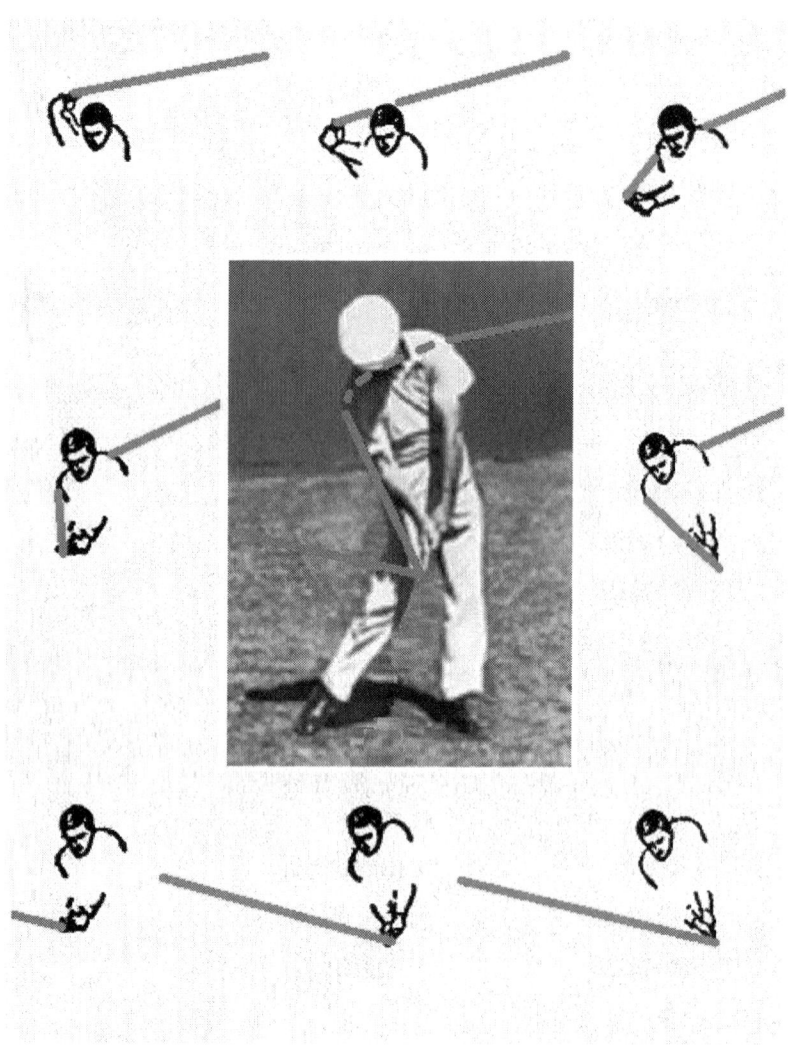

BOOK III - **THE DUTCHY GOLF SWING TRAINER**

CONTENTS

    LIST OF ILLUSTRATIONS

    FOREWORD   291

1   THE DUTCHY   295

2   POWER ISOMETRICS   301

3   SWING PLANE   303

4   SWING SPEED & RANGE OF MOTION   305

5   HYBRID CLUBHEAD DESIGN   309

LIST OF ILLUSTRATIONS

FIG.

1. Three different setups for the Dutchy
2. Two different setups for the door stop
3. Introduction to power isometric exercises
4. Introduction to swing plane exercises
5. Handkerchief with penknife attached
6. Mooring rope as stand-in for the Dutchy
7. Implications of different lie angles
8. Front and side views of the hybrid clubheads we tested

BOOK III - **THE DUTCHY GOLF SWING TRAINER**

FOREWORD

"What do we want to sell?" one of us asked in a time-to-change-the-subject frame of mind. We had just watched the Netherlands lose 2-1 to Germany in the 2012 European Football Championships being held in the Ukraine.

Whenever we meet, formally or informally (as on this Wednesday evening in June), we are the Dutchy Golf Team. A blending of diverse qualities and split personalities. The aspiring professional. The talented club fitter. The cancer survivor (through natural means). The promising county and university player from the 1960s who returned to golf this year after an unbelievable absence of over 35 years. The long drive fanatic, and the pitch and putt specialist. The retired sportsman who discovered golf.

We are most certainly not like-minded, with two exceptions. Firstly, each and every one of us shares a passion for this game called golf. Secondly, each one of us (in different ways) has been inspired by the thinking and teaching of Ernest Jones.

"What do we want to sell?" was the question raised. Until this evening, we thought we were in the business of producing and selling the Dutchy (Golf Swing Trainer) and hybrid golf club sets. A couple of hours discussion and a

BOOK III - **THE DUTCHY GOLF SWING TRAINER**

few drinks later found us in the early hours of Thursday morning, with a surprising answer to our question.

When we discuss the Dutchy (the nickname for our golf swing training aid) it seems that the focus of our discussion is the simple design and construction of the Dutchy, and the different exercise routines it was designed to cover. We have identified three groups of exercises that can be effectively be performed for 5-10 minutes each day:

- power isometric exercises
- swing plane exercises
- swing speed and range of motion exercises

When we discuss hybrid golf clubs (we are convinced that the hybrid golf club set has a hot future) it seems that the focus of our discussion is the simple design and construction of the clubheads, from long irons all the way through to the wedges, to facilitate the golf swing for players at all levels of the game. Not only as rescue clubs and replacements for the (more difficult to hit) long irons, but also their unique characteristics and benefits for the middle and short game.

So we have come to realise that what we want to sell, is not so much the end products such as the Dutchy and custom fitted hybrid clubs, as the thinking, the concepts and ideas, behind the designs of these products.

What we want to sell is contained in the following chapters of this book, namely:

- a description of the basic components of the Dutchy Golf Swing Trainer so that you can construct/build one for yourself;
- an overview of some basic exercises for the Dutchy covering the identified exercise groups: power isometrics, swing plane, swing speed and range of motion;
- some pointers on what to look for in the design of a hybrid clubhead.

And yes, we do sell the Dutchy and we do sell custom fitted hybrid golf clubs and sets. Yet our real passion, as we recently discovered, is in the information we share with you in the following chapters of this book – this training guide.

And we all share a passion for the pioneering work of Ernest Jones expressed in his method for teaching the golf swing, popularly known as "The Ernest Jones Method" and the thinking behind this book is strongly inspired by the thoughts of Ernest Jones (1887–1965).

This book would therefore not be complete without a description of the Ernest Jones Method. In the appendix you will find a complete reproduction of the original text and illustrations of his book "The Golf Swing - Ernest Jones Method (illustrated)".

BOOK III - **THE DUTCHY GOLF SWING TRAINER**

1 THE DUTCHY

Some inconvenient truths

The year is 2012 and we are inundated with a whole scala of exercises and tools to help us improve our golf game. Walter Simpson and Ernest Jones would have probably given us the same advice regarding how best to invest 20 minutes of our time - "Go out there and swing the club!" Our body and our golf club make up a whole, and the ability of that whole to perform the golf swing is a simple matter of balancing the different parts, the total performance being determined by the strength of the weakest link. In a balanced rhythmic swing the stronger components will temper and adjust to accommodate the weaker parts. If not, the result is usually unpredictable, jerky, not majestic to the eyes, and will eventually lead to injuries both on the mind and spirit as well as the body and (broken) clubs.

The following set of simple exercises are designed to help us identify the weaker parts and strengthen these weaker parts. The more the exercises involve all (as many of) the body parts that (try to) work together in the golf swing, the easier it is to work on the parts that need strengthening. And strengthening is a collective term for characteristics such as power, speed, coordination, timing, rhythm, elasticity, range of motion, etc.

The isometric exercises are about developing power. The swing plane exercises are about building coordination. The flexibility exercises are about increasing range of motion and speed (note: the rope exercise is fun in that performing for speed (fast) is less strenuous than performing for range of motion (slow). The slower the motion, the quicker the heart rate and breathing will tend to rise.)

In each and every-one of the following exercises, we will experience the weaker components of our body being put to work the most - at least until they are up to par with the rest. They are designed to give the most measurable benefit for the least feeling of effort. They are both effective as well as efficient. They are the exercises that we are most likely to stick to on a daily basis for 10-15 minutes each day.

Introduction to the Dutchy

The Dutchy is strongly inspired by the thoughts of Ernest Jones (1887–1965) who was an English professional golfer. His career included playing competitively on the European tour, head golf professional at several of America's most esteemed golf clubs, and a career of teaching both tour professional and amateur golfers. In the years after World War II, he conducted his instruction indoors at the Spaulding Building in New York City. He found that the could achieve better success with his students indoors because they would not be distracted by ball flight and instead focused on performing the swing correctly. Along with Harvey Penick, Tommy Armour, and Percy Boomer, he was inducted into the World Golf Teachers Hall of Fame in 1977.

The original thoughts of Ernest Jones Hammond were captured in The Golf Swing, The Ernest Jones Method. See Appendix for the illustrated version.

The average golder is apt to attach too much importance to power, and the result is that he manipulates his club ponderously and ineffectively, never for one moment realizing the idea of speed or touch, and usually failing to achieve his one objective power. His mental picture is ill-conceived, and therefore his action goes astray. His hands and fingers have failed to do their full share of the work, and consequently his body comes into the shot at the wrong time and in the wrong positions.

In golf the swing is the outcome of the mental picture. The Dutchy will help you visualize clearly a swing in which the motive force is applied by and through the hands and particularly the fingers. The Dutchy encourages you to cease caring what other physical processes are involved. Rest assured that if your brain prompts the hands and fingers to do their work, the other members of the body will probably do theirs. If you do this, you will be well on the way to achieving that crisp, decisive method of hitting a golf ball which makes the professional's game the despair of the ordinary amateur player.

Basic components of the Dutchy Golf Swing Trainer

The Dutchy Golf Swing Trainer is simple to make, and consists of the following basic parts:

- a golf training grip so that you can learn to position your hands correctly on the golf grip;
- a length of elastic tubing or bungie cord with connecting clip at one end, and a fixed cord connection at the other end (we use the cord connection by running it through the grip and fixing it with a connecting ring);
- and last but not least a door stop, so that we can anchor the Dutchy to any position (high or low) in a doorway.

BOOK III - **THE DUTCHY GOLF SWING TRAINER**

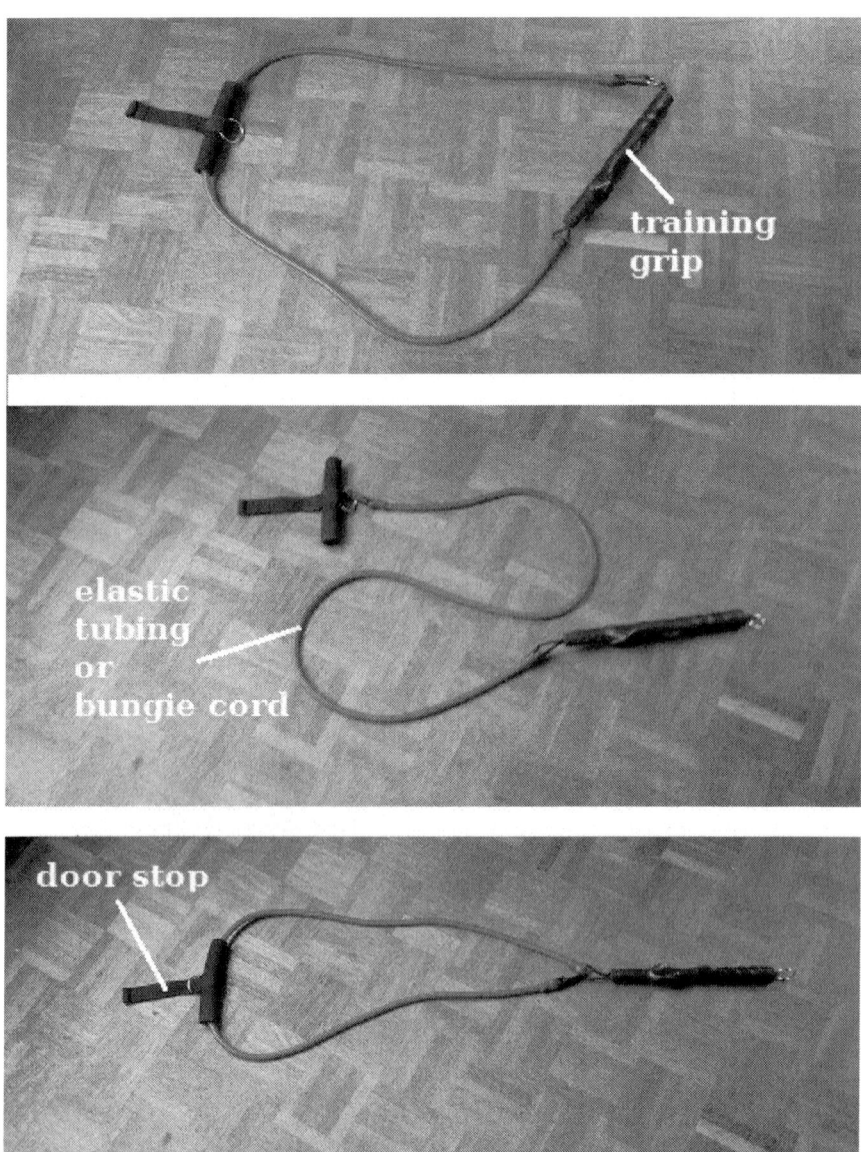

Fig 1. Three different setups for the Dutchy

CH. 1 – THE DUTCHY

We have fitted the door stop with a rubber sleeve and connecting ring, so that the tubing can either be clicked onto the connecting ring, or run through the sleeve and then clicked on to one of the training grip connectors. Running through the sleeve effectively doubles up the elastic tubing, thereby shortening the length of the elastic tubing for exercising in more confined areas, and doubling the resistance (for the same amount of stretch) of the elastic tubing, as a means of intensifying exercises.

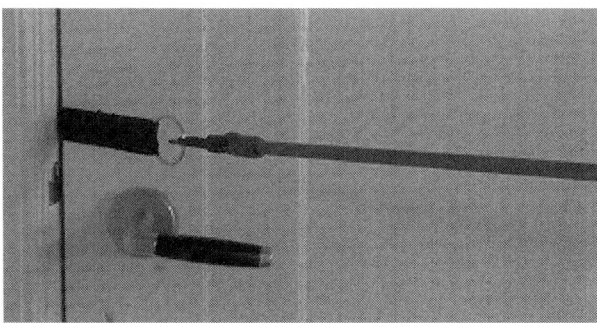

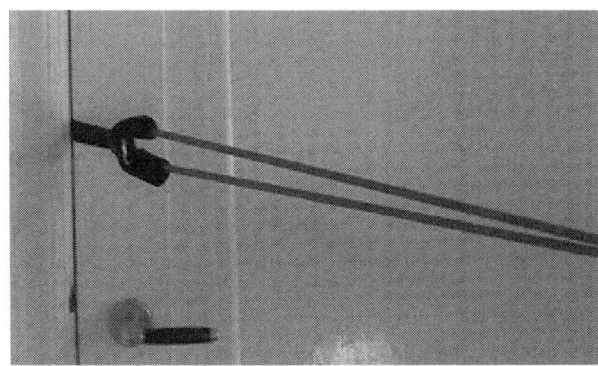

Fig 2. two different setups for the door stop

Some key highlights of the Dutchy Golf Swing Trainer

- a simple, affordable yet very effective training aid for golfers at all levels of the game;
- so compact you can take it with you anywhere and use it anywhere, from a corner of your hotel room or living room to the outdoors;

BOOK III - **THE DUTCHY GOLF SWING TRAINER**

- a standard training grip teaches your hands to adopt a correct basic position on the grip;
- the contours of the training grip actively involve the fingers during the Dutchy exercises;
- exercises can be performed with both hands as well as one hand at a time;
- exercises allow you to work both your left side as well as your right side;
- designed to allow you to vary the intensity of your exercises, from light through to heavy;
- encourages you to be creative and playful and develop your own exercise routines.

Get creative, follow your instincts, and develop your own power isometrics, swing plane, swing speed and flexibility exercises. Golf can be this simple!

2 POWER ISOMETRICS

Whether you swing left handed or right handed, try to perform the following exercises for both sides of the body, i.e. when you use one exercise to train the left hand/side, follow this exercise with its mirror image for the right hand/side.

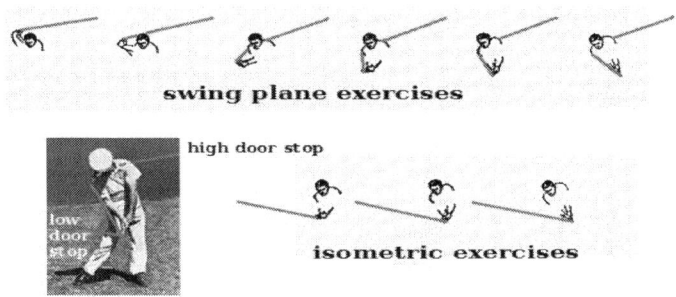

Fig 3. Introduction to power isometric exercises

By fixing the door stop at a lower position in the doorway, you can perform some isometric exercises. These are resistance exercises. The more you stretch the elastic tubing, the more you increase the intensity (resistance) of the exercise. You stretch slowly, then hold a position for 5-10 seconds, and then relax.

3-5 repetitions of each exercise performed 3-4 times a week is adequate.

You can perform these isometric exercises with both hands (as illustrated in the figure) and you can also repeat them with one hand at a time, e.g. perform the exercise with both hands, then repeat with the left hand only, and then repeat with the right hand only.

These kind of exercises are excellent for feeling how the different muscles of your body work together at the bottom of the downswing and through the impact area.

Isometric exercises are a good way to strengthen your golfing muscles without exhausting them. They are a good way to train your muscle memory, because you are working your golfing muscles together (as you would in the golf swing) and holding them in desired positions of the golf swing.

As you improve your swing mechanics and swing plane, the value of these isometric exercises will go up as well.

Get creative, follow your instincts, and develop your own power isometrics, swing plane, swing speed and flexibility exercises. Golf can be this simple!

CH. 3 – SWING PLANE

3 SWING PLANE

Whether you swing left handed or right handed, try to perform the following exercises for both sides of the body, i.e. when you use one exercise to train the left hand/side, follow this exercise with its mirror image for the right hand/side.

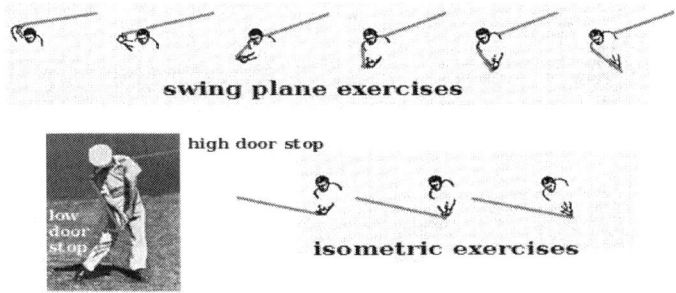

Fig 4. Introduction to swing plane exercises

These are simple relaxed exercises. By fixing the door stop at a height just above your head, you can go through the slow motions of your back swing, down swing and hitting through the ball area. This is not a strength exercise. This is a low resistance exercise. The purpose is to execute your swing in extreme slow motion, trying to sense the position of your hands and other factors that may affect your swing, such as shoulders, hips, weight distribution etc. The trick is to sense (feel) rather than to think. And the pressure of the elastic tubing (or bungie cord) on your neck or shoulders or back provides immediate feedback as to the nature of your swing plane.

Some swing planes are more up and down (vertical) in nature, whilst others tend to be flatter (more horizontal.) Your swing plane may well change from day to day, and even from stroke to stroke on the golf course, and even during the course of performing these exercises. Learn to observe these changes, and accept them as they are. Your swing plane at any given moment in time is not an objective for you to strive for, but the result of different conditions: how you feel, the lie of the land, the type of shot you want to play, etc.

Relax with this exercise and learn to feel what works best for you over time. The angle of your swing plane will affect the lie angle requirements for your golf clubs. You can read more about this in chapter 5, where we discuss hybrid golf clubs and custom fitting for lie angles.

Get creative, follow your instincts, and develop your own power isometrics, swing plane, swing speed and flexibility exercises. Golf can be this simple!

4 SWING SPEED & RANGE OF MOTION

Whether you swing left handed or right handed, try to perform the following exercises for both sides of the body, i.e. when you use one exercise to train the left hand/side, follow this exercise with its mirror image for the right hand/side.

It wasn't long before we started playing around with our Dutchy prototypes and swinging with them. And in so doing we hit upon the following exercises for swing speed and flexibility. Using the setup in fig. X we were able to simulate the pendulum type motion that Ernest Jones used to demonstrate with a handkerchief and penknife attached at one end (see fig. 5.) The best visual demonstration of a swinging action is the movement of a weight attached to the end of a string (or handkerchief) The string, being flexible, cannot transmit power through leverage. We create a similar situation using the Dutchy.

BOOK III - **THE DUTCHY GOLF SWING TRAINER**

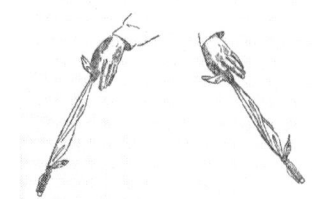

Fig 5. Handkerchief with penknife attached

We even developed an alternative aid using a mooring rope from one of our boats, which we folded twice (see fig. 6) into a swing-able length resembling the length of a short iron.

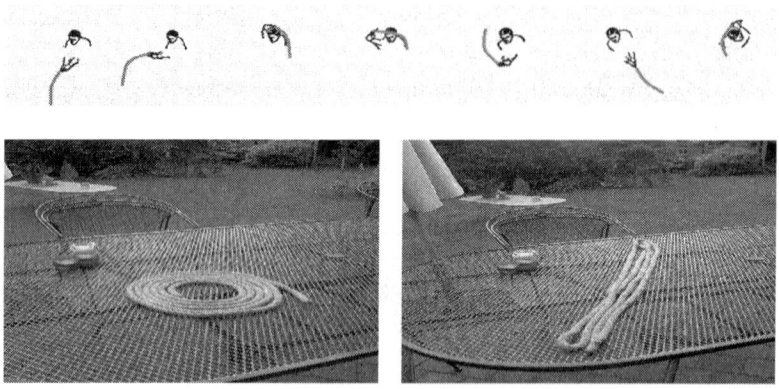

Fig 6. Mooring rope as stand-in for the Dutchy

Grip one end of the folded rope as you would a golf club and start swinging the rope back and forth until you are completing the back-swing and the follow-through. Get into a back and forth rhythm, where the follow-through of one swing becomes the back-swing for the next swing. The rope will come to rest on your back or shoulders (or even neck) at the completion of each back-swing and follow-through.

CH. 4 – SWING SPEED & RANGE OF MOTION

There is no right or wrong. Just feel the swing. Learn to observe.

Should the hands act forcefully on the back-swing or follow-through, then the rope may start whip-lashing into your back or shoulders. To soften these blows you may choose to soften the hand action. Alternatively, you may decide to maintain the hand action but to compensate by increasing the stretch and rotation of the rest of the body, so that the arc of your swing widens and the rope has more distance to travel and therefore more opportunity to slow down towards the end of each movement. You start to develop a sense of rhythm. The different muscles in your body start working together instead of against each other. You start working muscles that were not previously engaged in your swing. You start becoming aware of a build-up in your swing speed as you WHOOSH through the imaginary hitting zone. You will also be surprised at how deceptively simple exercise, after only a few minutes of gentle repetitions, can raise your heart beat and rate of breathing.

Your fast twitch muscles are engaged and trained.

Your shoulders and hips loosen up so that your ability to rotate increases.

ALL your muscles learn to work together for maximum speed and efficiency.

Your ears tune into the whooshing sound and pick up on the movements that produce the strongest whoosh (swing speed) through the hitting zone.

In the same way that every golfer feels the difference between a super swing and great ball strike, and a lesser swing and a lesser shot, you will be able to differentiate by feel between a smooth rhythmic swing with the rope, and one that is out of balance.

And when you start getting into that state of being when everything is as it should be, when the back and forth swinging motion feels powerful and gentle, fast and smooth, then you may engage your mind and allow your thoughts to wander to different parts of your body, BUT ONLY AS AN OBSERVER, and not as an active participant. By all means, observe the body movements that are produced by the swing. Do not allow your mind to drive your body movements as a means to producing a swing.

BOOK III - **THE DUTCHY GOLF SWING TRAINER**

Ernest Jones often said, "The trouble with the teaching of golf, is that one is taught what a swing produces [body movement], instead of how to produce a swing [club movement]."

Learn how to produce a swing and observe the body movements that a swing produces. For example, during one set of exercises you may observe how your balance is shifting from one foot to the next, or how your heels are (or are not) lifting from the ground, or how your forearms are rolling back and forth, etc.

Even with the Dutchy or a mooring rope in your hands, you can feel the action of your hands and fingers during the execution of the swing. Learn that feeling and try to replicate it when you are out there swinging the club(head.)

Ernest Jones was convinced that the golf swing could be readily taught and consistently performed only if it were conceived as one movement, that various members of the body (including the shoulders) were normally anxious to get busy too strenuously and too soon, and that the only way of insuring their working in due co-ordination with the other members of the body, notably the hands and the fingers, was to treat them as disastrous leaders, but as wholly admirable followers. The basis of the swing, as Jones had worked it out before the war, was the proper action of the hands and fingers.

5 HYBRID CLUBHEAD DESIGN

Introduction

"In these latter days, when golf clubs of all conceivable new materials and design have been indefinitely multiplied, and are being daily launched on the golfing world, backed by testimonials from many of our leading players, it is exceedingly difficult for the beginner to know what maker to patronise, and what particular clubs it would be advisable for him to purchase."

Extract from The World Of Golf 1898

Hybrid sets

The hybrid golf club was originally developed as a replacement for the long iron, particularly for the middle to high handicap player who found it difficult to hit the long irons well from a good lie on the fairway, and nigh impossible from a bad lie or the rough. So the hybrid club came to this golfer's rescue, hence the nickname "rescue club".

Yet the advantages envisaged for the middle to high handicap player were also recognised by the professional player, who has long learnt the advantages of tailoring/customising clubs to fit his/her swing, and personal preferences. And gradually the hybrid club started to appear in the golf bags of leading professional players. The rescue club is no longer for the middle and high handicap players, as its design has been evolved to meet the requirements of the top professional players.

We at Dutchy golf envisage these advantages being extended to the middle and to the short game. We expect the gradual emergence of hybrid middle irons and hybrid wedges from more and more manufacturers. We have tested a number of these emerging hybrid sets, and the hybrid clubs that best illustrate the do's and do nots, for lie angles and bounce angles, are the Cobra Baffler Rails, Acer XDS Reacts, Powerplay System Q and the Black Magic wedges.

Custom fitting

Whether you are just starting off in golf or you are a low handicap player, it seems that custom fitting has become a "must do" if you want to make the best of your golf game.

Lie angle

One required specification is the so-called lie angle. The more vertical the plane of your golf swing, then the smaller lie angles are recommended. The flatter your swing plane is, then the higher lie angles are recommended.

And yet there are hidden dangers in setting lie angles. The lie angle you adopt as a beginner will probably not be the lie angle most suited to your body when you discover your golf swing and try to improve. It can lock you in to your beginner mode, and hold you back from improving your swing and your game.

The top players seem to be able to play with golf clubs of varying lie angles, by adapting to the club in hand. They have learnt to play from uphill and downhill lies, from slopes where the ball is either located above their feet or below their feet. These differing lie situations come with differing lie angle requirements. And top players have learnt to play with their hands at the top of the grip, as well as moving their hands down the grip. Each hand position changes the lie angle.

CH. 5 – HYBRID CLUBHEAD DESIGN

And on some days we feel better than others. On a calm day we feel like standing more upright to the ball and swinging long and free, whereas on a windy day, we may prefer to crouch down a little more and adopt a shorter and more compact swing. These differing weather conditions can once again affect lie angles.

The ideal golf club would be one with a dynamic lie angle, whereby the lie angle easily adapts to varying factors that affect lie angle, such as the slope of the fairway and the location of the hands on the grip and the weather conditions of a specific day.

The golf club that meets the requirements of the ideal golf club with a dynamic lie angle, is the club with a rounded bottom edge as opposed to the fairly flat bottom associated with most irons. It would appear that the modern day hybrid club comes close to offering a dynamic lie angle.

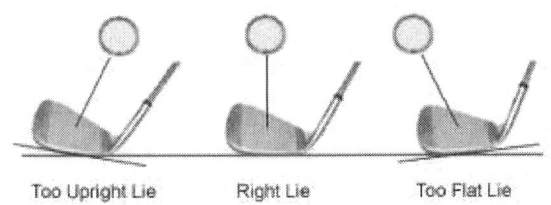

Fig 7. Implications of different lie angles

With a traditional golf iron, too upright a lie angle increases the risk of digging the heel of the club into the ground, and too flat a lie angle increases the risk of digging the toe of the club into the ground. Both lie angles respectively are associated with a tendency to hit left or to hit right of the intended line of flight. An upright lie angle means that you are standing too far away from the ball and that during the swing the heel of the club will hit the ground before the rest of the club. The result will be a pulling or hooking golf shot. If you have a flat lie angle then you are most likely standing too close to the ball. A flat lie angle will result in a push or a slice because the toe of your club sill come through first and hit the ground before the rest of the club.

With the more rounded bottom of the hybrid club, i.e a curved sole from the toe to the heel, the player does not need to worry about the heel or toe catching the turf. However, the evolving golfer learns to feel how a dynamic change in lie angle can be used to affect the flight of the ball.

The player learns to visualise the shot, to feel the swing that goes with that shot, and to swing the clubhead and make the shot. Golf can be this simple!

Bounce angles

Many of the hybrid clubs on the market, especially those sets that contain middle irons and short irons down to the pitching wedges and sand wedges, have been designed with the middle and high handicap players in mind. The wedges especially can come with an "exagerated" high bounce angle. The theory behind a high bounce angle is that it becomes virtually impossible for the player to dig the clubhead into the ground. Should the clubhead hit the ground before hitting the ball, a situation that with a normal golf iron would lead to a duffed shot, the hybrid should bounce or skid through to the ball, so that the resulting ball flight is closer to the intended shot than to a duffed shot. This is fine in theory, but in practice it comes with a number of setbacks.

The high bounce angle can result in a thinned shot that overshoots the target, particularly with the wedges off a tight lie or out of a divot. And the effective bounce angle increases the more the player tries to open the clubface, to play a higher pitch shot or play from a deep bunker, thereby limiting the shot making ability of the player. So there is room for hybrid clubhead designs to improve.

The ideal hybrid clubhead would be one that both protects the player from duffing a shot, as well as offering the player the versatility for opening the club face and shot making associated with the bladed irons. We consider the high bounce angles to be unnecessary, and envisage a hybrid clubhead

CH. 5 – HYBRID CLUBHEAD DESIGN

with a very low bounce angle. And we have tried out a number of hybrid clubs that are starting to incorporate this line of thought into their design.

We have tested a number of these emerging hybrid sets, and the hybrid clubs that best illustrate the do's and do nots, for lie angles and bounce angles, are the Cobra Baffler Rails, Acer XDS Reacts, Powerplay System Q and the Black Magic wedges.

Cobra

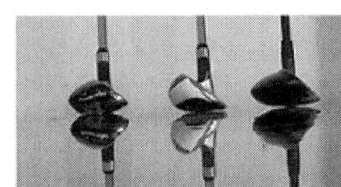
Powerplay #7 #9 PW SW

Powerplay - Cobra

Powerplay - Acer - Black Magic

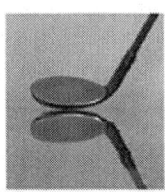
Black Magic

Cobra

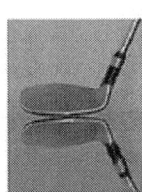
Acer

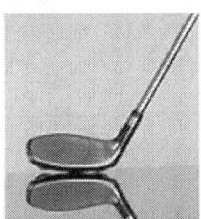
Powerplay

Fig 8. Front and side views of the hybrid clubheads we tested

The Cobra Baffler Rail hybrid and the Acer XDS React Hybrid heads have a fairly flat bottom with little bounce. The Powerplay System Q hybrid has a flat lie, but with a more pronounced bounce angle especially on the wedges. When it comes to the Pitching Wedge and Sand Wedge the bounce is a little overdone, with the leading edge raised higher than for the other irons in the Powerplay System Q Hybrid set. The Black Magic wedges have rounded bottoms, and depending upon the inclination of the shaft, the effective bounce can be easily increased or decreased.

When we look at the face of the hybrid clubs, from front to back, we see that the Black Magic wedges and the Cobra Bafflers have very rounded bottoms, whereas the Acers and Powerplays have less curved bottoms with sharply curved corners at the toe and the heel.

The above lie angle and bounce characteristics influence how the different clubs feel and play as follows:

- Cobra Baffler feels great and are fun to play, and the available club range is #2 - #6. Although the bottom of the clubhead is fairly flat with little bounce, the strongly curved face ensures that the club slides over the ground with no risk of the toe or the heel of the club digging in.
- Acer XDS React also has a flat bottom, but because the face has somewhat sharply curved toe and heel (relative to the other hybrids), the club is sensitive to lie angle and can dig in with the heel or toe (will affect the high handicap player).
- Power Play System Q is similar to the Acer XDS React with somewhat sharply curved toe and heel (relative to the other hybrids), and flattish bottom, but the raised front edge (higher bounce) makes the club very easy to play and the long/middle irons feel and play well. However, we find the bounce angle a little overdone (high leading edge) on the Pitching Wedge and Sand Wedge, which on the whole works fine for pitching and chipping, were it not for the occasional thinned shot creeping in. A lapse of concentration on short pitches and chip shots, and the raised leading edge will lead to a low trajectory and overshooting the green. We speak from experience during testing :) This high leading edge also limits the ability of the low handicap player to open up the clubface for bunker shots and higher flop shots. We have developed a love-hate relationship with the Powerplay System Q hybrids, in that we love the all the #2 - #9

irons, and would love the wedges if the leading edge were lowered a little.
- Black Magic Wedges really caught us by surprise. The rounded bottoms and rounded faces are ideal for all kinds of shot making. The player can vary the inclination of the shaft to increase or decrease bounce characteristics. There is no heel or toe to dig into the ground. Opening or closing the clubface for higher or lower trajectories is simple. Ball striking feels crisp, both on full pitches as well as short chip shots.

Our ideal set of hybrids would be a marriage between the Cobra Baffler or Powerplay System Q long hybrids #2 - #6, the Powerplay System Q middle hybrids #7 - #9 (only Powerplay covers this mid-range), and the Black Magic wedges PW-GW-SW-LW or modified Powerplay System Q with a lowered leading edge (still leaves sufficient bounce). The marriage would be based on the following design principles:

- well rounded faces;
- rounded bottom for wedges, becoming gradually flatter for the middle to long hybrid irons;
- to completely eliminate the risk of shanking (socketing) the ball: shaft aligned with top edge of the clubface.

Custom fitting for lie angles and bounce with the new generation of hybrid sets may offer some added value, but with hybrid clubs such as the Black Magic Wedges, the Powerplay System Qs and the Cobra Bafflers, custom fitting is about club length, grip size and shaft flex. Golf can be this simple!

PUBLISHED BY DUTCHYGOLF.COM 2012

Printed in Germany
by Amazon Distribution
GmbH, Leipzig